EXPLORING SCIENCE
INTERNATIONAL 11-14
CHEMISTRY

Mark Levesley, Iain Brand, Sue Kearsey, Sue Robilliard, Penny Johnson

Pearson

CONTENTS

HOW TO USE THIS BOOK

8Ee REDUCING POLLUTION

HOW CAN WE REDUCE POLLUTION FROM CARS EVEN FURTHER?

Air pollution from transport has been reduced by using filters, catalytic converters and new engines that use less fuel. To reduce it even further, people will need to change the way they travel.

Governments use a range of ways to persuade people to change their travel habits.

- Road tax: cars are taxed based on engine size, fuel type and carbon dioxide emissions. The lower the pollution, the less you pay.
- Annual tests: all cars over a certain age are tested for road-worthiness. If exhaust emissions are too high, the car must not be driven.
- Congestion charges: in some cities drivers must pay to use their vehicles at busy times of day.
- Fuel prices: higher taxes on fuel can make people decide to use cheaper forms of transport.
- Travel restriction: some countries restrict the number of days drivers can use their cars.

A | Electric cars reduce pollution from the car but electricity power stations release pollution.

Governments may make other changes. For example, the European Union has decided that at least 10 per cent of fuel used for transport should be **biofuel** (fuel made from plants).

1. Identify one advantage and one disadvantage, in terms of pollution, of choosing an electric car rather than a diesel or petrol one.

2. Give one advantage and one disadvantage of using hydrogen as a fuel for cars.

3. Some new cars have stop–start technology, where the engine stops when the car is not moving (such as at traffic lights). Explain how this is useful:
   a| for the driver   b| for the local population.

4. For each of the bulleted points in the list on the left, explain why this could help reduce pollution.

B | At this factory, waste material from making sugar is used to produce bioethanol (a biofuel). Using ethanol can reduce carbon dioxide emissions by up to about 70 per cent.

HAVE YOUR SAY

Should governments try to persuade vehicle manufacturers to make cars that produce less pollution, and how could they do this?

84

You should be able to answer the question at the top of the page by the time you have finished the page.

The **Key words** for the page are in bold. You can look up the meaning of these words in the **Glossary**, on pages 185–190.

If you are having trouble finding information about something, use the **Index**, on pages 195–197.

Questions are spread throughout the page so you can answer them as you go along.

Controlling pollutants

Exhaust gases can be treated to reduce pollution. Diesel vehicles usually have a **filter** to capture soot. Most vehicles also have a **catalytic converter** in their exhaust systems. This causes carbon monoxide gases to react with more oxygen to form carbon dioxide, and nitrogen oxides are broken down to oxygen and nitrogen.

carbon dioxide, water and nitrogen

carbon monoxide, nitrogen oxides and hydrocarbons

steel housing containing precious metals such as platinum

C | Catalysts are substances that speed up reactions but are not used up themselves. The catalysts in a catalytic converter cause exhaust gases to react more easily.

Controls: Neutralisation reactions are used to remove acidic gases from chimney smoke.

2 The gases dissolve in water vapour.

1 Sulfur dioxide and nitrogen oxides from vehicles, power stations and factories rise into the air.

3 Rain is more acidic than normal.

Controls: Acidic soil and water can be neutralised by adding substances such as calcium carbonate.

Controls: Catalytic converters on vehicles remove nitrogen oxides. Only low-sulfur fuel is burnt in engines.

4 Acid rain can harm plants and animals.

D | acid rain: its causes, effects and controls

Diagram D shows how the effects of acidic gases from fossil fuel combustion can be controlled. In many parts of the world, these controls are required by law. Parts of the world where industry is rapidly growing may have increasing air pollution problems.

6. Identify a trigger for asthma in vehicle exhaust gases.

7. a| Describe how burning fossil fuels in vehicle engines causes pollution.
   b| Describe how this pollution can be reduced.

8. a| What is acid rain and how is it caused?
   b| Explain how pollution from power stations is reduced.

FACT

In an asthma attack the tubes in the lungs get narrower, making it difficult to breathe. Attacks are usually caused by triggers, such as smoke, soot or pollen. Around the world, asthma affects over 300 million people and many animals. Using an 'inhaler' can make breathing easier.

E | asthma treatment

I can ...
- describe pollutants that are formed by burning fuels
- explain how these pollutants cause problems and how their effects can be reduced.

79

Fact boxes contain fascinating facts for you to think about.

I can ... boxes help you to reflect on what you have learned. Consider each statement carefully and think about how well this applies to you.

4

7Ea MIXTURES AND SEPARATION

To remain healthy, we need water. Your body loses water all the time and you can only live for a few days without drinking. Water for drinking must be clean, because dirty water can contain harmful substances and microorganisms.

In many dry parts of the world, people struggle to get enough suitable drinking water. Even in wetter parts of the world, there is sometimes too little rain to keep water reservoirs filled. Hosepipe bans can limit the water we use and make sure enough water is left for essential needs, such as drinking.

Water is a **liquid** in which many different substances can **dissolve**. Sources of water, such as rivers and streams, may also carry **solids** such as sand, gravel or mud. To make water safe and suitable for drinking, water must be treated in different ways to remove unwanted substances.

A | Around 800 million people in the world do not have clean water that is safe to drink.

B | This reservoir in South Africa supplies water for drinking and other needs to Cape Town. Sometimes rainfall levels are so low that the reservoir is at risk of running dry.

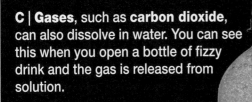

C | Gases, such as **carbon dioxide**, can also dissolve in water. You can see this when you open a bottle of fizzy drink and the gas is released from solution.

1 a| Give an example of a solid, a liquid and a gas.
 b| Describe how you can tell the difference between solids, liquids and gases.

2 A sample of water is collected from a stream. Suggest how you would separate out each of the following from the water:
 a| gravel   b| sand.

3 Sea water is a solution of water and dissolved substances, such as salt.
 a| Explain what 'solution' means.
 b| Describe how you would separate the dissolved substances from sea water.

4 a| Dissolving is a 'reversible change'. What does this mean?
 b| Give one other example of a reversible change.

FORENSIC
7Ea SCIENCE

HOW DOES A FORENSIC SCIENTIST PREPARE EVIDENCE FOR A COURT?

Forensic scientists collect materials from crime scenes. They may collect soil, burnt or broken materials, hairs and body fluids. The scientists then examine and test the materials in a lab. Their results can be used as evidence in a court of law. For example, the evidence could be used to show whether a person or vehicle was in a certain place.

Using knowledge of chemistry

Most forensic scientists have a university degree in forensic science, or other science followed by forensic science training. A forensic scientist needs a good understanding of the techniques used to separate and identify small amounts of substances (samples).

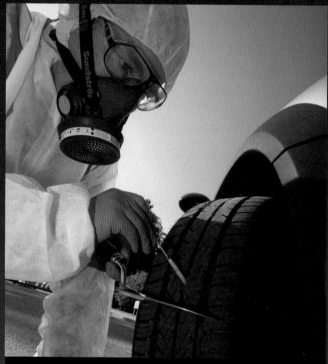

A | Samples of soil can be analysed to help identify where this car has been.

A common technique is **filtration**, which separates **insoluble** substances (the **residue**) from a liquid (the **filtrate**). When you filter a soil and water mixture, the filtrate contains substances naturally found in soil. These substances can be tested to find out what they are (e.g. by using chromatography, which you will learn about on page 16). The substances in a filtrate can be used to tell where some soil is from. Or the filtrate may contain substances from someone or something, such as a vehicle.

B | This apparatus can be used to separate soil from water.

1 Write down what you think forensic science means.

2 Give a reason why a forensic scientist needs to know how to separate the different substances in a sample.

3 Explain why filtration could help analyse where a soil sample originally came from.

Clear communication

Forensic scientists need to explain clearly what they have done. An important part of this is their **method**, which is a set of written instructions showing how an experiment is carried out. The method may also include a diagram of the **apparatus**. A clear method lets other scientists repeat an experiment exactly, to check the **results**. It also allows people in a court to understand easily what a forensic scientist has done.

The Method on the right can be used to filter a sand (or soil) sample using the apparatus in diagram C. It is clear because:

- it is done in steps, which each have a letter
- each step describes only one action
- each step begins with a command word (also called an imperative verb). This keeps the sentence simple.

Method

A | Fold a circular filter paper in half.

B | Fold the filter paper in half again to form a triangular shape.

C | Open out one layer of the paper to form a cone.

D | Place the filter paper cone into a filter funnel.

E | Stir the sand mixture with water so that all the sand is suspended.

F | Place the filter funnel into the neck of a conical flask.

G | Pour the sand and water into the filter paper.

---

4 Why is it important for forensic scientists to describe their methods clearly?

5 'Open' in step C is a command word because it tells you to do something. Identify three other command words in this Method. Explain your choices.

6 Suggest a part of this Method that could be made clearer by using a diagram rather than words.

7 Write a method to explain to someone how to set up the apparatus in diagram D. Use all the rules for writing a good method. Compare your method with one written by another student to see if your method could be improved to make it clearer.

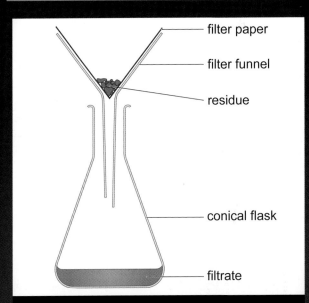

C | filtering apparatus

ACTIVITY

Use the Method above to carry out a filtering activity. As you carry out the Method, think about each instruction:

- is it written as clearly as it could be?
- is it given in the right order?

Try rewriting the method in a way you think makes it easier to carry out.

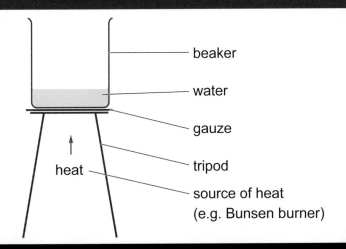

D | apparatus for heating water

7Ea MIXTURES

WHAT KINDS OF MIXTURES ARE THERE?

Water that carries waste materials needs to be treated in a water treatment plant so that it does not harm people or the **environment**. Waste water is not a single substance – it is not a **pure** substance. It is a **mixture** of water and solid substances.

Mixtures are grouped depending on whether the substances in them are solids, liquids or gases, and on how the substances can be separated.

- A **solution** is a mixture in which the solid dissolves in the liquid. This makes the mixture clear or **transparent**.

- A **suspension** is a mixture of two substances that separate if the mixture is not stirred. These two substances are often a solid and a liquid. When they are mixed, we say that one substance is suspended in the other. An example is sand mixed with water.

- In a **colloid**, one substance is **dispersed** in another substance and the two substances will not separate easily. Either substance may be a solid, liquid or gas. A colloid is cloudy or **opaque**, so it is easy to see that it is a mixture. Milk is a colloid of different milk solids dispersed in water.

Many mixtures we use are colloids, such as hair spray, hand cream, Styrofoam™ cups, paint and gel inks. Different kinds of colloid have properties that make them useful in different ways.

FACT

Fog is a colloid of water droplets dispersed in air.

A | Waste water from homes, offices and street drains contains large solids such as leaves, rubbish and lumps of human waste, as well as smaller solids. In the first stage of treatment, waste water passes through a screen, which acts as a **sieve**.

1   Why is waste water an example of a mixture?

2   a| Suggest what is removed from waste water during the first stage of water treatment.

   b| Describe how this is removed.

3   Describe one difference between a suspension and a solution.

4   What kind of mixture is the waste water that enters a water treatment plant? Explain your reasoning.

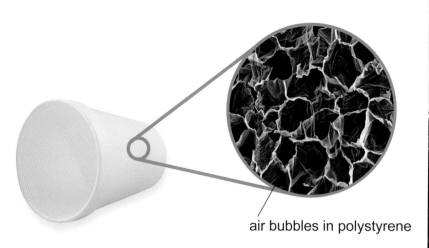

air bubbles in polystyrene

B | Styrofoam™ is a solid colloid of air and polystyrene.

After waste water has been screened at a water treatment works, it is passed through fine **filters** or left to stand in large 'settlement ponds'. This stage removes smaller suspended solids that eventually settle out when the water is still.

The water from the settlement ponds is not clean because very small solids are still dispersed in it. Special substances are added to make these solids stick together to form clumps. This makes it easier to separate them from the water (using more filters or another settlement pond).

D | The beaker on the left contains water after it has left the first settlement pond. On the right is the same water after substances have been added to stick the solids together.

C | Water, with fewer solids suspended in it, pours from the surface of a settlement pond. This water still contains dispersed and dissolved solids.

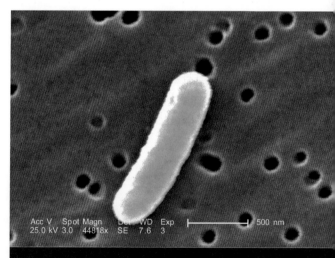

Acc V   Spot Magn   Det WD Exp   500 nm
25.0 kV 3.0 44818x   SE   7.6 3

E | Disease-causing microorganisms are too small to be removed by filters or settlement ponds. Drinking water may be treated with chlorine to kill them.

---

5   Explain why the Styrofoam™ cup in photo B is an example of a colloid.

6   Look at photo D. What kind of mixture is shown in the left-hand beaker? Explain your answer.

7   Suggest how waste water is cleaned after the special substances have been added to stick the remaining solids together. Explain your answer.

8   Draw a flow chart to summarise the stages of water treatment described on these pages. For each stage, give the name of the process used to clean the water.

I can ...

- classify mixtures
- describe how insoluble solids can be separated from a liquid.

7Eb SOLUTIONS

WHY DO SOME PEOPLE USE FILTERS FOR TAP WATER?

Tap water has been filtered and treated to make it safe for drinking but it does not contain only water. It is still a mixture, with many other substances dissolved in the water.

Some substances dissolve in a liquid to make a solution. In a solution, the dissolved substance breaks up into pieces so small that light passes straight through the mixture. Because of this, solutions are transparent. A solution may be coloured or colourless, depending on the substances in it.

B | Solutions, such as these, are transparent.

The liquid in a solution is called the **solvent**. The substance that is dissolved is called the **solute**. Water is a good solvent because it dissolves many solids, some gases and even some other liquids.

FACT

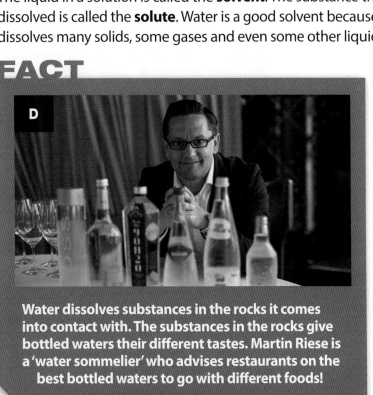

D

Water dissolves substances in the rocks it comes into contact with. The substances in the rocks give bottled waters their different tastes. Martin Riese is a 'water sommelier' who advises restaurants on the best bottled waters to go with different foods!

A | A water filter, like the one in the jug, removes some substances that are dissolved in drinking water.

1 What is meant when we say tap water is a solution?

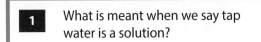
gills

C | This axolotl uses its gills to absorb **oxygen** dissolved in water.

2 Write down the names of two solids and one gas that dissolve in water.

3 Suggest two ways you could tell that a liquid was a solution.

A substance that dissolves in a solvent is said to be **soluble**. Substances that do not dissolve are insoluble. Nail varnish is insoluble in water but is soluble in a liquid called **propanone**, used in nail varnish remover.

When a solution is formed, there is **conservation of mass**. This means that the **mass** of the solution is the same as the mass of the dissolved substance plus the mass of the liquid at the start.

4 When propanone is used to remove nail varnish, which substance is the solvent and which is the solute?

5 20 g of sugar is stirred into 150 g of tea. What is the mass of the solution formed?

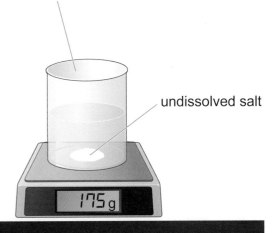

36 g salt

a saturated solution of table salt in water

If more than 36 g of salt is added to the 100 g of water, not all of the salt will dissolve.

undissolved salt

100 g   136 g   175 g

E | The total mass of a solution is the mass of the solid plus the mass of the liquid. A saturated solution is formed when 36 g of table salt is dissolved in 100 g of water.

The mass of solute dissolved in a certain volume of solvent is the **concentration** of the solution. The higher the concentration, the more solute is dissolved. There is a limit to how much solute you can dissolve in a particular volume of solvent. If you add more solute than this, the extra will sink to the bottom and stay undissolved. This type of solution is **saturated**.

The **solubility** of a solute is the mass that will dissolve in 100 g of a solvent. The solubility depends on the solvent. For example, 36 g of table salt (sodium chloride) will dissolve in water at 20 °C but only 0.1 g will dissolve in **ethanol** at the same temperature. The solubility also depends on the temperature, usually increasing with temperature: 37 g of sodium chloride dissolves in 100 g of water at 60 °C.

When a solution is made, no new substances are formed. A solution is a mixture. Changes in which no new substances are formed are **physical changes**.

6 The solubility of blue copper sulfate is 32 g per 100 g of water at 20 °C.

a| Which has the higher solubility in water, copper sulfate or sodium chloride?

b| State the largest mass of copper sulfate that would dissolve in 500 g of water at 20 °C.

c| A saturated solution of copper sulfate at 20 °C is cooled to 5 °C. Describe what you see as the solution cools. Explain your answer.

I can ...

■ describe how solutions are made
■ identify the solute and solvent in a solution
■ describe the effects of temperature and solvent on solubility.

SAFETY WHEN HEATING

HOW DO YOU HEAT TO DRYNESS SAFELY?

If a solution is left to stand, the solvent will slowly evaporate leaving the solids behind. If the solution is heated, the solvent will evaporate faster.

copper sulfate crystals

A | When the solvent in a solution evaporates, the solid is left behind.

barrel lifts the flame to a suitable height for burning

moveable collar opens and closes the air hole, so controlling the amount of air mixed with the gas

air hole allows air to mix with gas

wide base makes the burner stable on a flat surface

gas hose connecting burner to gas tap

B | The parts of a Bunsen burner have different functions.

Heating a solution until all the solvent has evaporated is known as 'heating to dryness'. In the lab, a Bunsen burner is usually used to heat a solution.

Turning the collar of a Bunsen burner allows different amounts of air to mix with the gas. This changes the temperature of the flame.

Using a Bunsen burner can be hazardous. A **hazard** is anything that could cause harm. When using a Bunsen burner you could burn yourself or others.

A **risk** is the chance that a hazard will actually cause harm. When working with a Bunsen burner you should plan to reduce the chances of burning yourself or others.

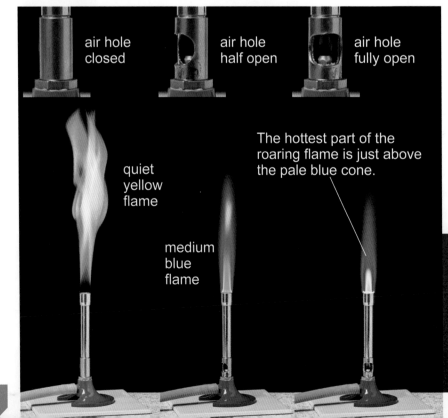

air hole closed

air hole half open

air hole fully open

quiet yellow flame

The hottest part of the roaring flame is just above the pale blue cone.

medium blue flame

C | The 'quiet yellow flame' is a 'safety flame' – it is not used for heating because it leaves a sooty layer on surfaces. The 'medium blue flame' is generally used for heating, especially tubes of liquid. The 'noisy blue flame' or 'roaring flame' is used for heating quickly.

Using a Bunsen burner safely

Bunsen burners must be used with care. Always follow the Method below to light a Bunsen, so that you work safely.

Method

A | Check the gas hose for breaks or holes. If it is damaged, return the burner and tubing to your teacher.

B | Tie back loose hair and any loose clothing, such as a tie or scarf. Remove everything from your working area except what is needed for the experiment.

C | Wear eye protection.

D | Place the burner on a heat-resistant mat, 30–40 cm from the edge of the bench.

E | Make sure the air hole of the Bunsen burner is closed.

F | Hold a lit splint about 2 cm above the top of the Bunsen burner.

G | Turn on the gas at the gas tap to light the burner.

H | When you have finished, close the air hole so that the flame is yellow. Then switch off the gas.

Heating to dryness safely

Heating to dryness increases risks because, when it has lost a lot of solvent, a solution often spits drops of very hot liquid.

The following safety rules help reduce these risks.

- Use a medium flame to heat the solution.
- Wear eye protection while heating.
- Do not fill an evaporating basin more than half-full with solution.
- If heating the liquid in a tube, make sure the open end of the tube does not point towards anyone.
- Always use tongs to hold or move hot things.
- When most of the liquid has evaporated, turn the burner off. Let the rest of the liquid evaporate more slowly.
- Always set the Bunsen burner to a safety flame when not in use and just before turning off.

---

1 What is a Bunsen burner used for?

2 Explain why the air hole of a Bunsen burner should be closed before the gas is lit.

3 Give two reasons why a medium blue flame is used for heating to dryness.

4 Look at photo E.

   a| Identify the hazards in this experiment when the Bunsen burner is lit.

   b| How could you reduce the risks of these hazards?

5 Plan an experiment to separate salt from salty water by heating to dryness. Include instructions that ensure the experiment is safe.

D | Hot equipment is a hazard when heating to dryness.

E | Working safely in an experiment reduces the risks from hazards.

I can ...

- describe how a Bunsen burner is used
- identify hazards and describe how to reduce risks.

7E c EVAPORATION

HOW DO YOU GET SOLIDS OUT OF A SOLUTION?

During **evaporation** of a solution, the liquid turns into a gas which escapes into the air. The evaporating liquid leaves behind the solids that were dissolved in it.

Evaporation can happen at any temperature, even when it is cold. However, the rate of evaporation increases as temperature increases.

A | Stalactites and stalagmites form from the water solution that slowly drips through the roofs of caves. Each drop of water that evaporates leaves behind a tiny amount of solid.

Producing salt

The table salt we use in food is a substance called sodium chloride. In some places, sodium chloride is found in thick layers of rock underground. This is called rock salt.

Rock salt can be dug up or mined, or water can be pumped into the layers of salt in the ground, dissolving the sodium chloride. The salt solution is called brine and this is pumped to the surface where it is heated to evaporate the water, leaving behind the sodium chloride.

Table salt can also be made by evaporating sea water.

FACT

Mined rock salt is spread on icy roads in cold countries in winter. The salt helps prevent ice forming and the bits of rock give extra grip for vehicle wheels.

B | rock salt being mined

C | Sea water is left in shallow ponds to form sea salt.

1 Look at photo C. The sea water is left in the ponds for a week or more.

  a| Describe what happens to the water.

  b| Explain why the salt is left behind in the ponds.

2 Would the rate of evaporation of water be greater in the cold cave in photo A or the warm salt ponds in photo C? Explain your answer.

3 Draw flow charts to show the two ways in which table salt is produced.

Boiling

Evaporation occurs when a liquid is turning into a gas at the surface of the liquid. **Boiling** is when liquid is turning to gas throughout all of the liquid. When a liquid boils you can see bubbles spread in all parts of it. These are bubbles of gas newly made from the liquid. The temperature at which a liquid boils is its **boiling point**.

Different liquids have different boiling points. For example, pure water boils at 100 °C and pure ethanol boils at about 78 °C . You can see if a liquid is pure by measuring its boiling point. You can also use boiling points to identify substances.

In the lab, we can use evaporation to recover solids that have been dissolved in a solution by heating to dryness.

4 Explain why a beaker of pure water will only boil when heated to 100 °C.

5 Explain, as fully as you can, what would happen if you heated a mixture of water and ethanol to a temperature of 80 °C.

6 How would you test whether a liquid was pure water?

7 Look at photo E.

  a| Suggest how the two samples were prepared.

  b| Describe what these samples show.

D | This geyser shoots high into the air because water underground is heated to boiling point, forcing the water out of the ground at high **pressure**.

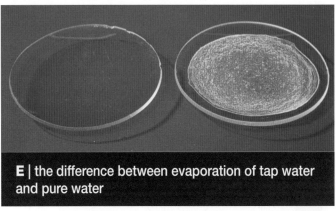

E | the difference between evaporation of tap water and pure water

I can ...

- describe how solutes can be separated from a solution by evaporation
- describe differences between evaporation and boiling.

7Ed CHROMATOGRAPHY

HOW CAN YOU SEPARATE SOLUTES FOR IDENTIFICATION?

After water has been cleaned at the treatment works, it must be tested before it can be used as drinking water. Tests for many different substances are carried out to make sure the water is safe.

Chromatography is one technique used in water analysis. Chromatography separates substances dissolved in a mixture. This makes it easier to identify and analyse each substance.

There are many different kinds of chromatography. **Paper chromatography** is the simplest method. It can be used to find out which colours are mixed together in different paints, dyes and inks. A **concentrated** dot of the mixture is placed near the bottom of special chromatography paper. The bottom of the paper is dipped into a solvent. The solvent carries the coloured substances in the ink or paint up the paper to form a pattern called a **chromatogram**.

The basic process of chromatography is the same, whether it is done with paper or by machine. Different substances in a mixture are carried by a gas or liquid solvent. The substances are carried at different speeds, which separates them out from each other.

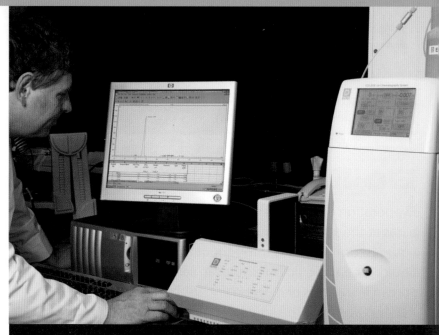

A | Chromatography is often done by complicated machines. The results of this water analysis are displayed as a graph showing a peak for each substance in the mixture. Peak height shows how much of the substance is in the sample.

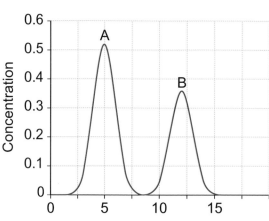

B | a sample chromatogram from water analysis

C | paper chromatography of two different inks

1   What is chromatography?

2   Look at diagram B. Which of the two substances had the higher concentration in the original sample? Explain your answer.

3   Look at photo C. Describe how this experiment was set up.

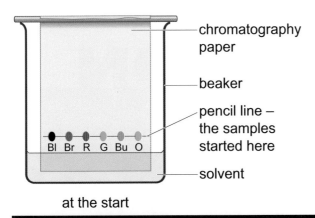

chromatography paper

beaker

pencil line – the samples started here

Bl Br R G Bu O

solvent

at the start

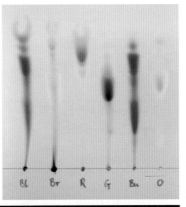

Bl Br R G Bu O

the chromatogram formed after the solvent has soaked up the paper

D | Six different inks were tested in this chromatography experiment: black (Bl), brown (Br), red (R), green (G), blue (Bu), orange (O).

Chromatography can be done with colourless substances. The chromatogram that is produced is then treated to make the substances coloured. Alternatively, ultraviolet light might make the substances glow. This makes the substances visible so the chromatogram can be analysed.

7 Diagram E shows the results of chromatography on three different orange drinks and some food colourings.

a| Which food colourings are found in the three kinds of orange drink?

b| Tartrazine is thought to make some children over-active. Which orange drink would be safe to give to an over-active child? Explain your answer.

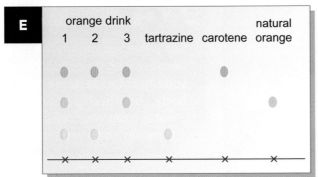

E	orange drink					natural
	1	2	3	tartrazine	carotene	orange

8 Give two examples of how chromatography is used in industry.

9 Compare the results of paper chromatography with the results of the water analysis chromatography shown in diagram B.

a| How are they similar?

b| How are they different?

c| Suggest why the method shown in photo A is used to analyse water rather than paper chromatography. (*Hint:* Think about why drinking water is analysed.)

4 Look at diagram and photo D.

a| Identify the colours in the different inks.

b| Which colour was carried the fastest?

5 Explain why chromatography separates the substances in the mixture.

6 Why can't you just evaporate a liquid to find out which substances were dissolved in it?

FACT

Chromatography is used to identify the contents of many kinds of mixtures, including water, food, urine, blood, sweat, soil and the atmosphere. During international athletic competitions, chromatography can be used to test blood and urine samples for banned drugs. It is also used in the forensic analysis of crime scenes to identify specific mixtures, such as colours in a lipstick or in a black ink.

I can …

■ describe how chromatography can be used to identify substances in a mixture

■ explain how chromatography works.

7Ee DISTILLATION

HOW DO WE MAKE SEA WATER DRINKABLE?

In many countries, drinking water comes from rain water that collects in rivers, lakes and reservoirs. However, drier countries need to get their drinking water from other sources.

1	Why is rain water usually safe to drink?
2	Why do many parts of the world need sources of water different from the ones used in the United Kingdom?

Over 70 per cent of the Earth's surface is covered in water. Most of this is sea water, which contains too many solutes to be safe to drink. Drinking water can be made from sea water using a process called **desalination**. Desalination removes most of the salts from the water. This requires expensive equipment and a lot of space, so it is only suitable in some places.

A | Fresh rain water contains only small amounts of dissolved substances. This means it is usually safe to drink.

B | The Jebel Ali desalination plant in the United Arab Emirates produces over 800 million litres of drinking water each day.

FACT

Sea water is dangerous to drink because it contains high levels of sodium chloride (table salt). In your body, sodium chloride removes water from your cells, which makes you even thirstier!

One of the ways in which sea water is desalinated is called **distillation**. The sea water is heated so that the water evaporates to form **steam**. The steam is collected and cooled so that it **condenses** back into liquid water. This distilled water is pure; it contains no solutes because the solutes in sea water cannot evaporate and are left behind.

3	What does desalination mean?
4	Explain why desalination plants are usually built next to the sea.
5	One of the products of distilling sea water is drinking water. Suggest another product from this process. Explain your answer.

The steam rises and then goes down the inner tube of the Liebig condenser.

The flask contains a solution. When the flask is heated the water turns into steam, leaving dissolved solids behind.

Anti-bumping granules stop violent boiling, which could blow the bung out of the flask.

thermometer

cold water out

cold water in

heat

The outer tube of a Liebig condenser is filled with cold water, flowing from a tap. This keeps the inner tube cold.

In the condenser the steam is cooled and condenses into a liquid.

Pure (distilled) water runs into the beaker.

C | This apparatus can be used to distil mixtures in the lab, including solutions such as salty water.

6 Use diagram C to help you draw a flow chart that describes how sea water is distilled in a desalination plant to produce drinking water. Use suitable scientific words in your descriptions.

7 Describe how anti-bumping granules reduce the risk of harm from a hazard.

! If the tube from the distillation apparatus is submerged in the collected liquid, it must be removed from the liquid as soon as you stop heating. Otherwise, suck-back may occur in which the cooling air in the apparatus contracts and cold liquid flows into the hot glassware. This can cause the glass to break.

The apparatus shown in diagram C is sometimes called a still. Stills can use **energy** from the Sun. In 1872, Charles Wilson invented the solar-powered water still, to supply drinking water to a large mining community in Chile, South America. The solar-powered still is a cheap way of providing clean water in poor areas of the world. Diagram D shows how it works.

Today solar-powered stills can be important for providing emergency clean water in remote places and at sea.

D | a basin solar still

transparent cover

sunlight

Water vapour condenses under the cover.

evaporation

pure water collecting chamber

dirty water

insulated evaporation chamber

8 Explain why a solar-powered water still might be useful:

a| on a ship that has broken down at sea

b| in a country where the drinking water contains bacteria that cause diseases.

9 Compare the basin solar still in diagram D with the still apparatus in diagram C.

a| Identify any similarities and differences in the way they work.

b| Suggest which still is better for getting the most pure water out of salty water. Explain your reasoning.

E | An inflatable solar still may be part of the emergency supplies on the life rafts of an ocean-going ship.

I can ...

- explain how distillation can be used to separate a solvent from a solution
- give examples of where distillation is used.

SAFE DRINKING WATER

7Ee

CAN WE MAKE SAFE DRINKING WATER FOR EVERYONE?

One in eight of the world's population do not have a water supply that is free from harmful substances and disease-causing microorganisms. Climate change and increases in the number of people may make safe water supplies more difficult to access for everyone.

A | Disasters, such as flooding and earthquakes, damage water and waste pipes. Rising sea levels caused by climate change will make flooding much more common in many places.

B | In low-income countries, an average of 5 million people each month move into cities to find work. Many live in slum areas where there is no safe drinking water.

C | The filtering system in the LIFESAVER® jerrycan removes dirt and disease-causing microorganisms, and leaves water safe to drink. A smaller bottle system is ideal for emergency situations.

1 Suggest why safe drinking water could become more of a problem in more countries in the future?

2 The LIFESAVER® system uses a range of filters to clean the water.

a| Describe how the filters clean the water.

b| One of the filters in the system has extremely small holes. Suggest what this filter removes from the water to make it safe to drink. Explain your reasoning.

c| One of the filters contains a substance that can remove dissolved solids. Explain why this is needed.

3 List the different ways in which safe drinking water can be made. Briefly explain how each one works and describe where it might be most useful. Explain your answers.

HAVE YOUR SAY

Can we make sure there is safe water for everyone?

CHEMISTRY IN THE HOME

Chemical substances are all around us in our homes. In a kitchen, the cleaning products, containers, and the pots and pans we use to cook are all made using chemistry. Even a lot of your food and drink will be made using chemical processes.

Many chemical substances can be dangerous and need to be handled with care. Information to help us use substances carefully is found on their containers. You should use this information to make sure you know how a substance can cause harm and how to stop this from happening (e.g. by wearing gloves).

child lock

A | Many substances in your home can be dangerous, particularly to young children, and should be kept in places that young children cannot reach. Nearly 4000 children die each year in Europe due to substances found at home.

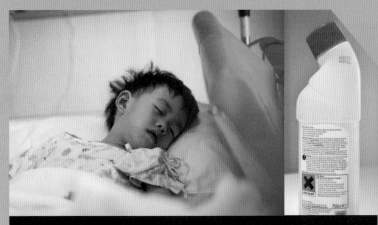

B | Bleach is useful because it kills microorganisms that can make us ill. It is also harmful if used wrongly, such as by drinking it or spilling it on your **skin.**

If a large amount of a dangerous substance is spilt, it could cause harm to a lot of people. Firefighters receive special training in how to deal with spills of dangerous substances.

1. Write down the names of two solids and one gas that dissolve in water.

2. State two ways in which children might have an accident with bleach.

3. Suggest two ways to reduce the risk of children being hurt by bleach.

4. a| Why is it useful to have information on the sides of containers about what they contain?

   b| Even with this information, why must people keep cleaning products out of reach of young children?

C | Firefighters wear protective clothing and gas masks to protect them from the dangers of spilt chemicals as they clear up this spill. The label on the side of the drum shows what the substance is and how to deal with it.

7Fa HAZARDS

HOW DO WE DEAL WITH HAZARDOUS SUBSTANCES?

Something that can cause harm is a **hazard**. The type of harm that can be caused is often shown using a hazard symbol.

Acids and **alkalis** are common substances found in homes and laboratories. They can be **corrosive**. This means they can attack certain materials like **metals**, stonework and skin. Great care must be taken when handling corrosive substances as they can destroy living **tissue** and cause permanent damage.

corrosive hazard symbol

A | The sulfuric acid in car batteries is diluted but still corrosive.

B | Drain cleaner is a corrosive alkali. It contains sodium hydroxide.

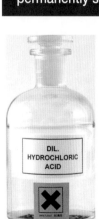

C | If you spill acid on you, your skin may be permanently scarred.

Acids and alkalis used in the laboratory are often **diluted** with water to make them less dangerous. Although not corrosive, dilute acids used in the laboratory can be **irritants**. These solutions are unlikely to cause serious injury but can cause skin inflammation and soreness. The vinegar we use on our food contains about 5–8 per cent ethanoic acid in water. It is not a hazard but stings if you get it in a cut. Above 10 per cent, ethanoic acid is an irritant and above 25 per cent it is corrosive. A solution of 5–10 per cent ammonia in water (a common household cleaner) is an irritant. Above 10% ammonia solution is corrosive.

D | Concentrated hydrochloric acid is corrosive. Dilute hydrochloric acid can be an irritant.

1 a| How can an acid be diluted?
   b| Explain whether car battery acid is a pure substance or a mixture.

2 Name an acid used in the laboratory and one used in everyday life.

3 a| Name two substances that will be attacked by a corrosive acid.
   b| Name one substance that is not attacked by a corrosive acid.

4 How are corrosive and irritant substances different?

We like the sour taste of acids and so they are often found in foods and drinks. Many sour-tasting fruits (such as lemons) contain a lot of citric acid. All fizzy drinks are also acidic. In general these acids will not cause damage and so do not carry a hazard symbol. However, these types of food and drink may help cause tooth decay.

Table F shows internationally agreed symbols that warn of different hazards. All countries are being encouraged to use these.

E | Many drinks contain natural and artificial acids.

FACT

Chemists from around the world work at the International Union of Pure and Applied Chemistry (IUPAC). One of this organisation's jobs is to give chemical substances names that are agreed internationally. However, some acids and alkalis are still often called by their old names, such as acetic acid (ethanoic acid), caustic soda (sodium hydroxide) and aqua fortis (nitric acid).

International hazard symbol	Hazard description
	Dangerous to the environment: This can cause long-term damage to animal and plant life.
	Toxic: This is poisonous and can cause death if swallowed, breathed in or absorbed through the skin.
	Corrosive: This attacks certain substances like metals, stonework and skin.
	Explosive: Heating may cause an explosion.
	Flammable: These substances catch fire easily.
	Caution: Although similar to toxic and corrosive this is a less serious hazard, e.g. may cause skin irritation.

F | international hazard symbols

5 How do acids in food and drink taste?

6 a| Name an acid found in fizzy drinks.
   b| Why do acidic foods not carry hazard symbols?

7 Which international hazard symbols will be displayed on the following household chemicals:
   a| turpentine – damages pond life, causes headaches and sickness, can catch fire if heated
   b| soap powder – causes irritation to the skin?

8 Phosphoric acid is delivered to a drinks factory in concentrated form. Why do you think the acid is not diluted before transporting it?

I can ...

- recognise some common hazard symbols
- explain why hazard symbols are necessary
- recognise some common acids.

CONTROLLING
7Fa RISK

HOW CAN WE REDUCE RISKS WHEN CARRYING OUT EXPERIMENTS?

A hazard is anything that could cause harm. A **risk** is the chance a hazard will cause harm.
By using chemicals carefully and protecting yourself and others, you can reduce the risk of harm.
For example, there is always a great risk of splashing when heating an acid. Wearing eye protection
and protective gloves is a sensible **precaution** for reducing the risk of damage to eyes and skin.

A | potential hazards in a school laboratory

---

1 Copy and complete the table below. Name six more potential hazards shown in cartoon A. Also describe the risks and the precautions that could be taken to reduce them.

B

Hazard	Risk is increased because ...	Precaution to reduce risk
Corrosive acid	bottle is at edge of bench and could be knocked over and harm students.	Remove bottle of corrosive acid from bench and store safely.
Fumes from chemicals	fumes could cause damage to student's nose and lungs when inhaled deeply.	Smell by slowly waving a hand over the flask to carefully move some vapour towards nose.

Planning for hazards and risks

Here is a set of instructions for a teacher to demonstrate what happens when sulfuric acid is added to sugar. For the experiment, concentrated sulfuric acid is used. 'Concentrated' means that it has very little or no water added to it.

Method

Warning: This method is for teacher demonstration only. Wear eye protection or a face shield, use a fume cupboard and wear chemical-resistant gloves.

A | Place a 100 cm³ beaker on a white tile inside a fume cupboard. Add 50 g of table sugar to the beaker.

B | Add concentrated sulfuric acid to just saturate the sugar, and no more.

C | Observe what happens. Beware that sulfur dioxide and carbon monoxide gases are formed. Do NOT touch the carbon that forms.

D | Allow the beaker to cool for at least 20 minutes in the fume cupboard (the beaker will reach temperatures of over 100 °C).

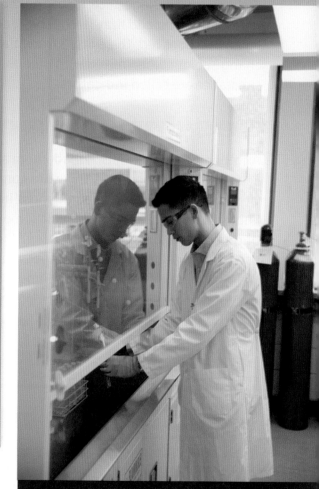

C | Common ways of reducing the risks of harm when using chemical substances include gloves, eye protection, wearing a lab coat and using a fume cupboard.

2
a| What corrosive substance is used in this experiment?
b| What does corrosive mean?
c| How do you know that substances such as this are corrosive?
d| Suggest a way of reducing the risk of harm from this substance.

3
a| What is the hazard in step C of the Method?
b| What safety instructions in the Method reduce the risk from this hazard?

4
a| What is the hazard in step D?
b| What safety instructions in the Method reduce the risk from this hazard?

I can ...

- plan and explain safety precautions
- recognise hazards and explain how the risks can be controlled.

7Fb INDICATORS

HOW CAN WE USE INDICATORS TO CLASSIFY SOLUTIONS?

Red cabbage can be stored in vinegar. The juice from the 'pickled' cabbage is red. If you mix soap with the red cabbage juice, it changes colour and goes blue. If you add fizzy lemonade, it changes again and goes red. The colours from plants that change colour when mixed with different types of substance are called **indicators**.

Testing for acids

Another indicator, litmus, is made from a type of lichen (shown in photo C). The word comes from 'lit-moss', which meant 'coloured moss' in medieval English. Litmus can be red, blue or sometimes purple (blue and red mixed together). It can be used as a solution or as litmus paper. Most acids, like vinegar and fruit juices, turn litmus red.

A | Different substances have been dropped into red cabbage indicator.

1 Name two organisms that can be used as indicators.

2 What colour is car battery acid mixed with:
a| red cabbage juice   b| litmus?

Testing for alkalis

In ancient Arabia, people took ashes from fires and mixed them with water. This liquid was boiled with animal fats to make the first soap. In Arabic, the ashes were called *al quali*. We use the word alkali to describe a group of substances that feel soapy. However, many alkalis are corrosive and are too dangerous to feel. This is because they attack the natural oils in your skin. Your skin can start to turn into soap!

Alkalis turn litmus indicator blue. Alkalis can be irritants, harmful or corrosive, just like acids, and in some ways they are more dangerous, especially if you get them in your eyes.

3 A few drops of litmus solution are added to some toothpaste. The litmus turns blue. What does this tell you about the toothpaste?

4 Mayuree has made some red cabbage indicator by crushing up red cabbage leaves with a mixture of water and ethanol. She now needs to separate the juice from the leaves. How could she do this? Draw a diagram to explain how your method works.

B | Ashes from the fire contain alkalis

Oven cleaners often contain alkalis. The grease in the oven is attacked by the cleaner and the grease turns into soap. This helps the cleaning process.

Many solutions are neither acidic nor alkaline. Examples include **pure** water, salt and sugar solutions. These are **neutral**. Neutral solutions do not change the colour of indicators. However, being neutral does not mean that a substance is safe. Some neutral solutions are **toxic**, and some are corrosive (but in a different way from acids and alkalis).

C | the lichen from which litmus indicator is made

D | Many household cleaners are alkaline.

E | some common indicators and their colours with acids and alkalis

Indicator	Colour with acidic solutions	Colour with alkaline solutions
litmus	red	blue
methyl orange	red	yellow
phenolphthalein	colourless	pink

Other indicators include phenolphthalein (*feen-ol-***fthay-leen**) and methyl orange. Their colour changes are shown in table E.

5 State whether these substances are acidic, alkaline or neutral.
   a| vinegar   b| water   c| salt solution
   d| lemon juice   e| sugar solution   f| soap

6 Which substance(s) in question 5 will turn phenolphthalein pink?

7 a| What colour would methyl orange turn with:
      i| grapefruit juice   ii| oven cleaner?
   b| Will the colour of methyl orange change if pure water is added to it? Explain your answer.

8 Litmus paper has litmus indicator soaked into it. It comes in two forms, red and blue. Copy and complete table G.

Substance added	colour of red litmus	colour of blue litmus
lemon juice		
ammonia solution		
pure water		

G

FACT

F

Lake Van, the largest lake in Turkey, is so alkaline that the water naturally forms a lather and you can wash clothes in it without using detergent.

I can ...

- name examples of indicators made from plants
- describe how indicators can be used to test for acidic, alkaline or neutral solutions.

7Fc ACIDITY AND ALKALINITY

HOW CAN WE MEASURE HOW ACIDIC OR ALKALINE A SOLUTION IS?

An indicator like litmus can show us whether something is an acid or an alkali. However, it cannot tell us how much acidity or alkalinity there is. A Danish chemist, called Søren Peder Sørensen (1868–1939), solved this problem. In 1909, he invented the **pH scale** as a way of measuring how acidic a solution was. This scale measures acidity and alkalinity in numbers, which is more precise than describing it in words.

The main pH scale runs from 0 to 14. Substances with a pH of 7 are neutral, while acids have a pH lower than 7 and alkalis have a pH above 7. The lower the pH the more acidic the solution and the higher the pH the more alkaline the solution.

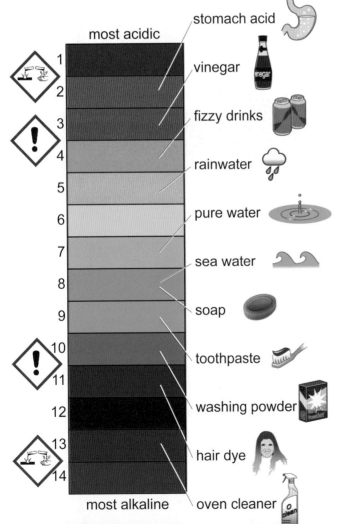

most acidic

1
2 — stomach acid
3 — vinegar
4 — fizzy drinks
5 — rainwater
6 — pure water
7 — sea water
8
9 — soap
10 — toothpaste
11
12 — washing powder
13 — hair dye
14 — oven cleaner

most alkaline

B | using the pH scale

A | The pH of a solution is often measured using a meter or test papers. The pH is written with a small p and a capital H (which stands for hydrogen).

We can use a **universal indicator** to measure pH. This is a mixture of indicators that gives a range of colours depending on the pH of the solution. The precise colours depend on the indicators in the mix but most brands show red, orange, yellow, green, blue and purple. Using a pH meter like the one in photo A is a more accurate way of measuring pH. However, universal indicator, as paper or solution, is often a quicker and simpler way of estimating pH.

Being able to measure the pH of solutions is important in many industries. Measuring the pH is also important in the environment, where we need to keep a check on rain and water quality. The pH of water is checked regularly to make sure it falls within safe limits. This is particularly important near factories that produce acidic waste. The pollution from them can cause **acid rain** and harm wildlife and waterways.

C | The testing of chlorine and pH levels in a swimming pool is important.

1 a| What is the pH of a substance that turns universal indicator orange?

b| Would it be an acid or an alkali?

c| Would the substance be very acidic or alkaline or not very acidic or alkaline?

2 Copy and complete table D.

D Name of chemical	Colour of universal indicator	Acidic, alkaline or neutral	pH
hydrochloric acid		very acidic	
			7
sodium hydroxide	purple		
carbon dioxide solution		not very acidic	

Swimming pools need to be kept at about pH 7.4. This pH matches the pH of the liquids in your eyes. If the swimming pool water becomes too acidic, it hurts your eyes. If the water becomes too alkaline, the chlorine does not kill microorganisms very well.

3 Estimate the pH of the following items.

a| stomach acid   b| toothpaste

c| fizzy drinks   d| soap

4 Look at chart B. Describe the link between the pH number and the hazard rating of the substances. Give as much detail as you can.

5 If you added some washing powder to sea water, would the pH go up, down or stay the same? Explain your answer.

6 A sample of river water taken near to a factory shows a pH of 5.

a| Do you think this represents a pollution problem? Give reasons for your answer.

b| What other evidence might you need to consider before reaching a conclusion?

7 Describe one way in which the man in photo E is reducing the risk of harm. Mention one hazard in your answer.

E | An alkali is needed to help dyes stick to some fabrics, such as cotton.

I can ...

- name some common examples of acids and alkalis
- describe the pH scale and how it is useful
- describe how pH can be measured.

7Fd NEUTRALISATION

WHAT HAPPENS WHEN AN ACID IS ADDED TO AN ALKALI?

Farmers and gardeners test the pH of their soils so they know which types of plants will grow best. Table A shows the best pH for growth in some common crops.

A	Plant	Best pH range
	cabbage	5.6–6.6
	cauliflower	6.0–7.0
	onions	6.2–6.8
	leeks	5.0–6.0
	mushrooms	7.0–8.0
	potatoes	5.8–6.5

If a soil is too acidic then farmers can add an alkali called lime to their fields. The alkali cancels out the acids, making the soil more neutral. This is **neutralisation** and it happens when any alkali and acid are mixed together.

> **1** a| Which pH values indicate an acidic soil?
> b| Which pH values indicate an alkaline soil?
>
> **2** a| Which plants grow well in a neutral soil?
> b| Which crop is least likely to need lime in the soil?

Neutralisation can be carried out in the laboratory as shown in steps 1–5 in photo D. The pH is measured using universal indicator. If the alkali (sodium hydroxide solution) is added carefully to the hydrochloric acid in flask X, you can find the precise amount of acid and alkali needed to obtain a neutral solution.

The solution is **neutral** in step 4. As more alkali is added, the solution becomes alkaline (shown in step 5).

> **3** a| Does flask X contain acid or alkali?
> b| How can you tell?
>
> **4** a| What does the precise colour in flask X tell you?
> b| What is the approximate pH of the solution in step 5?

B | testing the pH of soil

C | Lime is used to cure an acid soil.

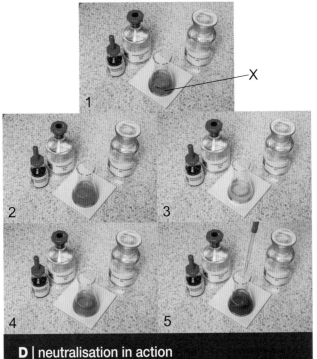

D | neutralisation in action

The neutralisation of an acid and an alkali forms new substances and is an example of a **chemical reaction**. If the neutralisation of hydrochloric acid and sodium hydroxide is repeated without the indicator, a clear solution is produced.

If we evaporate the solution, we are left with a white solid, which is sodium chloride (common salt). The other new substance produced in the reaction is water.

The chemical reaction can be written as:

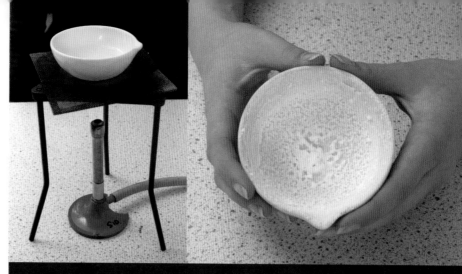

E | Sodium chloride solution is formed in a neutralisation reaction.

hydrochloric acid + sodium hydroxide → sodium chloride + water

This is called a **word equation**. Word equations are used to model (describe) chemical reactions. The **convention** (set of rules) for writing word equations is:

- the starting substances, the **reactants**, are written on the left
- then there is an arrow, pointing to the new substances formed
- the new substances, the **products**, are written on the right.

The general word equation for the reaction of acids with alkalis is:

acid + alkali → salt + water

Neutralisation produces substances called **salts**. Different acids and alkalis produce different salts. Hydrochloric acid produces chloride salts, sulfuric acid produces sulfate salts and nitric acid produces nitrate salts. Lithium chloride, sodium sulfate and potassium nitrate are all examples of salts produced by neutralisation. Only **sodium chloride** is called common salt (or table salt).

F | Ammonium nitrate fertiliser is a salt made in factories using ammonium hydroxide and nitric acid.

---

5 a| What pH is neutral?

b| How can you tell when just enough alkali has been added for neutralisation?

6 From the word equation for the reaction between hydrochloric acid and sodium hydroxide, select substances that are:

a| alkaline b| acidic c| neutral d| reactants e| products.

7 Copy and complete these word equations:

a| lithium hydroxide + hydrochloric acid → _____ + _____

b| _____ + sulfuric acid → sodium sulfate + _____

8 Which acid and alkali would react to produce ammonium sulfate?

9 Suggest how you could make spilled concentrated acid safe to be mopped up.

I can ...

- describe what happens during neutralisation
- write word equations for neutralisation reactions
- explain the pH changes taking place during neutralisation.

31

THE CHEMICAL INDUSTRY

WHAT SKILLS DO CHEMISTS IN THE CHEMICAL INDUSTRY NEED?

Many different types of chemist work in the chemical industry. They help to improve our lives by developing new materials, paints, dyes, medicines, cleaning products and even some foods.

> **1** a | What does the chemical industry do?
> b | Name four products of the chemical industry.
> c | Name two types of cleaning product.

Research chemists develop new products. They have to be inventive. First, they identify a 'need'. This may be a product that people want or one that will be useful. They then plan a way to develop that product.

For example, bleach has been used for many years to remove stains and as a disinfectant. Unfortunately, many bleaches can harm humans and our environment. So, research chemists are trying to develop new types of bleach. When trying to invent something like this, they first look at ways in which they could change the existing product. If this does not work, then they look at ways of creating a new product that does the same job.

A | Research and development chemists work together on discovering new products.

> **2** Many paint removers release fumes, which can be harmful. A team of research chemists are looking at developing a paint remover that releases less fumes.
> a | What need have the chemists identified?
> b | Suggest what they should try to do first.
> c | Explain why you think the chemists should do this first.

Quality control

Quality control technicians monitor the production of a new bleach. These scientists check a product after it has been made. They test and analyse it to make sure it contains the exact combination of substances it is meant to. If this job is not done, a new product may not work properly or it may cause harm and be dangerous to use.

Quality control technicians plan experiments to test new products and analyse the data from those tests. They have to collect and record data carefully. They have to know how often to repeat their experiments, to obtain reliable results (results that they can be sure are correct).

B | A quality control technician tests samples of the product. The more samples tested, the greater the reliability of the results.

3 Why do quality control technicians:

a | test the bleach produced in a factory

b | analyse more than one sample of the bleach?

4 A factory produces a bleach. Some of its quality control analysis is shown in table C.

a | What colour would universal indicator turn in a sample of bleach?

b | Which shift produced a non-standard bleach at one point? Explain your answer.

c | Which shift was having problems with how often they were taking samples?

Morning shift samples		Day shift samples		Evening shift samples	
Time taken	pH of bleach	Time taken	pH of bleach	Time taken	pH of bleach
01.15	10.3	08.30	10.2	16.30	10.2
02.10	10.0	10.00	10.2	18.00	8.1
04.50	10.0	12.10	10.0	20.15	10.3
05.20	10.2	14.05	9.9	22.00	9.9

C

5 A quality control technician is given four samples of sea water and asked to find the amount of salt in 100 cm³ of each of the samples. List the apparatus needed to carry out this analysis.

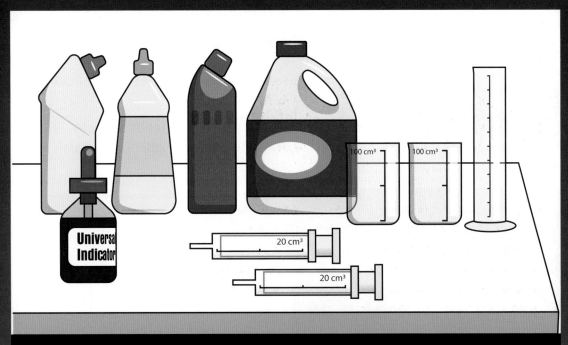

D | apparatus to investigate the amount of alkali in samples of bleach

PRACTICAL

Describe how you could use the apparatus shown to investigate the amount of alkali in the different samples of bleach. (*Hint*: Look at the previous page.)

Your teacher may choose to test your plan by demonstrating this investigation.

7Fe NEUTRALISATION IN DAILY LIFE

HOW CAN WE MAKE USE OF NEUTRALISATION?

An alkali can be described as a **soluble base**. A base is any substance, soluble or **insoluble**, that neutralises an acid forming a salt and water. Metal oxides and metal hydroxides are common examples of bases.

acid + base → salt + water

Acids, alkalis and bases are common substances and many neutralisation reactions occur in nature and our homes. It is important we understand these reactions so we can use these substances properly.

The hydrochloric acid in your stomach has a pH of 1 or 2. If you produce too much acid, you may get indigestion or heartburn. Some indigestion treatments, such as Milk of Magnesia, are **antacids**. An antacid contains bases, such as magnesium hydroxide, to neutralise some of the acid and help keep the balance right. For example:

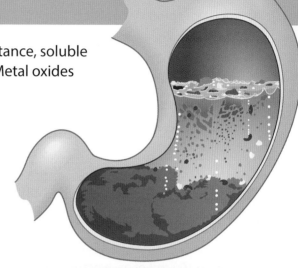

A | Stomach acid helps to break down your food.

magnesium hydroxide + hydrochloric acid → magnesium chloride + water

Indigestion treatments are not very alkaline (usually about pH 9) so that they do not lessen the acidity in your stomach too much.

The food you eat causes acid to be produced in your mouth. These can cause your teeth to decay. Toothpastes often contain bases such as magnesium hydroxide and calcium hydroxide. These bases react with the acids in your mouth to reduce acidity.

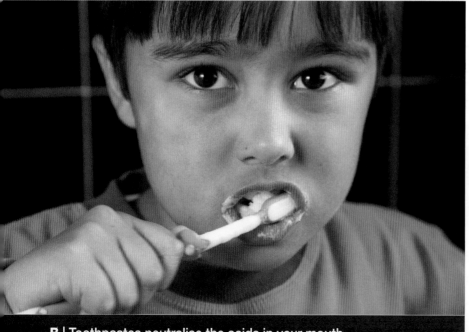

B | Toothpastes neutralise the acids in your mouth.

1   a| What kind of substance is Milk of Magnesia?
    b| What might be its pH?

2   What do you call the reaction between magnesium hydroxide and hydrochloric acid?

3   Why is it not a good idea to use sodium hydroxide, with a pH of 13, to neutralise excess stomach acid?

4   Explain why toothpaste might contain magnesium hydroxide.

5   Some toothpastes contain aluminium hydroxide. Write a word equation for this base reacting with hydrochloric acid.

An old treatment for bee stings was supposed to work by neutralisation. When a bee strings you, it injects an acidic venom (pH 5.0–5.5). Applying a base, such as baking soda, to the sting was supposed to reduce the pain by causing a neutralisation reaction. However, it is the actual substances in the bee venom that cause the pain and not its pH.

FACT

A bee sting is known to contain acids like methanoic acid and even a single sting can be very painful. It is also estimated that 1100 stings from a honey bee could be fatal. However, it is not really the acids that cause the problem but a combination of some of the 60 other nasty substances in the sting that cause the pain.

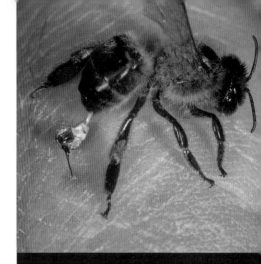

C | The sting of some bees stays in their victim and the bee dies.

Acid can be used to clean **metals**. Objects made of iron and steel can form rust (iron oxide) on them. Sulfuric acid can attack the rust and remove it from the surface via a neutralisation reaction. For example:

sulfuric acid + iron oxide → iron sulfate + water

Acidic waste **gases** from some industries are neutralised by sprays of calcium hydroxide before they are released into the atmosphere. This reduces the possibility of creating harmful **acid rain**.

D | using acid to clean off rust

E | Power stations that burn coal can release sulfuric acid as a waste gas.

6 An old treatment for wasp stings was 'to neutralise the venom with vinegar'. Wasp venom has a pH of 6.8–6.9. Explain why this remedy will not neutralise wasp venom.

7 Why is the man in photo D wearing gloves?

8 Write a word equation for the reaction between calcium hydroxide and the acid gas released by power stations.

9 Indigestion tablets reduce acidity in the stomach. Write down the steps for an experiment to find out which indigestion tablets work best.

I can ...

- describe some examples of everyday acids and bases
- describe and explain some everyday neutralisation reactions

7Fe DANGER AT HOME

HOW DANGEROUS ARE CHEMICALS IN THE HOME?

(i) (ii) CORROSIVE (iii) DANGEROUS FOR THE ENVIRONMENT (iv) HARMFUL

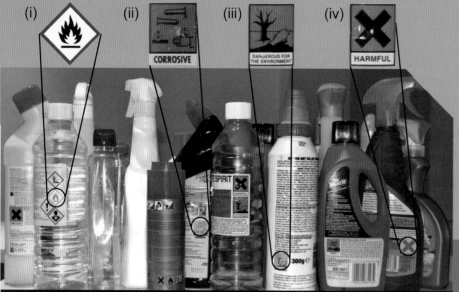

A | Hazard symbols around the world are all being changed to the newer international symbols, which have a diamond shape.

In most houses you will find a range of chemicals with a variety of uses. We buy specialist chemicals for decorating, cleaning, car maintenance, gardening and more. Often we use them just once and store what is left for another day. The problem is that many of these chemicals present particular hazards. We need to understand some of the science behind these chemicals so we can use and store them safely.

1 Describe the dangers represented by the four hazard symbols, i to iv in photo A.

2 Name a household chemical that could be:
a| an acid   b| an alkali
c| flammable   d| corrosive.

3 a| Describe how you could test a household chemical to find out its pH.
b| What do the pH numbers tell you about a chemical?

4 Look at photo B. Two of the chemicals Joseph mixed, before they got hot, were sodium hydroxide (drain cleaner) and sulfuric acid (rust remover).
a| What was the sign that a chemical reaction had taken place?
b| What do you call the type of reaction that occurs between these two chemicals?
c| Write a word equation for the reaction that occurs.

5 Use the information in this unit to design a safety information leaflet for parents on the dangers of household chemicals.

B | This is Joseph, aged eight. He does not know much about chemicals but he has decided to mix some together. Suddenly the glass gets very hot and he drops it. The glass breaks and the chemicals splash across the worktop. Luckily, no damage is done and an adult clears away the mess safely.

HAVE YOUR SAY

A council proposes to ban all household chemicals with a pH higher than 10. Discuss what you think of this statement, listing the advantages and disadvantages of such a ban.

36

7Ga SORTING RUBBISH

Every year we use more of the world's **resources** to make goods that we throw away. On average each person in Europe causes the production of 5 tonnes of waste, each year. This includes the waste from the industries that make the things we use. Over half of that rubbish ends up in landfill sites.

We need to recycle more of our waste, to save resources and **energy**.

B | The mark tells us the type of plastic (polypropylene). Symbols like this help us to sort rubbish and make recycling easier.

A | aerial view of a landfill site in the state of Veracruz, Mexico

Like all matter, waste comes in different states that have different **properties**. **Solids** are easiest to dispose of in landfill sites, as they stay in one place. **Liquids** are more difficult, as they flow and can leak away. **Gases** are the most difficult, as they can spread out in all directions.

1 a| What are the three states of matter?

b| Divide the following materials into three groups depending on their state:

carbon dioxide, cardboard, clothing, cooking oil, copper scrap, food scraps, glass bottles, heated air, methane, milk, paint, petrol, plastic containers, scrap wood.

2 Some <u>soluble</u> solids cause problems in landfill sites as they <u>dissolve</u> in rainwater.

a| Explain the meaning of each underlined word in the sentence above.

b| Describe how a soluble fertiliser dumped in a landfill site can get into our water supply.

3 How do you think the amount of rubbish produced in the area where you live is likely to change in the future? Explain your answer.

C | Sorting rubbish into groups makes it easier to recycle.

7Ga SOLIDS, LIQUIDS AND GASES

HOW ARE SOLIDS, LIQUIDS AND GASES DIFFERENT?

The different properties of waste materials have to be considered when recycling or disposing of the waste. **Corrosive**, **flammable** and **toxic** materials present particular **hazards** and have to be handled carefully.

Waste materials exist in all three **states of matter** (solids, liquids and gases) and have different properties. Therefore they have to be handled differently, during recycling and disposal.

Solids

In general, solids do not **flow** or change their shape. Solids stay in one place, unless they are pushed or pulled.

As most of it is solid, most waste going to landfill sites stays where it is put. Solid waste, such as **metals**, paper and plastic, is often easy to transport in open lorries.

The **volume** of an object is the amount of space that it takes up. It can be measured in **cubic centimetres (cm³)**. The volume of a solid does not change much and so, even when squeezed, solids cannot easily be **compressed** (squashed into a smaller volume).

> **1** Describe the properties of a solid.
>
> **2** What property allows solid waste to be left in piles at landfill sites?

Liquids

Liquids can change their shape and flow. So liquids take the shape of their container. However, liquids do not change their volumes and they cannot be easily compressed.

As they are able to flow, liquid wastes can be pumped along pipelines. It would be very difficult to transport liquids in an open truck like the one in photo B. The liquid would slosh about as it was moved and could spill.

A | Symbols warn of hazardous substances.

B | scrap metal being transported for recycling

C | Waste cooking oil can be converted to biodiesel.

FACT

Waste cooking oil from restaurants can be converted to biodiesel. In the Europe all diesel contains 5–10 per cent of biodiesel.

Gases

Gases can change their shape and their volume. They can spread out in all directions and they can also be easily compressed into a smaller volume. The gas cylinders in photo D can contain a lot of gas that has been squeezed into them under **pressure**. They are stored away from other areas in the recycling plant as there could still be gases in the cylinders that are flammable and could cause an explosion or major fire.

D | Gases can be compressed into a small volume.

> **3** Draw a table to show the differences between solids, liquids and gases. Use these headings: Keeps its shape, Keeps its volume, Able to flow, Able to be compressed.
>
> **4** Look at photos B and C. Why do solid and liquid wastes need to be transported in different ways?

Many waste gases are released directly into the atmosphere where they can cause harm to the **environment**. Factories and power stations that burn **fossil fuels** produce large amounts of acidic gases.

It is not always easy to identify the state of a substance using its properties. For example, sand is a solid but it flows like a liquid as it is made up of small pieces.

> **5** A cuboid block of wood measures 4 cm high by 5 cm deep by 10 cm long. What is its volume, in cubic centimetres (cm³)?
>
> **6** Look at photo F. How can a sponge be described as a solid if it can be squashed like this?

E | waste gases released into the atmosphere

Density

Density is the mass of a certain volume of material. It is measured in units such as kilograms per cubic metre (kg/m³) or grams per cubic centimetre (g/cm³). Iron has a density of 7.9 g/cm³. This means that 1 cm³ of iron has a mass of 7.9 g.

Iron is denser than water, which has a density of 1 g/cm³. 1 cm³ of iron is much heavier than 1 cm³ of water. In general, solids are denser than liquids and liquids are denser than gases. The density of gases can be changed by squashing them.

F | Some objects are difficult to categorise as solids, liquids or gases.

> **7** Put these materials in order of their density. Start with the least dense: gold, carbon dioxide gas, water.
>
> **8** What is the mass of 5 cm³ of:
>
> a| water   b| iron?

I can ...

- describe and compare the properties of the three states of matter
- state what is meant by density, and recall its units.

7Gb HYPOTHESES AND THEORIES

HOW DO SCIENTISTS THINK AND WORK?

Many people notice that different items are placed in different areas of a household waste recycling centre because they have different properties. However, a scientist will also ask *why* certain items have certain properties.

> **1** Look at photo A. Write down two observations about liquids.

Scientists usually answer their questions using the **scientific method**. This may involve a scientist thinking up an idea about how or why something happens. This idea is called a **hypothesis**. The hypothesis can then be used to make a **prediction** about what will happen in an experiment. Sometimes scientists may also use an existing hypothesis to make a prediction. An example of how scientists use hypotheses and predictions is shown in cartoon B. The phrase 'depends on' is often used when writing a hypothesis while a prediction can be formed around the phrase, 'if … then …'.

A | How can we explain how liquids change shape?

B | scientific method

Salty water takes longer to boil than tap water.

Observation

The boiling point of water *depends* on the mass of salt added.

Hypothesis

Let's test it.

Experiment

If I add more salt to the same volume of water, *then* the boiling point will increase.

Prediction

After the experiment has been carried out, the **results** can be analysed. If the **data** matches the prediction, this is **evidence** that the hypothesis is correct. We say that the data supports the hypothesis.

Theories

When all the data from many experiments supports a hypothesis, the hypothesis becomes a theory. A **theory** is a hypothesis or a group of hypotheses with lots of supporting evidence.

However, as more data is collected, a theory may not be strengthened. Some evidence may be found that does not support the theory, and the theory may need to be changed or even scrapped altogether.

2 Look at cartoon C.

a| What observation is the person trying to explain?

b| What is her hypothesis to explain the observation?

c| How well does her idea explain the observation?

A good theory is one that:

- has been tested;
- allows us to make predictions and
- explains **observations**.

A theory may be formed from the work of different scientists and may contain many hypotheses.

C

Observation: If you heat ice, it disappears and water runs away from it.

Idea: Ice is made of lots of little boxes with water in them. The heat breaks open the boxes, so the water can run out.

3 What is the difference between a hypothesis and a theory?

4 Draw a flow chart to outline the different stages in the scientific method.

Explaining the observations of the different properties of solids, liquids and gases is one of the most important theories in science. Our modern theory about the states of matter combines many hypotheses from many observations, such as those in photos D–G.

5 What observation is made about photo D?

6 Write down a scientific question about the observation in photo E.

7 Write down an observation and a scientific question for each of the photos F and G.

D | It is easy to compress a gas.

E | As you dilute an orange drink the colour and the flavour get weaker.

F

G

I can ...

- identify scientific questions, hypotheses and predictions
- describe how evidence is used to develop a hypothesis into a theory.

7Gb PARTICLES

WHAT IS THE PARTICLE THEORY OF MATTER?

Scientists have developed a theory to explain the different properties of solids, liquids and gases. This theory has been improved over many years using scientific methods of investigation. It is called the **particle theory** or **particle model** of matter.

The particle theory states that:

- all matter is made up of tiny **particles**
- the particles are moving all the time
- there are **forces** of attraction holding the particles together
- the forces vary in strength in the different states of matter.

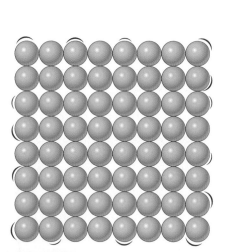

A | solid

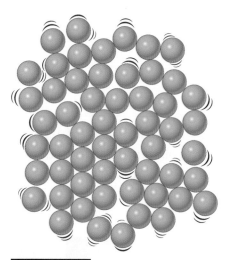

B | liquid

C | gas

In solids the particles are held closely together, by strong forces of attraction. The particles cannot move over each other, but **vibrate** (wobble) back and forth.

The particles in liquids are also held closely together by fairly strong forces of attraction. However, the particles in liquids can move past each other.

The particles in a gas are far apart from each other. The forces of attraction between the particles are weak, so gas particles are free to move about in all directions.

1. What is all matter made up of?

2. What determines whether something is a solid, a liquid or a gas?

3. Solids have fixed volumes and shapes. How could you describe liquids and gases in terms of their volumes and shapes?

FACT

At room temperature the particles in air are moving in all directions at a speed of about 500 m/s. That is faster than a jet aeroplane.

Using the theory

Solids have a fixed shape as the particles are held closely together by strong forces of attraction. The position of the particles cannot change so the shape stays the same unless a force is applied. The particles are very close together and so solids cannot be **compressed** (squashed into a smaller volume).

> **4** Most solids, like plastics, can change shape when heated. What do you think heating does to the particles?

Liquids can change their shape because although the particles are close together they can move over each other. This allows the liquid to flow and so it takes the shape of the container. However, the particles are very close together and so liquids cannot be compressed. When **soluble** solids **dissolve** in liquids, the tiny solid particles are separated from one another and spread through the liquid. Since the **solute** particles are so spread out, you can then see through the **solution**.

Gases have no fixed shape or volume, as their particles are free to move in all directions. This allows gases to spread out and fill all the space in a container. However, gases are fairly easy to compress. Their particles are far apart, so they can be squeezed closer together, to reduce the total volume. If the volume of a gas is reduced, its density increases.

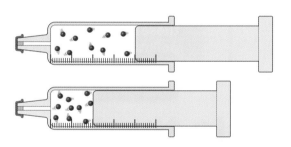

F | Gases can be compressed.

Rotting rubbish can involve all three states of matter, as solids break down in time forming different solids, liquids and gases. While the solid waste stays put, the liquids will slowly flow away, and any gases formed will escape into the air so they may be smelled some distance away.

D | Solids have a fixed shape.

E | Liquids can flow into different shapes.

G | Solids and liquids in rubbish behave differently.

> **5** How does the particle theory explain:
>
> a| why gases spread out to fill a container
>
> b| why sugar disappears when stirred into some water?
>
> **6** Describe how the particles move in solids, liquids and gases.
>
> **7** Explain, using particle theory, how liquids can leak slowly out of rubbish when left in landfill sites.

I can ...

- recognise that all matter is made up of particles
- describe, draw and recognise the arrangement of particles in solids, liquids and gases
- use the particle theory to explain the properties of the three states of matter.

7Gc BROWNIAN MOTION

WHAT EVIDENCE ALLOWED ALL SCIENTISTS TO ACCEPT THE PARTICLE MODEL?

Scientific theories are always changing. Through new experiments and observations, scientists can improve their ideas and explanations. Sometimes scientists even use the results of experiments from the past to further develop their ideas.

In 1827, the Scottish scientist Robert Brown (1773–1858) was using a microscope to study pollen grains in water. He observed that the pollen grains moved about randomly in different directions. He discussed his observations with other scientists but they could not think of an explanation for the movement, which came to be called **Brownian motion**.

Brownian motion has now been observed in many other situations. For example, it can be seen with specks of smoke in air and fine dust in liquids other than water.

If we were to watch one individual pollen grain or smoke speck, we would see it moving jerkily in different directions. Drawing C is a typical **trace** of the movement of a particle showing Brownian motion over a short time interval.

A | Artists and musicians use Brownian motion as a source of inspiration. This piece, by textile artist Barbara Nepom, is called *Brownian Motion*.

FACT

Understanding Brownian motion is important for many scientists, including those working on air pollution, paints and electronics.

1. Describe Brownian motion.

2. Why do you think Robert Brown talked to other scientists about his observations?

Explanation using particle theory

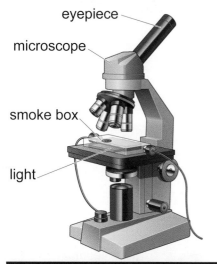

eyepiece

microscope

smoke box

light

B | observing Brownian motion within air with specks of smoke

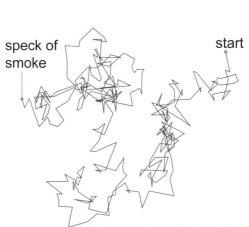

speck of smoke

start

C | the plotted smoke speck tracks, showing Brownian motion

Later scientists, including Albert Einstein (1879–1955), used the particle theory to explain Brownian motion. This added a lot of evidence in support of the particle model. The theory had not been accepted by all scientists up to that time.

The particle model says that air consists of tiny particles, moving about in all directions. Air particles therefore hit specks of smoke. If many particles hit one side of a smoke speck, they push the speck in that direction.

However, the air particles are moving about randomly and so the direction in which a smoke speck is pushed will change all the time. We therefore see Brownian motion as random movements.

The same thing happens with pollen grains in water, with moving water molecules hitting the grains. Einstein developed a hypothesis to explain this. He used his hypothesis to make a prediction about how far a pollen grain would be moved by water **molecules**. This was tested by J.B. Perrin (1870–1942). His data matched Einstein's prediction, which was further evidence in support of the particle theory.

The nanoscale

Although many pollen grains and smoke specks are too small to be seen without a microscope, they are more than 100 000 times larger than the particles in water or air. When dealing with such small particles, we use nanometres as the unit of measurement: 1 nanometre (nm) is 0.000 000 001 metres (m).

D | The moving air particles are constantly colliding with the speck of smoke, causing it to change direction.

speck of smoke

air particles

3 Write a letter to Robert Brown explaining Brownian motion. (Remember that he would not have our knowledge of particle theory, so you need to explain this carefully.)

4 How did the evidence from Brownian motion affect another scientific theory?

5 Explain why the moving particles of air do not push us about, like the specks of smoke.

6 How many nanometres are in a metre?

7 Diagram D is a model which can be used to explain how Brownian motion occurs. In what ways does the diagram represent Brownian motion:

a| well   b| poorly?

water particle
0.3 nm
(0.000 000 3 mm)

sugar particle
1 nm
(0.000 001 mm)

virus
65 nm
(0.000 065 mm)

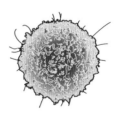

pollen grain
20 000 nm
(0.02 mm)

dot on paper
500 000 nm
(0.5 mm)

football
220 000 000 nm
22 cm (220 mm)

E | measuring on the 'nanoscale'

FACT

You can fit about 33 500 000 000 000 000 000 000 000 water particles in a 1 litre bottle.

I can ...

- explain how Brownian motion supports the particle model
- explain how scientific theories evolve
- convert between nanometres and metres.

7Gd DIFFUSION

WHY DO SOME THINGS SPREAD OUT?

A lot of waste ends up in landfill sites. These sites are expensive to run and use up valuable land. They are often ugly and sometimes smelly. Even if you cannot see the rubbish dump you know it is there by the smell!

When waste rots it naturally gives off gases (including smelly ones), which spread through the air even if there is no wind. This happens because the particles of the smelly gas are moving all the time. They move in all directions and mix in between the particles of air. Eventually, they spread out until they reach your nose – that is when we know they are there!

When particles of one substance spread out and mix with the particles of another, we call this **diffusion**. You smell a substance when some of the particles from the smelly substances are inside your nose. This happens because the particles of the smelly substances are moving and spreading about in all directions.

Diffusion is an important process inside our bodies. Diffusion allows particles of essential substances in our food to pass through the wall of the **small intestine** and into the blood. The blood then carries them around our bodies, where they diffuse into the **cells** of the body. Waste products are also removed by diffusion.

A | Some landfill sites are sprayed to lessen the smell.

FACT

B | sign banning durian fruit

No durians

No pets
No animals

Fine $500

Durian fruit is banned from most public places because of its disgusting smell, which may best be described as a mixture of rotten eggs, onions and gym socks.

1 a| What is diffusion?

   b| Give an example of diffusion in everyday life.

2 Describe what happens to the particles of smelly substances in rubbish that allows you to smell the rubbish from far away.

Diagram C shows diffusion. The brown gas and the clear gas mix together until the gases in both gas jars look the same. The particles of both gases are moving randomly in all directions, and so they eventually all mix up together. Notice that the particles of the brown gas gradually move from where there are a lot of them (high **concentration**) to where there are fewer of them (lower concentration). Diffusion always occurs in this direction (from higher concentration to lower concentration).

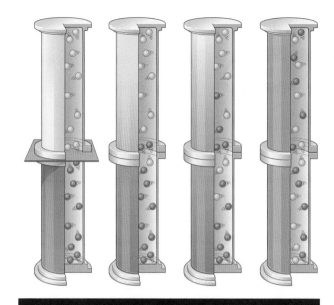

C | We can use the particle theory to model how diffusion occurs in a gas.

> **3** a| Explain how diffusion occurs in gases.
>
>   b| Describe the overall movement of the particles of the colourless gas in diagram C, in terms of concentration.
>
> **4** How could you measure the speed of diffusion in gases?

The particles in liquids are closer together and cannot move as freely as the particles in gases. As diffusion is caused by the movement of particles into the spaces between other particles, using these hypotheses you would predict that diffusion would be slower in liquids than in gases. Scientists have shown that this is what happens, which is more evidence to support the particle theory.

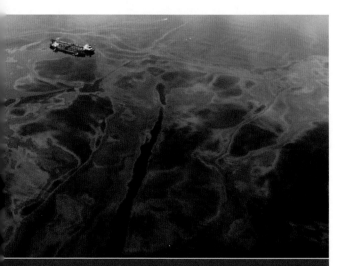

D | Liquid pollution can spread through still water by diffusion.

E | The coloured dye has diffused into the icing.

> **5** Use particle theory to explain how the liquid substances from the oil tanker in photo D will spread.
>
> **6** a| What state of matter is diffusing in photo E?
>
>   b| Would diffusion in solids be slower or quicker than in liquids? Explain your answer.
>
> **7** Explain how observations of diffusion help support the particle model.

I can ...

- state what is meant by diffusion and recall some of its effects
- use the particle model to explain diffusion in liquids and gases
- use the particle model to explain why diffusion is faster in some materials than in others.

7Ge AIR PRESSURE

WHAT IS AIR PRESSURE?

We are surrounded by air and its particles are hitting us all the time. **Air pressure** is just the force of these particles hitting a surface. We do not normally feel this pressure but it is always there and we can sometimes see its effects.

Air pressure is an example of **gas pressure** (a pressure caused by gases). Gas pressure inside a car tyre, pushing out, keeps the tyre inflated. The more particles that hit a certain area of a surface, the greater the gas pressure. Adding more air particles into a tyre will increase the gas pressure inside it. Squashing the tyre to make its volume smaller will also increase the gas pressure.

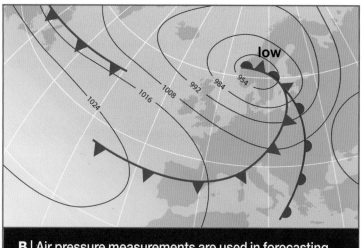

B | Air pressure measurements are used in forecasting weather. High air pressure usually produces more settled weather than low air pressure.

particles of air inside the tyre

tyre wall

particles of air hitting inside of tyre wall

particles of air outside the tyre

A | The gas pressure inside a car tyre is greater than outside the tyre because there are more particles hitting the inside of the tyre than the outside.

1 How can air produce a pressure?

2 Why does gas pressure increase when you pump up a tyre?

The vacuum pump in photo C can be used to remove the air from inside a metal can. A **vacuum** does not contain anything, not even air. When the air is removed, the can is pushed in by the air particles hitting the outside of the can.

The outside air pressure was always there, but before the pump was used there was also air inside the can. The inside gas pressure balanced the outside air pressure. With the air inside removed, the outside pressure is strong enough to crush the can. This is another example of how the particle theory can explain something we see happening.

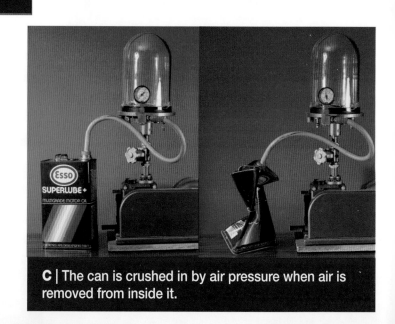

C | The can is crushed in by air pressure when air is removed from inside it.

A 1 litre bottle of most fizzy drinks contains nearly 3 litres of pressurised **carbon dioxide** gas. This gas pressure can sometimes cause these bottles to explode.

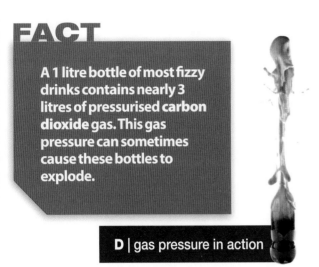

D | gas pressure in action

3. Use particle theory to explain:
   a| why a tyre gets bigger as you pump it up
   b| why a tyre gets smaller as you let the air out
   c| why the can is crushed in photo C.

4. In your own words, explain how air pressure helps you drink through a straw.

Many common observations can be explained using air pressure and particle theory. Sucking up liquids through a straw works because of air pressure. When you suck, you reduce the pressure inside the straw. So the air pressure outside the straw acting on the liquid is greater than the pressure inside the straw and the liquid is pushed up the straw.

All gases apply a pressure to the surfaces around them. Rotting waste in landfill sites produces the **flammable** gas methane. This can be dangerous in several ways. Gas particles move in all directions and so the methane can flow through a landfill site and collect in pockets. As more gas collects, the increasing pressure causes the pockets to expand. This can crack the surface of a landfill site. Sparks can cause the gas to explode. Therefore, it is important to get the methane out of landfill sites.

E | Air pressure helps you to suck drinks through a straw.

air pressure

5. Explain how methane can crack the surface of a landfill site.

6. Explain why the gas pressure inside a full can of spray deodorant is greater than the gas pressure inside a half-empty can.

7. Use diagram G and the particle theory to explain how a 'sucker' sticks to a smooth surface.

G | When a sucker is pressed onto a surface, some of the air is squeezed out from under it.

F | Chimneys are used to vent and burn methane at landfill sites.

I can ...

- say what is meant by gas pressure and recall some of its effects
- describe the cause of gas pressure using particle theory.

FORECASTING THE WEATHER

7Ge

HOW DO METEOROLOGISTS WORK?

Meteorologists are scientists who study the weather. They also make weather forecasts, which they need to communicate to others. Weather forecasts are important for many kinds of business, such as airlines, farms and shipping companies. Weather forecasts can help people to prepare for dangerous conditions, such as floods or typhoons.

A | These people are taking precautions against a typhoon that has been forecast.

> **1** Explain why the following people need accurate weather forecasts:
> a | farmers
> b | pilots.

Weather forecasting

The weather depends on the pattern of air pressure around the world, which determines how the winds blow. Weather also depends on the temperature of the air and the oceans, which affect how much moisture is in the air.

Meteorologists cannot make changes to air pressure and temperature patterns to see how they affect the weather! Instead, they use their knowledge of how liquids and gases behave to make computer models of the atmosphere.

A **model** is a way of representing something else. Computer weather models use information about the current weather conditions and make predictions about what will happen to the atmosphere in the future.

Meteorologists test the predictions made by their models by comparing the forecasts with what actually happens to the weather. If the predictions are not accurate, then the computer model will need changing.

B | Weather forecasters can use satellite images and computer technology to track typhoons and tornadoes.

> **2** Suggest three different measurements that need to be put into a computer weather model.

> **3** Compare how a scientist and meteorologist work with diagram B on page 40.

50

Careers in meteorology

People who want to be meteorologists go to university when they leave school. They may study meteorology, or they might study computer science, mathematics, physics or physical geography.

Meteorologists need to develop many skills. They must be able to understand and use computer models to make predictions, and carefully analyse how well predictions match what actually happens. They need to communicate information clearly with other scientists and with people who use weather forecasts.

4	Suggest why a university degree in computer science is useful for a meteorologist.
5	Explain why good communication skills are essential for a meteorologist.
6	Why do you think meteorologists need to communicate with people in other countries?

C | Weather apps use symbols to show the weather.

Forecasts

Meteorologists use symbols to communicate a lot of complicated information in a clear way, which is easy to understand.

The charts being used by the weather forecaster in photo B use uses diagrams and symbols to give information about air pressures and temperatures. Diagram C uses symbols to present a weather forecast.

Chart D is a different kind of weather chart. Each little dot and its tail shows the wind speed and direction in different places. Pilots use this kind of chart to help to work out how the wind will affect their flight.

D | pilots' weather chart

7	Why are there different kinds of weather chart?

ACTIVITY

1 Make two large copies of map E and label one 'morning' and one 'afternoon'.

2 Add symbols to your maps to represent the weather forecast below. Make a key to show what your symbols mean.

It will be a sunny morning in the north, and a cloudy afternoon with heavy rain. The south will have some sunshine and some rain, and a dry, cloudy afternoon. Strong winds will blow from the south all day.

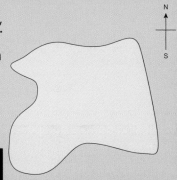

E

7Ge WASTE

There are many ways in which we can deal with our waste but they all have their problems. Recycling is better for the environment but can be expensive. Landfill sites are good for getting rid of a lot of rubbish but are ugly, take up a lot of space and can cause pollution.

There are other methods of dealing with waste. Incineration burns waste at high temperatures. The energy released can be used elsewhere – to generate **electricity**, for example. However, it is expensive, and the gases produced have to be controlled or they could cause problems.

A | Incineration releases waste gases.

B | Glass can be recycled over and over again.

Waste plant material can be composted (rotted down). This can be done on a large scale, and the compost that is produced can be used to improve soil and reduce the use of fertiliser. However, composting can also cause problems. The rotting plant material produces heat and methane gas, which can catch fire.

1 a| What is the main advantage of incineration?

b| Explain, using particle theory, why gases released by incinerators cause problems.

2 Look at photo B. Explain in terms of particles how the recycled glass can be moulded.

3 Explain why soot particles (from a fire) appear to 'dance' about, if you examine them through a microscope.

4 Look at this hypothesis: The particles in a gas are very far apart (unlike in liquids and solids). Make a prediction from this hypothesis and outline an experiment to test this prediction.

C | hosing down a compost heap to put out fires

HAVE YOUR SAY

In the UK, to dump waste at a landfill site, companies may need to pay a landfill tax. To avoid this, some companies just dump their waste anywhere. This is called fly tipping. In some countries, people can be fined for fly tipping and/or go to prison. Do you think this is reasonable?

7Ha OUR MATERIAL WORLD

Our Earth and its atmosphere contain a **mixture** of materials with different **properties**. Over time we have learned to use these materials to make objects to improve our lives. Sometimes, however, we misuse our material world.

Some substances can be used just as they are found, or they can be shaped to make useful objects. Rocks can be used to make building blocks for houses and wood can be formed into furniture.

Sometimes we need to use **physical changes** to separate useful materials from mixtures. For instance, we can get salt from sea water by **evaporation**. Sometimes we use physical changes to make materials into more useful shapes, such as when we mould **metals** into different shapes by melting them. Physical changes do not make new substances and they can often be reversed quite easily.

A | our source of materials

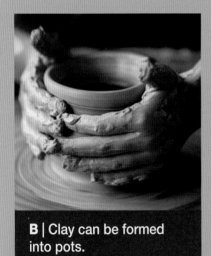

B | Clay can be formed into pots.

C | melting gold to make jewellery

D | Chemical reactions have been used to make soap for thousands of years. An alkali (such as sodium hydroxide) is mixed with fat, and a reaction produces a new substance – soap.

Chemical reactions make new substances with different properties and different uses. For example, an **alkali** can react with fats to make soap. Chemical reactions always make one or more new substances and they are often difficult to reverse.

1 What happens in all chemical reactions?

2 State whether the following changes are chemical or physical:
   a| boiling a kettle to make steam
   b| mixing sand and water
   c| frying an egg
   d| iron railings rusting
   e| water freezing.

3 Explain why liquid gold can flow while solid gold cannot.

4 Describe how you could obtain solid salt from sea water.

SORTING
7Ha RESOURCE DATA

HOW CAN WE RECORD AND PRESENT SCIENTIFIC DATA?

Scientists answer questions by carrying out investigations and collecting **data**. The data can be **qualitative** (in words) or **quantitative** (in numbers). Quantitative data can be **discontinuous** or **discrete** (a limited choice of numbers) or **continuous** (any number between two limits).

To make sense of data it has to be recorded, sorted and presented. The type of presentation used depends on the type of **variable** and what you want to show. Some common types of presentation are shown in table B.

number of tablets added – quantitative and discrete

temperature of water – quantitative and continuous

type of salt tablets – qualitative

volume of water – quantitative and continuous

A | different types of data

B	Method of presentation	When used ...
	tables	to show exact values / to order a list / to show best and worst / to sort data into groups
	bar charts	to compare qualitative or discrete variables / to compare continuous data that has been put into groups
	pie charts	to show the proportions of a total made up by different items
	line graphs	to show how one variable changes with time (or with another gradually changing variable)
	scatter graphs	to look for a relationship (link) between two quantitative variables

Gases in air	%
nitrogen	78.08
oxygen	20.95
argon	0.93
carbon dioxide	0.039
neon	0.002
helium	0.0005

The air contains a mixture of **gases**, which have different uses. Different ways of presenting this data are shown in figure C. The **bar chart** and **pie chart** are more visual than the table and give an instant impression of the proportions of gases. However, the table shows the exact percentages of the gases and is more useful when there are large differences in the numbers. For example, the table includes data about the other gases that cannot be shown in a pie chart or bar chart.

Percentages of different gases in air

(bar chart: y-axis Percentage (%) 0–100; x-axis nitrogen, oxygen, other gases)

1. Explain why the amount of carbon dioxide in air cannot be shown easily on the pie chart or bar chart on the right.

2. Table D contains information on how long certain metal resources will last if we keep using them at the current rate.
   a| How could you sort this data in the table?
   b| Draw a bar chart of the data.
   c| Explain why you would not draw a line graph of this data.
   d| Use the data to explain why we should recycle more metals.

Metal	Years left
nickel	90
copper	61
silver	29
zinc	46

D

Relative composition of air

(pie chart)
78% nitrogen
1% other gases
21% oxygen

C | presenting information about air

Investigating air

Candles use the **oxygen** in air when they burn and will go out when the oxygen is used up. The Method given here, and photo E, describe an investigation in which a candle is burnt in different **volumes** of air (using beakers of different sizes) to discover how the volume of air affects the time the candle will burn for.

Method

A | Place a tea light/candle on a heat-resistant mat.

B | Light, and immediately, but carefully, place a beaker over the candle.

C | Time how long it takes for the candle to go out.

D | Record the volume of the beaker and the time for the flame to go out.

E | Repeat steps A to D, changing the size of the beaker used.

3 The burning candle experiment is looking for a relationship between two variables.

a| Are these variables quantitative or qualitative?

b| Which method of presenting the results would be best to use? Explain your choice.

Results

To analyse the results, they are first recorded in a table and then converted into a **scatter graph**.

Volume of air in beaker (cm³)	Burning time of candle (s)
100	5.1
200	7.5
400	13.0
600	17.9

How burning time depends on the volume of air

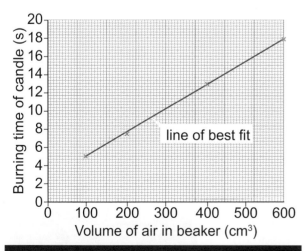

F | table and scatter graph of results

E | the burning candle experiment

Conclusion

The points on the scatter graph follow a pattern and so there is a **relationship**. We can make the relationship clearer by drawing a **line of best fit**, as shown in graph F.

4 What is the relationship between the volume of air and the time it takes for the flame to go out?

5 Describe how you draw a line of best fit on a scatter graph.

6 How could you change this investigation to be more sure of the conclusion?

I can ...

- draw, use and interpret tables, bar charts, pie charts and scatter graphs
- identify the best way to present different types of data.

7Ha THE AIR WE BREATHE

WHAT KINDS OF PARTICLES ARE FOUND IN AIR?

Like all matter, air is made up of tiny **particles**. However, the air is not **pure**. It contains a mixture of gases, including about 78% nitrogen, 21% oxygen, 0.9% argon and 0.1% other gases (including **carbon dioxide**). These different gases have different properties because they are made up of different types of particle.

The simplest particles of matter are called **atoms**. We can imagine that an atom looks like a tiny ball. Argon gas is made up of atoms like the ones shown in diagram B.

In many substances the atoms are held together in groups called **molecules**. Oxygen molecules have two oxygen atoms joined together. All the molecules of a certain substance always contain the same type and number of atoms.

All substances are made up of atoms. If they are made up of one kind of atom, like argon, oxygen and nitrogen, they are called **elements**. Atoms and elements are the building blocks of all matter. There are about 90 different types of atom found naturally. So there are only about 90 different naturally occurring elements. They are listed in the **periodic table** (see page 191).

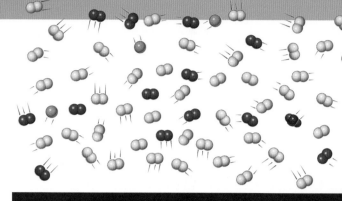

A | Air contains a mixture of particles.

1	Describe the arrangement of particles in all gases.
2	a| State the percentage of each gas shown in diagram A.
	b| Explain why it is wrong to use the term 'pure air' in science.

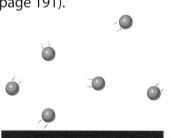
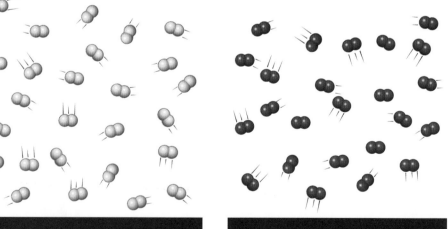

B | atoms of argon

C | molecules of nitrogen

D | molecules of oxygen

The word 'elementary' means simple. Elements are simple substances. You cannot split an element into anything simpler using a chemical reaction. Most substances, however, can be broken down because they contain more than one kind of atom. If different kinds of atoms are joined together in a substance, the substance is a **compound**. Of the four important gases in air only carbon dioxide is a compound. It contains molecules made up of two elements, carbon and oxygen, joined together.

E | molecules of the compound carbon dioxide

To make a compound, the atoms of the elements have to be joined together. If they are not joined, then it is a mixture of elements. Diagram F shows the difference between a mixture of elements (on the left) and a compound (on the right).

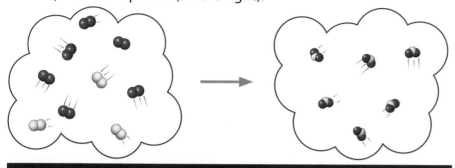

F | A chemical reaction can turn a mixture of nitrogen and oxygen into a compound called nitrogen dioxide. The mixture is not a pure substance but the nitrogen dioxide is.

The 90 elements can be joined together in different ways to form many different compounds, just like the 26 letters of the English alphabet can make millions of different words.

3 Use the periodic table on page 191 to find out which of the following substances are elements: zinc, plastic, sea water, chlorine, gold, lead, wood, magnesium, granite and iodine.

4 Describe the difference between:
a| elements and compounds
b| atoms and molecules.

5 How many different kinds of atom are there in diagram A?

FACT

There are now 28 manufactured elements to add to the 90 natural elements. The newest element is number 117 in the periodic table. It is called Tennessine. It was named after the American state of Tennessee, where many of the scientists who helped to make it worked.

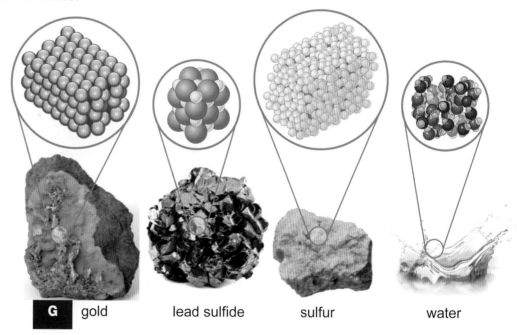

G gold   lead sulfide   sulfur   water

6 Which of the substances in diagram G are elements and which are compounds? In each case briefly explain your choice.

7 The water of our seas and oceans covers over half the surface of the Earth. Each water particle is formed by joining two atoms of hydrogen to one atom of oxygen. The sea also contains dissolved substances, including sodium chloride (salt) and oxygen gas, which supports all sea life.

Using examples of substances from the above passage explain the difference between pure substances and mixtures, elements and compounds, and atoms and molecules.

I can ...

- recognise the difference between atoms and molecules
- identify elements, mixtures and compounds from descriptions and particle diagrams.

7Hb EARTH'S ELEMENTS

WHY ARE DIFFERENT ELEMENTS USED FOR DIFFERENT PURPOSES?

The periodic table (see page 191) lists the names and **symbols** of all known elements. Chemical symbols have one or two letters, starting with a capital letter. The symbols are a **convention**, agreed and used by scientists all over the world. Symbols make it easy for scientists to communicate about elements even if they do not speak the same language.

Diagram A shows the symbols and abundance of elements in the **Earth's crust**.

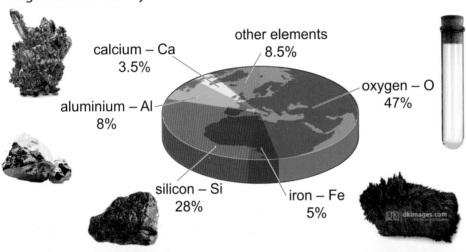

calcium – Ca
3.5%

other elements
8.5%

oxygen – O
47%

aluminium – Al
8%

silicon – Si
28%

iron – Fe
5%

dkimages.com

A | elements in the Earth's crust

Naturally occurring elements are usually found in compounds. A few (e.g. gold) are found on their own. Others (e.g. copper, tin) can be got out of their compounds easily, using simple chemical reactions. These elements have been known and used for thousands of years.

1	What is all matter made up of?
2	What is the difference between a mixture of elements and a compound?
3	What are the symbols for the two elements that make up about 75 per cent of the Earth's crust?
4	Find out one use for four of the gases in the air. Present your research as a table.

The **properties** of an element describe what it looks like and how it behaves. The gases in the air all look the same – they are all colourless gases. However, they behave differently. Oxygen makes things burn more quickly and so is used to help make very high-temperature flames in some tools. Argon, nitrogen and carbon dioxide can all stop things burning and so are used in fire extinguishing systems.

FACT

John Dalton (1766–1844) developed a system of symbols, using circles, marks and letters, to represent the elements. At the time other scientists found his symbols awkward and they were not widely used.

ELEMENTS

☉	Hydrogen	1	Strontian	46
	Azote	5	Barytes	68
●	Carbon	54	Iron	50
○	Oxygen	7	Zinc	56
	Phosphorus	9	Copper	56
⊕	Sulphur	13	Lead	90
	Magnesia	20	Silver	190
⊖	Lime	24	Gold	190
	Soda	28	Platina	190
	Potash	42	Mercury	167

B | Dalton's symbols for elements

C | Oxygen helps the gas in this tool to burn at 3500 °C, which is hot enough to cut through metals.

5 Which elements were described by the following symbols by Dalton:

a| a circle with a cross

b| a circle with an upside-down Y

c| a circle with a dot?

6 Sodium is an element that was discovered in 1807. Iron was probably discovered about 4000 years ago. Suggest a reason for this difference.

D | the elements in a smart phone

Modern technology uses many different elements. Diagram D shows the elements needed to make a smart phone. Some of these elements, such as indium, gallium and antimony, are now in short supply. If we continue to use them at the current rate, our sources will run out in the near future. Reducing waste and increased **recycling** is one way of saving our **resources**. For example, it is thought that there are £150 million worth of valuable metals in discarded mobile phones in the UK.

The properties of an element depend on its atoms and how they are arranged. The uses of an element are linked to its properties.

The element carbon can be found in two different forms that contain the same atoms. Diamond is one of the hardest natural substances, while graphite is the soft **solid** used in pencil leads. The different properties are due to the different ways the atoms are joined together.

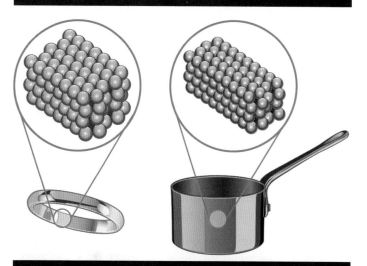

E | The uses of elements, such as gold (Au) and copper (Cu), depend on the properties of their atoms.

7 a| Using the periodic table on page 194, find two elements in diagram D where the first letter of the element's name and its symbol are not the same.

b| Explain why symbols are useful.

8 a| Define an element in two different ways.

b| Using one named element as an example, explain why we must increase recycling.

9 Suggest some properties for the following elements with these uses:

a| gold to make jewellery

b| diamonds to make glass cutters.

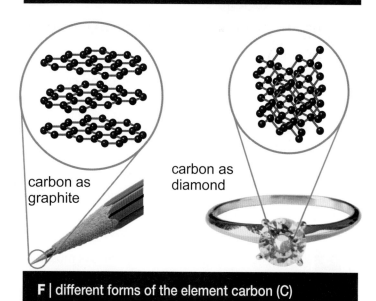

carbon as graphite

carbon as diamond

F | different forms of the element carbon (C)

I can ...

- use chemical symbols for common elements and explain why they are an international code
- recall that different elements have different properties and uses
- explain that our resources of elements are limited and can run out.

7Hc METALS AND NON-METALS

WHAT IS THE DIFFERENCE BETWEEN METALS AND NON-METALS?

Chemists classify elements into two main groups, **metals** and **non-metals**, depending on their properties. Three-quarters of all elements are metals.

When we look at elements we can often guess if they are metals or non-metals. Metals are often grey or silver in colour. However, appearances can be misleading and not all grey solids are metals. Look, for example, at silicon in photo E.

> **1** What is similar about the appearance of most metals?
>
> **2** Give the names and symbols for three metal and three non-metal elements.

A | The steam train and rails are made from metals, mainly iron. The blackness in the smoke is caused by a non-metal called carbon.

The common physical properties of most metals are:

- solids with high melting points
- **ductile** (can be stretched into wires)
- **malleable** (can be hammered into shape)
- shiny (when polished)
- good **conductors** of heat and electricity.

Some metals have properties that others do not have. Most elements are unaffected by magnets but iron, nickel and cobalt can be made to attract each other. They are **magnetic**.

> **3** Write down three physical properties of most metals.
>
> **4** What properties make the following suitable for their uses:
>
> a| aluminium for lightning rods b| iron for house radiators?

Non-metals have different properties. Most non-metals are:

- substances with low melting points
- **brittle** (when solid)
- not shiny
- **insulators** (poor conductors) of heat and electricity.

B | Iron can be separated from sand using magnets in some places, such as in the rivers in San Marcelino, in the Philippines.

Sulfur, a typical non-metal, is a yellow brittle solid that melts at 115 °C. It is a poor conductor of heat and electricity. Most sulfur is used as compounds like sulfuric acid. Sulfur is also used in matches, where it burns with a pale blue flame to form the acidic gas sulfur dioxide. This is the gas you smell if you light a match.

> **5** Describe two properties of sulfur shown in photo C.
>
> **6** Iodine is a dull blue/black non-metal solid, which has several uses in medicine. Describe three other possible properties of the element iodine.

Every element has unique properties and uses – not all metals and non-metals fit all the general properties of their group. Photos D, E and F show some unique elements.

C | burning molten sulfur flowing down the inside of a volcano

D | Mercury is the only metal element that is a **liquid** at room temperature. As it remains a liquid over a wide range of temperatures, mercury can be used in thermometers.

E | Non-metallic silicon can be shiny like a metal. It also has some unique conducting properties that make it useful to make silicon chips for the electronics industry.

F | The two forms of carbon, graphite and diamond, both have very high melting points for non-metals. Unlike most non-metals graphite conducts electricity and is used in batteries and electric motors.

> **7** Describe two properties that make these metals suitable for their uses.
>
> a| copper wires in electrical cables   b| iron fridge magnets
>
> **8** The properties of two elements, X and Y, are compared in table G.
>
> | Property | X | Y |
> |---|---|---|
> | melting point | 1083 °C | 98 °C |
> | boiling point | 2567 °C | 883 °C |
> | reactivity | unreactive | reacts with water |
> | conductor of heat | good | good |
> | conductor of electricity | excellent | good |
>
> G
>
> a| Explain how you would know whether elements X and Y are metals or non-metals.
>
> b| Which element would make better cooking pots? Give two reasons for your choice.

FACT

In the late 19th century, aluminium was called the metal of kings as it was more expensive to produce than gold. We now know how to make aluminium cheaply and it is used to make 200 billion drinks cans each year.

I can ...

- describe and identify metals and non-metals by their properties
- relate the use of an element to its properties.

WHAT FACTORS AFFECT THE PROFITABILITY OF MINING?

Rocks from which metals can be obtained are called ores. Geologists are scientists who investigate rocks and have the skills to find ores. However, mining is very expensive, and so is getting the metal out of an ore. Before a mine is built, a project team collects data to work out if it will make a profit. Some factors that affect the amount of profit are shown in diagram A.

1 Look at diagram A. Suggest how the following might affect the profit made by a mine:

a | depth of the mine

b | distance to where the metal will be sold

c | environmental problems

d | how easy it is to get the metal out of the ore.

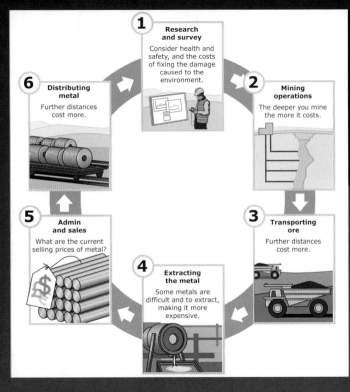

1 Research and survey
Consider health and safety, and the costs of fixing the damage caused to the environment.

2 Mining operations
The deeper you mine the more it costs.

3 Transporting ore
Further distances cost more.

4 Extracting the metal
Some metals are difficult and to extract, making it more expensive.

5 Admin and sales
What are the current selling prices of metal?

6 Distributing metal
Further distances cost more.

A | Different scientists and experts provide advice for each stage involved in the extraction of a metal.

2 Outline why the mine in photo B makes a profit.

Careers in mining

Different scientists are needed to estimate the cost of producing a metal from a particular mine. Analytical chemists test ores to find out how much metal they contain. The more metal an ore contains, the more valuable it is. Mining engineers work out the cost of getting the ores out of the ground. Chemical engineers design ways of getting the metals out of their ores. These experts all have different knowledge, experience and skills.

B | This gold mine is profitable.

Mining for profit

The final decision on which mines will be opened, will be made by **financial analysts**. These experts have special training in a subject such as economics and finance. Many financial analysts work in banks.

An important part of their job is to evaluate the data to see if they have enough good quality information to be able to make conclusions. For example they will need to know the amount of metal that can be obtained from each ore.

C | This mine did not get any further than drilling some test holes because the percentage of metal in the ore was too low.

magnetite 72% iron

goethite 63% iron

limonite 55% iron

D | A higher percentage of metal in an ore makes it more valuable.

3 Look at flowchart A. Identify the type of scientist involved in each stage.

4 Look at the ores shown in photo D.

a | Explain which ore is likely to be the most profitable.

b | How much useful iron could be obtained from 200 g of magnetite ore?

5 Give a reason why a hundred years ago copper ores containing less than 5% copper would not have been used, but today we use ores containing 0.5 to 1% copper.

ACTIVITY

The data in table E is about a proposed copper mine.

a Do you have all the data that you need? Look back at diagram A to check.

b Calculate the total cost of handling 1000 kg of the copper ore.

c Show that the mine is not going to make a profit.

d What would the selling price need to be to avoid making a loss?

E

The amount of copper that can be obtained from the ore is 1%. The present selling price of copper is £4.50 per kg.	Costs per 1000 kg of ore handled
	survey and research = £11.00
	mining operations = £19.50
	transport of ore = £10.00
	extracting metal = £31.00
	admin and sales = £14.00
	distribution of metal = £4.50

7Hd MAKING COMPOUNDS

HOW DO ELEMENTS FORM COMPOUNDS?

Compounds make up most of the materials in the land and seas around us. The most common compound in the Earth's crust is silicon dioxide. Like most natural substances, it is usually found mixed with other compounds and has several different forms.

FACT

Carbon makes up more compounds than all the other elements put together. Carbon compounds are the basis of life and over 10 million different carbon-containing compounds have been identified.

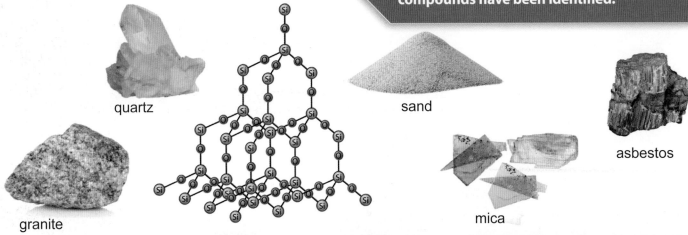

quartz

sand

asbestos

granite

mica

A | All these materials contain forms of silicon dioxide, which is a compound made of silicon and oxygen atoms. Many forms of silicon dioxide are used for building.

Forming compounds

The first stage in forming compounds often involves heating a mixture of elements. Though not all combinations of elements react with one another, many do. For example, iron and sulfur react easily: heat is needed to start the reaction but, once started, you can take the test tube out of the flame and it will keep on glowing and giving out heat. **Energy** is often given out when elements react to form compounds.

During a reaction, atoms are re-arranged and joined together in new ways. In the reaction in photo B, the atoms of iron and sulfur join together to form a compound called iron sulfide. We say that new **bonds** have formed between sulfur and iron the atoms, which are now bonded together.

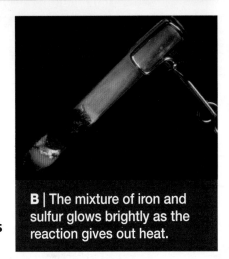

B | The mixture of iron and sulfur glows brightly as the reaction gives out heat.

1   What percentage of the Earth's crust is made up of silicon and oxygen? (See page 58.)

2   Describe one difference between silicon dioxide and one of its elements.

3   After iron and sulfur are heated, what observation tells you the reaction has started?

Notice in photo C that the atoms in iron sulfide are joined to form a large regular structure. A piece of iron sulfide has billions of atoms bonded together.

Iron sulfide, like most compounds, is very different from its elements. It looks different and has different properties.

4 Why is the iron sulfide structure not described as molecules?

5 How is the arrangement of atoms different between iron sulfide and a mixture of iron and sulfur?

6 Describe how iron sulfide is different from its elements in terms of:

a| appearance b| properties.

iron

sulfur

iron sulfide

C | The reaction between iron and sulfur bonds their atoms together.

D | Iron can be separated from sulfur by using a magnet. Iron sulfide is not magnetic.

Most of the compounds found on Earth were formed millions of years ago. This includes the rocky **ores** that contain valuable compounds called **minerals**. We get metals from minerals.

Naming compounds

Compounds are often named after their elements:

- if one of the elements in the compound is a metal, its name goes first

- the non-metal at the end of the compound's name has its name changed so that it ends in –*ide*.

For example, chlorine reacts with copper to form copper chloride. Silicon and hydrogen are both non-metals and they react to form silicon hydride.

galena, an ore containing a mineral compound of sulfur and lead

cassiterite, an ore containing a mineral compound of tin and oxygen

covellite, an ore containing a mineral compound of copper and sulfur

E | metal ores contain valuable minerals

7 Why are metal ores useful?

8 Name the useful compounds in the ores shown in photo E.

9 When some powdered aluminium is mixed with crystals of iodine, nothing happens. If a few drops of warm water are added, flames and purple fumes are produced and a white solid is left.

a| What tells you a reaction has occurred?

b| What is the name of the compound formed?

I can ...

- describe changes that occur when compounds are formed
- identify elements, compounds and mixtures from descriptions and particle diagrams
- name simple compounds.

7He CHEMICAL REACTIONS

HOW CAN WE USE CHEMICAL REACTIONS?

Unlike a **physical change**, a **chemical reaction** always forms one or more new substances. Signs of a chemical reaction include: a colour change, a gas being given off, a solid forming, heat being given out. We use these signs as **criteria** to decide whether a chemical reaction is occurring.

Many chemical reactions occur in everyday life. Some work just by mixing the right substances together. Others need an input of energy to get them started or a constant supply of energy to keep them going. Photo A shows some chemical reactions.

A | the reactions involved in burning, cooking and rusting

> **1** What happens in all chemical reactions?
>
> **2** Which of the reactions shown in photo A:
> a| needs a constant supply of energy
> b| just needs energy to start it off
> c| works without any energy input?

Chemical reactions can be described using models called **word equations**. The **reactants** (what you start with) are shown on the left. An arrow points to the **products** (the new substances formed) on the right. The word equation for the reaction between iron metal and powdered sulfur is:

$$\underbrace{\text{iron} + \text{sulfur}}_{\text{reactants}} \rightarrow \underbrace{\text{iron sulfide}}_{\text{product}}$$

> **3** Write word equations for the following reactions.
> a| Hot copper metal reacts with chlorine gas to form solid green copper chloride
> b| Non-metal carbon burns in oxygen gas to form only carbon dioxide gas.

Thermal decomposition

Elements can form compounds in chemical reactions and the reverse can also happen. When heat is used to break down a compound the reaction is called a **thermal decomposition**. This type of reaction is used in many industries, including the extraction of metals from their minerals (in ores).

When mercury oxide is heated (as in photo B) blobs of liquid mercury can be seen on the side of the test tube and oxygen gas escapes from the tube. The word equation for the reaction is:

mercury oxide → mercury + oxygen

Some compounds can decompose to form other *compounds*. Metal **carbonates** do this. They are compounds containing a metal, carbon and oxygen. Many metal carbonates are found naturally and have many uses. For example, calcium carbonate is found in limestone, chalk and marble.

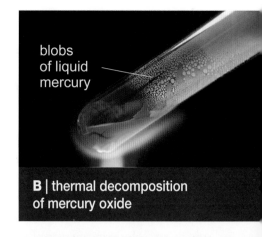

B | thermal decomposition of mercury oxide

blobs of liquid mercury

C | These cliffs are mostly calcium carbonate.

The **apparatus** used to investigate the thermal decomposition of copper carbonate is shown in photo D. The limewater turns milky if carbon dioxide is formed. (This is the test for carbon dioxide.) The word equation for the reaction is:

     copper carbonate → copper oxide + carbon dioxide

Many metal carbonates break down to form similar products.

More about names

If a compound contains two elements plus oxygen, the ending of the name of one element is changed to *–ate*. The *–ate* means 'with oxygen'. For example, a compound of zinc, sulfur and oxygen is zinc sulfate.

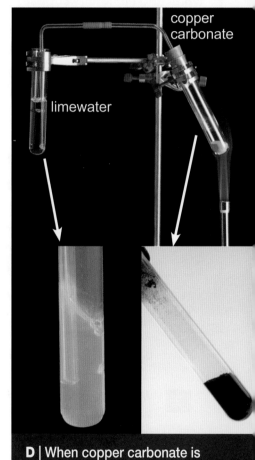

copper carbonate

limewater

D | When copper carbonate is heated, black copper oxide is formed together with carbon dioxide gas.

I can ...

- use and understand word equations for chemical reactions
- describe examples and uses of decomposition reactions.

7He PROBLEMS WITH ELEMENTS

WHAT PROBLEMS CAN BE CAUSED BY GETTING METALS?

The mining and extraction of metals is important for many low-income countries because it provides income for the economy and work and training for the **population**. It also introduces new technologies and brings about improvements to transport systems and services like water and electricity supplies.

Lead, which is mainly used to make batteries, is produced in many developing countries. Its ores usually contain lead sulfide or lead oxide and the extraction involves several stages.

B | Lead is also used as a roofing material.

A | Workers in lead production are exposed to lead dust and other poisons.

These stages include reactions to remove impurities like sulfur, and free the pure lead metal from its compounds. The processes use extremely high temperatures and release dust and smoke. The waste materials contain lead and other **toxic** metals, such as arsenic and mercury.

C | In some countries, children work in metal production and face hazardous conditions.

1. a| Name all the elements and compounds mentioned in the text above.
   b| What is the difference between an element and a compound?

2. Write a word equation for the reaction between lead sulfide and oxygen forming solid lead oxide and sulfur dioxide gas.

3. What do you call a reaction that breaks down a compound using heat?

4. Why is the waste produced during the isolation of pure lead so dangerous?

5. What are the benefits and problems of lead production in a low-income country? Write your ideas in a table like the one below.

D	Benefits of lead production	Problems of lead production

HAVE YOUR SAY?

Some people think that the mining and extraction of metals in low-income countries takes advantage of workers. Do you think that we should find alternative sources for these metals?

It is estimated that there are 1.2 billion cars in the world. Cars are self-propelled vehicles, which means they carry their source of energy with them. The energy is transferred from the energy source to the wheels so that the car moves.

The first self-propelled vehicle was powered by steam, which was produced by burning wood to heat water until it evaporated (photo A). The steam passed into the engine to produce movement that drove the wheels. In 1807, the first engine was built that burnt the **fuel** inside the engine. The fuel was hydrogen gas, but later designs used liquid fuels such as petrol. **Combustion** is another word for burning, so these kinds of engine are known as internal combustion engines.

steering controls   boiler: where fuel is burnt to produce steam

engine: where energy from the steam causes movement that is transferred to the wheels

A | Nicolas-Joseph Cugnot built the first self-propelled vehicle in 1769 to carry cannons, but it was too slow and heavy to be useful.

B | The Benz Patent-Motorwagen of 1886 was the first modern car. Its engine ran on petrol.

Many fuels release gases and other substances that cause **pollution** and damage the environment. New car engines are designed to limit the pollution they cause.

1. What does combustion mean?

2. Why do cars need a source of energy?

3. Give two examples of fuels that are, or have been, used in vehicles.

4. Explain how the fuel in a car is used to make it move.

5. Why are the fuels used in most modern cars harmful to the environment?

6. Cugnot's steam vehicle had an external combustion engine. Compare how it worked with the way an internal combustion engine works.

C | Several car manufacturers are developing hydrogen-fuelled cars. These cause less pollution than petrol and diesel vehicles.

8Ea BURNING FUELS

WHAT FORMS WHEN A FUEL REACTS WITH OXYGEN?

A fuel is a chemical substance from which stored energy can be transferred usefully to make things happen. Hydrogen is a gas that can be used as a fuel. Most hydrogen-powered vehicles use fuel cells, in which energy is released from hydrogen in a carefully controlled manner and reacts with oxygen.

We can model the chemical reaction in a fuel cell using a **word equation**:

hydrogen + oxygen → water

Remember: **reactants** are the substances that react together in a reaction and **products** are the substances that are formed.

> 1 Define the word 'fuel'.
>
> 2 What is the product of the reaction in a hydrogen fuel cell?

A | In the hydrogen fuel cell in this bus, hydrogen fuel releases energy that is transferred to electricity to make the bus move.

FACT

In the 1930s, airships were built to carry passengers long distances. Many were filled with hydrogen, which made them float in air. In May 1937, the *Hindenburg* airship burst into flames. The flames quickly spread as the hydrogen reacted with oxygen in the air. The accident killed 35 of the 97 people on board.

B

Hydrogen combustion

Combustion does not happen in fuel cells, but hydrogen does also combust with oxygen. For this to happen, energy from a spark or a flame is needed to start the reaction. The reaction then continues without needing any further input of energy. Instead, energy is released and transferred to the surroundings.

Some of the energy is transferred by heating, which we feel. Some is transferred by light, which we see. If the reaction is very vigorous, we may even hear the transfer of energy by sound. For example, if you put a lighted splint into a boiling tube full of hydrogen, it burns with a 'squeaky pop' sound. This can be used as a test for hydrogen. A combustion reaction continues until one or both reactants have been used up.

> 3 Suggest what could have started the combustion reaction on the *Hindenburg*.
>
> 4 Give three ways in which energy can be transferred from a fuel to the surroundings during a combustion reaction.

Most fuels used in car engines also transfer energy during combustion reactions with oxygen. Petrol and diesel are **fossil fuels** because they are produced from oil that was formed from living organisms that died millions of years ago. Petrol and diesel are also **hydrocarbons**, because their molecules contain only carbon and hydrogen.

During combustion, the carbon and hydrogen atoms react with oxygen. The carbon reacts to produce carbon dioxide.

We can identify the products of the combustion of a hydrocarbon in air using tests. A test for water uses copper sulfate. If blue hydrated copper sulfate crystals are heated, **thermal decomposition** occurs. Water is given off (the **water of crystallisation**), leaving a white powder (anhydrous copper sulfate). Adding water produces blue copper sulfate again. This is one test for water. Other tests are shown in photos D and E.

C | This 1861 Thomas Rickett steam carriage used coal as the fuel.

5 Coal is a hydrocarbon fossil fuel. Explain what this means.

6 Write a word equation to model the reaction of carbon with oxygen.

7 Write a word equation to model the reaction of coal with oxygen.

D | The test for carbon dioxide involves bubbling the gas to be tested through limewater.

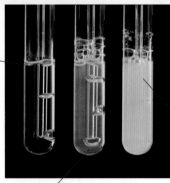

limewater before carbon dioxide is added

limewater after some carbon dioxide has bubbled through it

limewater after a lot of carbon dioxide has bubbled through it

Wear eye protection when carrying out these experiments.

E | White, anhydrous copper sulfate and blue cobalt chloride can both be used to test for water.

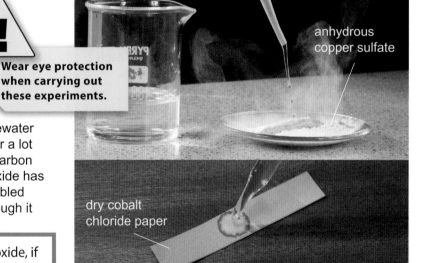

anhydrous copper sulfate

dry cobalt chloride paper

8 What happens in the test for carbon dioxide, if the gas is present?

9 Describe two tests for water.

10 If you touch bubbles that are full of hydrogen with a lighted splint, they catch fire. The flames continue when the lighted splint is removed but then go out. Explain these observations.

I can ...

- describe the combustion reactions of hydrogen and hydrocarbons
- describe tests for hydrogen, carbon dioxide and water.

8Eb OXIDATION

HOW DO METALS REACT WITH OXYGEN?

Water is so familiar that we use its everyday name. A chemical name that refers to the elements in it would be hydrogen oxide. This name makes it easier to see that hydrogen reacts with oxygen to form a compound called an **oxide**. This kind of reaction is known as **oxidation**.

1	Carbon reacts with oxygen to form an oxide.
	a| What is the name of the oxide?
	b| What is a reaction like this called?
2	One carbon atom reacts with one oxygen molecule to produce one molecule of the product. Draw a diagram like diagram A to show this reaction. (*Hint*: A carbon atom is shown as a single ball).

Hydrogen and carbon are both **non-metals**. However, many **metals** also react with oxygen to produce **metal oxides**:

metal + oxygen → metal oxide

3	Write word equations for the reaction of each of these metals with oxygen:
	a| magnesium b| iron c| copper.
4	Describe one way in which energy is transferred when magnesium combusts.

Conservation of mass

Mass is never gained or lost in a chemical reaction. This idea is the **law of conservation of mass**. No new atoms are created and no atoms disappear. The **bonds** between the atoms in the reactants are broken, and the atoms are rearranged. New bonds form between the rearranged atoms, forming new substances (the products).

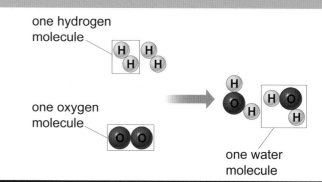

one hydrogen molecule

one oxygen molecule

one water molecule

A | During the oxidation of hydrogen, two molecules of hydrogen react with one molecule of oxygen to produce two molecules of water.

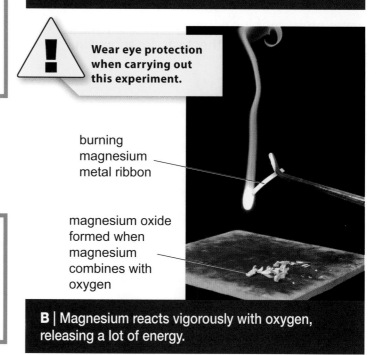

Wear eye protection when carrying out this experiment.

burning magnesium metal ribbon

magnesium oxide formed when magnesium combines with oxygen

B | Magnesium reacts vigorously with oxygen, releasing a lot of energy.

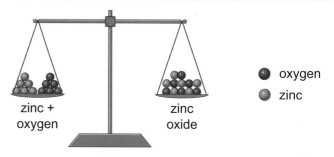

zinc + oxygen

zinc oxide

● oxygen
● zinc

C | The masses of zinc and oxygen (on the left) before they react are the same as the mass of the zinc oxide (on the right) that is produced in the reaction.

In some reactions mass may seem to increase. For example, when you heat zinc in air you get a white powder. The mass of the white powder is greater than the initial mass of zinc. This increase in mass is because the zinc has combined with oxygen from the air to form zinc oxide. The mass of the zinc and of the oxygen that reacted is the same as the mass of the zinc oxide formed.

Where a product is a gas that can easily escape into the air, the mass may seem to decrease during the reaction.

> **5**
> If a mass of 2.4 g of magnesium is burnt in air, 4.0 g of magnesium oxide is formed.
>
> a| What kind of reaction is this? Explain your answer.
>
> b| What was the mass of oxygen that reacted with the magnesium? Explain your answer.

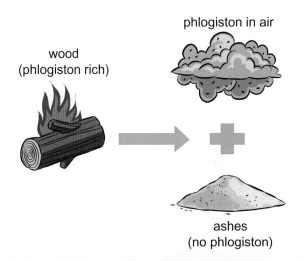

D | Three grams of zinc metal react with oxygen to form 3.7 g of white zinc oxide powder.

Phlogiston

Until 1772, many scientists thought that substances contained something they called **phlogiston** ('*flo-jist-on*'). When the substances burned, the phlogiston escaped leaving a solid ash called a calx. This theory explained why the mass after burning fuels was less than the original mass.

Careful experiments that measured the masses of gases showed that the phlogiston theory was wrong. This led to the discovery of oxygen. However, some scientists continued to believe in phlogiston. They thought this explained the heat and light given off in combustion reactions. Today we see this as evidence of the transfer of energy to the surroundings.

wood
(phlogiston rich)

phlogiston in air

ashes
(no phlogiston)

E | Substances that combust were once thought to contain phlogiston.

> **6**
> A supporter of the phlogiston theory says that when petrol burns in air phlogiston is lost to the air so the mass decreases. Write a letter to this person explaining why the phlogiston theory is wrong.

FACT

Antoine Lavoisier (1743–1794) was the first to prove that oxygen gas was the cause of an increase in mass during oxidation. He burnt jets of hydrogen and oxygen in a sealed jar and showed that fixed masses of the gases produced a predicted mass of water.

I can ...

- describe oxidation reactions of metals and non-metals
- explain changes in mass seen in oxidation reactions
- compare how phlogiston and oxygen explain combustion.

8Ec FIRE SAFETY

HOW DO YOU STOP A COMBUSTION REACTION?

Combustion reactions are **exothermic**, which means they release energy that we can feel as heat. This transfer of energy increases the temperature of the surroundings, which is measured using a **thermometer**. Some fuels release more energy than others, and so will increase the temperature of the surroundings more than other fuels.

> **1** Why is a combustion reaction exothermic?

Once started, a combustion reaction usually continues even if the initial source of heat (such as a flame or spark) is removed, because heat from the burning fuel makes unburnt fuel start to react.

A | temperature being measured using an infrared thermometer

B | A grassland fire spreads as the grass (the fuel) is heated to a temperature at which it combusts.

Three factors allow combustion to continue and these are shown in the **fire triangle**. To put out a fire, you must remove at least one factor.

C | the fire triangle

> **2** Which three things are needed for a fire?
>
> **3** Use the fire triangle to help explain why the fire in photo B has gone out in the burnt area.

Substances that are particularly likely to cause fires are labelled with a **hazard symbol** to show why they are dangerous.

FACT

Large forest fires can be controlled by starting more small fires in front of the main fire. This 'back burning' clears dry wood and grass so that, when the main fire reaches the area, there is no fuel left to burn.

flammable (easily bursts into flames)

oxidising (releases oxygen)

explosive (contains enough stored energy to explode if not handled correctly)

D | Fire is particularly dangerous when using substances labelled with these hazard symbols.

4 Look at diagram D. For each symbol, explain as fully as you can why a substance labelled with that symbol should be kept away from fire.

Fire extinguishers

Fire extinguishers work by cooling a fire or by stopping oxygen getting to the fuel. It is important to choose the right type of fire extinguisher for each type of fire. Using the wrong type may be dangerous and can even make the fire spread.

Water can put out fires because it takes away the heat, but it should never be used on burning oil. The water sinks through the hot oil and turns to steam. The steam rises quickly, pushing the burning oil out of the way and making the fire spread out. Petrol or oil fires should be extinguished with foam or a fire blanket, to keep oxygen away.

Water should also never be used on an electrical fire because it conducts electricity, and so you may get a serious electric shock. The electricity should be turned off at the mains, and the flames covered using a powder or carbon dioxide gas extinguisher. Carbon dioxide is heavier than air, so it pushes the air (containing oxygen) away from the flames.

E | Different types of fire extinguisher have different coloured bands.

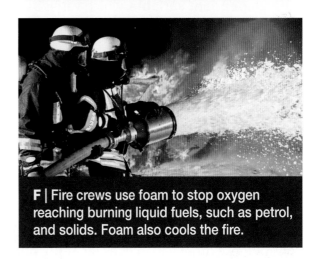

F | Fire crews use foam to stop oxygen reaching burning liquid fuels, such as petrol, and solids. Foam also cools the fire.

5 Which side of the fire triangle is taken away if you put out a fire with:

a| water   b| a fire blanket?

6 Explain why an oil fire should not be treated with a water-filled fire extinguisher.

7 Use the fire triangle to explain why carbon dioxide puts out an electrical fire.

8 How should each of these kinds of fire be put out? Explain your choices fully:

a| a chip pan full of burning fat

b| a bonfire of wood and paper

c| a fire caused by sparks from a damaged electrical cable.

G | This trained firefighter is demonstrating in a controlled environment that water added to burning fat or oil can cause a fire to spread explosively. Do not attempt this.

I can ...

- use the fire triangle to explain how to control a fire
- identify hazard symbols for substances likely to cause fires.

8Ec FAIR TESTING

WHY ARE FAIR TESTS CARRIED OUT?

A **variable** is any factor that can change and have different values. In an experiment you are usually interested in two variables:

- the **independent variable**, for which you choose the values
- the **dependent variable**, which varies as the independent variable changes and is the variable you are measuring.

different volumes of the same fuel to be burnt

A | Two variables in this experiment are the volume of fuel burnt and the time it takes for all the fuel to burn.

> **1** In the experiment shown in photo A, which is the independent variable and which is the dependent variable? Explain your answer.

In many experiments, you want to test the effect of a single variable on another. You want to find out how the independent variable affects the dependent variable. So, you do not want any other variables affecting the dependent variable. It is important to control these other variables as far as possible, and so they are called **control variables**.

Controlling variables is also very important in industry. MMT is a substance added to petrol to reduce pollution. Scientists found the best way of making MMT by changing the amount of one reactant and measuring how much MMT was produced. They also discovered that it was important to control the temperature during this reaction. In 2007, in Florida, USA, something went wrong with an MMT factory cooling system. The temperature rise caused an explosion that spread debris up to a mile away.

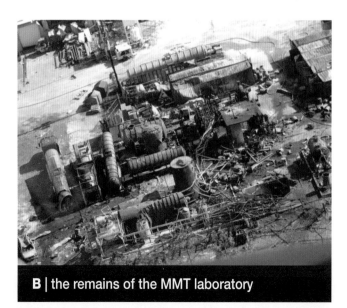

B | the remains of the MMT laboratory

> **2** Look at photo A.
>
> a| One variable that should be controlled is the type of fuel. Explain how using different fuels might affect the dependent variable.
>
> b| Describe one other variable that should be controlled in this experiment and what effect it might have if it were not controlled properly.

> **3** In the experiments to find the best way to make MMT:
>
> a| which was the independent variable
>
> b| which was the dependent variable
>
> c| which variable was not controlled properly and caused the explosion?

Planning a fair test

A **fair test** is an experiment in which all the control variables are controlled. This means that these variables do not change, and so cannot affect the dependent variable. Fair tests produce **valid** data. Something that is valid does what it is supposed to do. By controlling all other variables, data from a fair test only shows the effect of the independent variable on the dependent variable.

When you plan an experiment, you first identify the independent and dependent variables. Then you must identify all the other variables that could affect the dependent variable. Finally, you need to plan how to control these other variables.

The Method below describes how to carry out an experiment using the equipment in photo C.

Method

A | Place one tea light on a heat-resistant mat and another tea light on a block on a heat-resistant mat.

B | Measure the height between the surface and the base of the wick of both tea lights and record the values.

C | Light both tea lights and cover them both immediately with heat-resistant glass containers. Start the stopwatch.

D | Measure the time taken for each flame to go out and record the values.

C

! Wear eye protection when carrying out this experiment.

You usually record results from experiments in a table (see table D). It is a convention that the independent variable goes in the left-hand column.

independent variable | Do not forget the units! | dependent variable

D

Height of wick (cm)	Length of time it burned (s)
1	
2	
3	
4	

4 Identify the independent and dependent variables in the experiment described in the Method above.

5 Use your answer to question 4 to state the question this experiment is set up to answer.

6 a| Suggest two other variables that could affect the dependent variable.

b| Explain your answer to part a.

c| Describe how you could control each of the variables you identified in part a, in order to collect valid data.

I can ...

- identify control variables in an experiment and describe how to control them
- explain why it is important to carry out a fair test.

8Ed AIR POLLUTION

HOW CAN BURNING FUELS CAUSE POLLUTION?

When carbon burns in plenty of air, only carbon dioxide is formed. This is called **complete combustion** because all the carbon reacts as fully as it can with oxygen. However, if there is not enough oxygen, the carbon will undergo **incomplete combustion**. This can happen in vehicle engines.

Incomplete combustion of carbon results in a mixture of products:

- carbon dioxide gas from carbon that reacts completely with oxygen
- **carbon monoxide** gas from carbon that reacts partly with oxygen
- **soot** particles, made up of carbon that has not reacted with oxygen.

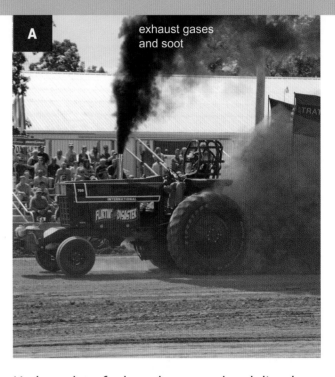

A | exhaust gases and soot

1 Name the carbon-containing compounds produced by an engine in which there is incomplete combustion of a hydrocarbon fuel.

2 Explain why the tractor in photo A is producing a lot of soot in its exhaust.

B | Pollutants from vehicle exhausts can form a hazy smog – a harmful mixture of particles and gases.

- *Carbon monoxide* is poisonous and can kill.
- *Carbon dioxide* is linked to global warming and climate change.
- *Sulfur dioxide* and *nitrogen oxides* are acidic gases that can cause **acid rain**.
- *Soot particles* can damage lungs and trigger **asthma** (a breathing problem).

Hydrocarbon fuels such as petrol and diesel contain **impurities**, which are small amounts of other substances. These impurities also react in the very hot conditions in engines. For example, sulfur is a common impurity and is oxidised to **sulfur dioxide** gas.

High engine temperatures also cause nitrogen and oxygen from the air to react and form several kinds of **nitrogen oxide**.

Many of the products of burning fuels in vehicle engines are **pollutants**. This means they can harm living things and damage the environment.

3 Write a word equation for the formation of sulfur dioxide in an engine.

4 a| Suggest an example of a nitrogen oxide and draw a diagram of it.
   b| Explain why vehicle engines produce nitrogen oxides.

5 What is meant by a pollutant?

Controlling pollutants

Exhaust gases can be treated to reduce pollution. Diesel vehicles usually have a **filter** to capture soot. Most vehicles also have a **catalytic converter** in their exhaust systems. This causes carbon monoxide gases to react with more oxygen to form carbon dioxide, and nitrogen oxides are broken down to oxygen and nitrogen.

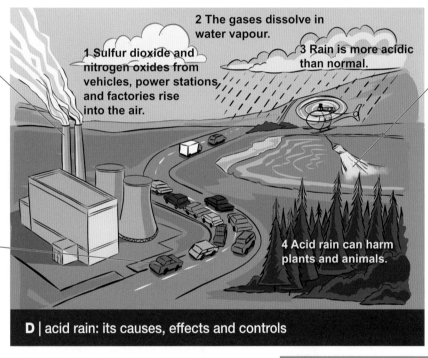

carbon dioxide, water and nitrogen

carbon monoxide, nitrogen oxides and hydrocarbons

steel housing containing precious metals such as platinum

C | Catalysts are substances that speed up reactions but are not used up themselves. The catalysts in a catalytic converter cause exhaust gases to react more easily.

Controls: Neutralisation reactions are used to remove acidic gases from chimney smoke.

2 The gases dissolve in water vapour.

1 Sulfur dioxide and nitrogen oxides from vehicles, power stations, and factories rise into the air.

3 Rain is more acidic than normal.

Controls: Acidic soil and water can be neutralised by adding substances such as calcium carbonate.

Controls: Catalytic converters on vehicles remove nitrogen oxides. Only low-sulfur fuel is burnt in engines.

4 Acid rain can harm plants and animals.

D | acid rain: its causes, effects and controls

Diagram D shows how the effects of acidic gases from fossil fuel combustion can be controlled. In many parts of the world, these controls are required by law. Parts of the world where industry is rapidly growing may have increasing air pollution problems.

6 Identify a trigger for asthma in vehicle exhaust gases.

7 a| Describe how burning fossil fuels in vehicle engines causes pollution.
b| Describe how this pollution can be reduced.

8 a| What is acid rain and how is it caused?
b| Explain how pollution from power stations is reduced.

FACT

In an asthma attack the tubes in the lungs get narrower, making it difficult to breathe. Attacks are usually caused by triggers, such as smoke, soot or pollen. Around the world, asthma affects over 300 million people and many animals. Using an 'inhaler' can make breathing easier.

E | asthma treatment

I can ...

- describe pollutants that are formed by burning fuels
- explain how these pollutants cause problems and how their effects can be reduced.

8Ee GLOBAL WARMING

IS POLLUTION CAUSING CLIMATE CHANGE?

Most of the energy that causes the Earth's surface to warm up is transferred to the Earth from the Sun. Some of the energy is trapped within the Earth's atmosphere by **greenhouse gases**, including carbon dioxide. This warming effect is called the **greenhouse effect**. Without it, the surface of the Earth would be too cold for most living things.

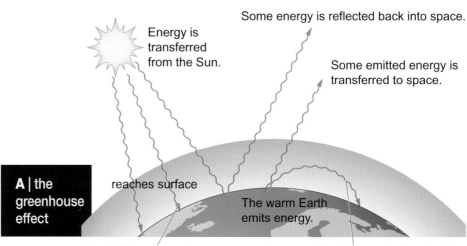

A | the greenhouse effect

Energy is transferred from the Sun.

Some energy is reflected back into space.

Some emitted energy is transferred to space.

reaches surface

The warm Earth emits energy.

Most of the energy is absorbed, causing an increase in temperature.

Some emitted energy is absorbed by carbon dioxide and other greenhouse gases and can be transferred back to the Earth's surface.

1. Where does most of the energy that warms the Earth's surface come from?

2. What is meant by the greenhouse effect?

3. Explain how carbon dioxide in the air helps to cause the greenhouse effect.

FACT

About 36 000 million tonnes of carbon dioxide are released into the air each year. China and the United States together release more than 40 per cent of this. The largest source of carbon dioxide in industrialised countries is from burning fossil fuels to generate electricity and in vehicles.

The temperature of the Earth's surface varies over time for many reasons. These include the tilt of the Earth's axis and the amount of energy that is transferred from the Sun to the Earth.

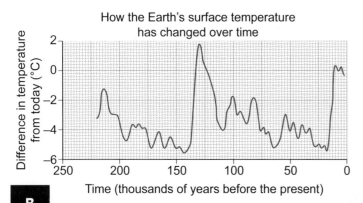

B
How the Earth's surface temperature has changed over time

Difference in temperature from today (°C) vs Time (thousands of years before the present)

4. Look at graph B.
a| What does 0 on the x-axis mean?
b| How long ago was the Earth's highest temperature according to this graph?

5. Humans only started to change the environment a few thousand years ago. What is the most likely explanation for the shape of graph B?

The burning of large amounts of fossil fuels began in the late 1700s, when coal was used as a fuel in factories. Since then, the amount of coal and other fossil fuels being burnt has greatly increased. This has led to an increase in the amount of carbon dioxide released into the air. Cement production also adds carbon dioxide to the atmosphere.

As carbon dioxide is one of the greenhouse gases, scientists predict that increasing the amount of it in the air will increase the greenhouse effect and so make the Earth's surface warmer. This increase in the greenhouse effect is known as **global warming**. This could lead to **climate change**, including changes to weather patterns, causing more storms, floods or droughts.

There is now plenty of evidence that global warming is happening. This evidence includes an increase in average temperatures of the atmosphere and oceans. We can also see the effect this is having on ice caps and glaciers. Most scientists agree that global warming is mostly due to the release of large amounts of greenhouse gases from human activity.

How global emissions of carbon dioxide have changed since 1900

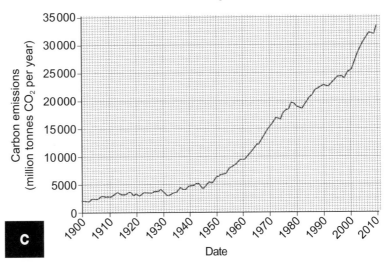

C

---

6   Use graph C to describe fully how the amount of carbon dioxide in the air has changed since 1900.

7   Suggest a reason for the change shown in graph C.

8   What is meant by global warming?

---

9   Describe changes that may be caused by global warming.

10   Explain how human activity could be causing global warming.

M.R. Campbell photo, USGS, 1911

D | Two photos of the same glacier in the USA show melting over 100 years.

E | Rising sea levels as a result of global warming could flood many major cities of the world, including London.

I can ...

- describe the greenhouse effect and how it is caused
- explain how human activity may be causing global warming.

HOW CAN WE REDUCE OUR CARBON FOOTPRINT?

A 'carbon footprint' is a measure of the masses of greenhouse gases (especially carbon dioxide) put into the atmosphere by people or organisations.

Companies that burn a lot of fuels to manufacture and transport goods have a large carbon footprint. Companies that do not use a lot of energy, and supply services and goods through the internet, have a small carbon footprint.

1 What is the 'carbon footprint' of a business or organisation?

2 Look at graph A.

a | Describe the **correlation** (relationship) between the amount of carbon dioxide in the atmosphere and global temperatures.

b | Give the approximate year in which carbon dioxide levels start to rise steadily.

c | Suggest a reason for the start of this rise.

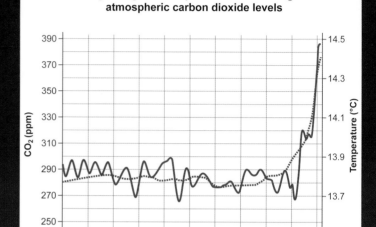

Changes in global temperatures with changes in atmospheric carbon dioxide levels

A | Atmospheric carbon dioxide concentrations are in blue (dotted line) and average global temperatures are in red.

Sustainability managers

We should all try to reduce our carbon footprints. Diagram B shows some ways we can all help to reduce our carbon emissions.

Large businesses now employ sustainability managers to carry out careful surveys (audits) of their carbon footprints. Sustainability managers then suggest ways to reduce carbon footprints.

For example, in some companies the transport of goods is the main source of carbon emissions. The sustainability team would collect data and suggest possible solutions. They might suggest using more efficient engines, alternative fuels, or hybrid or electric vehicles. They might also encourage staff to use public transport or share rides in their cars.

3 Suggest how changes in the following areas could reduce your carbon footprint:

a | travelling to school

b | recycling materials

c | using electrical appliances

d | drinking water.

REDUCE YOUR CARBON FOOTPRINT

USE PUBLIC TRANSPORT RATHER THAN THE CAR

EAT LOCAL PRODUCTS

RECYCLE

USE RECYCLED MATERIALS

DRINK TAP WATER (NOT BOTTLED)

TURN OFF ELECTRICAL APPLIANCES WHEN NOT IN USE

WALK TO SCHOOL

B | ways to reduce your carbon footprint

Diagram C shows part of a company's 'carbon audit'. This is used to suggest ways to reduce the carbon footprint. The suggested changes have disadvantages as well as advantages, so sustainability managers need good communication skills to convince business managers to accept their plans. They use diagrams, charts, graphs, posters and presentation software to display their data and make their proposals clear.

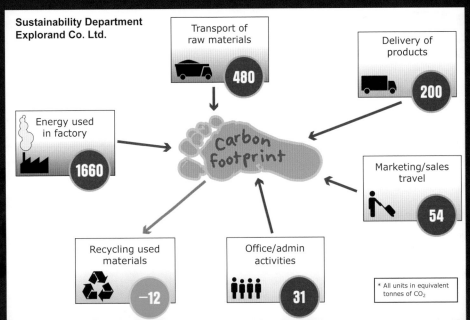

Sustainability Department Explorand Co. Ltd.

Transport of raw materials — 480

Delivery of products — 200

Energy used in factory — 1660

Carbon footprint

Marketing/sales travel — 54

Recycling used materials — −12

Office/admin activities — 31

* All units in equivalent tonnes of CO_2

C | part of a carbon audit

THINK GREEN!

CLICK

Click for more information

D | A sustainability manager needs to communicate ideas clearly.

4 Suggest a reason why the 'Recycling used materials' box in diagram C has been given a different colour.

5 Suggest one advantage and one disadvantage of using hydrogen instead of diesel as a fuel for a company's trucks.

6 Table E shows data about a school's travel arrangements.

Travel by ...	Number of students	Carbon cost (kg of CO_2 / pupil / year)	E
walking	160	0	
bicycle	40	5	
bus	350	65	
car	90	540	

a | What is the total mass of carbon dioxide released (in kg of CO_2 per year) for school travel?

b | Half of those who are driven to school in cars changed to take the bus. What percentage of the carbon dioxide released is saved?

ACTIVITY

1 | Suggest why eating locally-grown food reduces your carbon footprint.

2 | Find out how far some of your food has travelled (its food miles).

3 | Use your data to explain one way to reduce your carbon footprint.

4 | Work in a group to prepare a poster or presentation slide for your school's management team on how to reduce your school's carbon footprint. Start by identifying ways in which your school causes the release of greenhouse gases into the atmosphere. If possible, collect and use data in your poster.

REDUCING POLLUTION

HOW CAN WE REDUCE POLLUTION FROM CARS EVEN FURTHER?

Air pollution from transport has been reduced by using filters, catalytic converters and new engines that use less fuel. To reduce it even further, people will need to change the way they travel.

Governments use a range of ways to persuade people to change their travel habits.

- Road tax: cars are taxed based on engine size, fuel type and carbon dioxide emissions. The lower the pollution, the less you pay.

- Annual tests: all cars over a certain age are tested for road-worthiness. If exhaust emissions are too high, the car must not be driven.

- Congestion charges: in some cities drivers must pay to use their vehicles at busy times of day.

- Fuel prices: higher taxes on fuel can make people decide to use cheaper forms of transport.

- Travel restriction: some countries restrict the number of days drivers can use their cars.

A | Electric cars reduce pollution from the car but electricity power stations release pollution.

Governments may make other changes. For example, the European Union has decided that at least 5.75 per cent of fuel used for transport should be **biofuel** (fuel made from plants).

1. Identify one advantage and one disadvantage, in terms of pollution, of choosing an electric car rather than a diesel or petrol one.

2. Give one advantage and one disadvantage of using hydrogen as a fuel for cars.

3. Some new cars have stop–start technology, where the engine stops when the car is not moving (such as at traffic lights). Explain how this is useful:

   a| for the driver   b| for the local population.

4. For each of the bulleted points in the list on the left, explain why this could help reduce pollution.

B | At this factory, waste material from making sugar is used to produce bioethanol (a biofuel). Using ethanol can reduce carbon dioxide emissions by up to about 70 per cent.

HAVE YOUR SAY

Should governments try to persuade vehicle manufacturers to make cars that produce less pollution, and how could they do this?

Elements and compounds combine during **chemical reactions** in fireworks to produce amazing displays. The energy released by these reactions makes rockets fly into the air, bangers explode and shells produce starbursts of bright light.

Most fireworks contain a mixture, called black powder, as their main source of energy. This is the same as gunpowder and is a mixture of carbon (as charcoal) and sulfur, together with saltpetre (potassium nitrate).

Through a series of chemical reactions, the black powder releases energy and large volumes of gas. Inside mortars and firecrackers this causes explosions. In rockets and shells, the same reactions produce the force to push them into the air.

The reactions in fireworks need oxygen. Most of this is supplied not by the air but by the potassium nitrate, which is known as an **oxidiser**. The carbon and sulfur in black powder react with oxygen to form carbon dioxide gas and sulfur dioxide gas.

Many fireworks also contain powdered metals such as magnesium, which burns to produce a brilliant white light:

magnesium + oxygen → magnesium oxide

A | spectacular chemical reactions

B | Black powder or gunpowder was invented in China over 2000 years ago.

C | Magnesium flares can be used by military aircraft to confuse heat-seeking missiles.

1. What happens in all chemical reactions?

2. Describe the difference between an element and a compound.

3. In certain fireworks, carbon, sulfur and aluminium react with oxygen.
   a| Write word equations for these three reactions.
   b| What are these kinds of reaction called?
   c| What is the source of oxygen for the reactions?

4. What causes the explosion that occurs when black powder reacts inside a sealed container?

8Fa DALTON'S ATOMIC MODEL

WHAT ARE ATOMS LIKE?

The idea that all **matter** is made up of tiny particles started over 2400 years ago. The Greek thinker Democritus wrote about this and called the particles *atomos*, meaning 'indivisible'.

> **1** How did Democritus explain the different properties of substances?
>
> **2** Describe what we now know about the spacing and movement of particles in ice, water and steam.

In 1805, the English chemist John Dalton (1766–1844) published his atomic theory or model, which said:

- all matter is made up of tiny particles called **atoms**
- the atoms in an **element** are all identical (but each element has its own type of atom)
- atoms are indestructible and cannot be created or destroyed
- in **compounds**, each atom of an element is always joined to a fixed number of atoms of other elements
- during **chemical reactions**, atoms rearrange to make new substances (and there is no change in mass).

B | The scanning, tunnelling electron microscope can now show us images of atoms and provides further evidence for Dalton's theory.

a silicon atom

(magnification x 35 000 000)

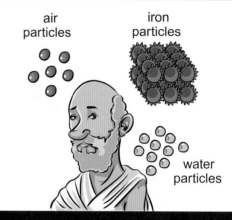
air particles
iron particles
water particles

A | Democritus thought these particles had different sizes and shapes, which explained the different properties of substances.

> **3** Use Dalton's model to describe what an element is like.
>
> **4** Suggest a difference between how Democritus and Dalton worked out their ideas.

FACT

Atoms are extremely small. There are about 50 167 000 000 000 000 000 000 000 atoms in a 500 cm³ bottle of water.

Physical properties

Dalton's atomic model says that all the atoms in an element are identical but that each element has its own type of atoms. The differences in the atoms give each element its own, specific **properties**.

The properties that describe a substance on its own are its **physical properties**. Examples include:

- colour
- melting point
- boiling point
- density
- **ductility**
- **malleability**
- conduction of heat
- conduction of electricity.

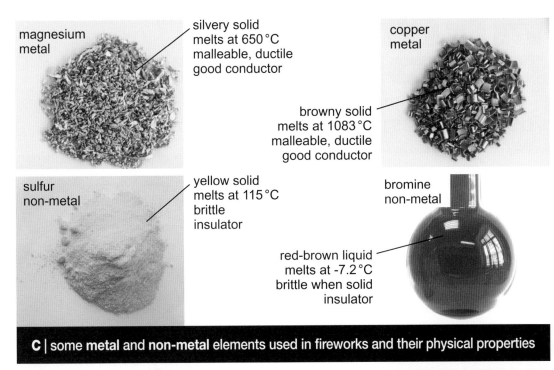

magnesium metal — silvery solid melts at 650 °C malleable, ductile good conductor

copper metal — browny solid melts at 1083 °C malleable, ductile good conductor

sulfur non-metal — yellow solid melts at 115 °C brittle insulator

bromine non-metal — red-brown liquid melts at -7.2 °C brittle when solid insulator

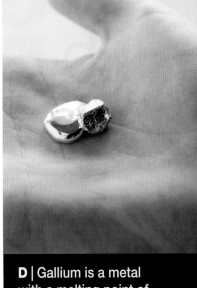

D | Gallium is a metal with a melting point of 30 °C. It will melt in your hand!

C | some **metal** and **non-metal** elements used in fireworks and their physical properties

5 Draw a table to compare the four physical properties of metals and non-metals.

6 Which physical properties allow us to work out the state of an element at room temperature?

mercury liquid

mercury gas

E | Mercury evaporates when heated. On cooling, the change reverses and droplets of liquid mercury form by condensation.

Physical changes, like physical properties, only involve one substance. During a physical change (such as the changes of state shown in photos D and E) there is no change in mass and no new substances are formed. Physical changes are often easy to reverse.

Symbols

To show different atoms, Dalton introduced **symbols** to represent them. The modern symbols are similar but consist of one or two letters (the first letter being a capital), e.g. C for carbon and Cl for chlorine. They have been agreed by the International Union of Pure and Applied Chemistry (IUPAC). All countries use the same symbols so that all scientists can communicate with each other, even though they may use different languages.

7 a| What change will occur if liquid gallium is removed from the hand in photo D?

b| Explain three other changes of state.

F | Dalton's symbols

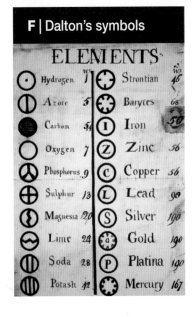

8 a| Draw Dalton's symbols for the elements:
  i| strontium   ii| hydrogen
  iii| phosphorus   iv| oxygen   v| lead.

b| Give one IUPAC symbol for an element.

c| Why are international symbols useful?

I can ...

- describe Dalton's atomic theory
- describe elements using physical properties
- write and identify the chemical symbols for elements.

8Fb CHEMICAL PROPERTIES

HOW DO SCIENTISTS DESCRIBE SUBSTANCES?

In physical changes, no new substances are formed. New substances are formed in chemical reactions (**chemical changes**). During a chemical reaction you may observe a colour change, a gas being formed or energy being released. It is often difficult to reverse chemical changes.

The **chemical properties** of a substance describe how it reacts with other substances. Flammability and reaction with acids are examples.

> 1 What observations show chemical changes in photo A?
>
> 2 List two chemical and two physical properties of calcium metal.

A | chemical reactions of the element calcium with water and oxygen

Reactions of elements

Unlike Democritus, John Dalton used a **scientific method** to develop his atomic theory. He developed a **hypothesis**, which he tested by making **predictions** and carrying out experiments. He formed his theory only using the hypotheses that were supported by evidence.

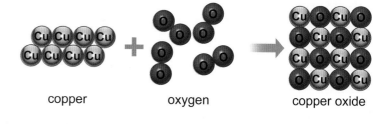

copper   oxygen   copper oxide

B | The total mass of the copper (Cu) and oxygen (O) atoms does not change in this reaction.

One prediction made from Dalton's ideas is that the mass of the products of a reaction will be the same as the mass of the reactants. And this is what is found. Dalton's theory explains this by saying that since atoms cannot be created or destroyed, there is no change in the number of atoms and so there can be no change in the overall mass.

Dalton also noticed that the masses of elements always reacted in the same proportion or **ratio**. For example, when copper disulfide is made, whatever mass of sulfur you start with, the reaction always uses twice as much copper.

> 3 When 4 g of zinc react with 1 g of oxygen, what mass of zinc oxide is produced?

> 4 To produce copper disulfide, how many grams of:
> a| sulfur react with 15 g of copper
> b| copper react with 10 g of sulfur?

Dalton showed that this was still true even when elements formed more than one compound. For example, carbon and oxygen react to form two different compounds and it takes twice as much oxygen to make one compound as it does to make the other. This is explained by Dalton's model, which says that in a certain compound all the atoms of one element are joined to a *fixed* number of the other atoms.

Each carbon atom is always joined to two oxygen atoms.

carbon dioxide

Each carbon atom is always joined to one oxygen atom.

carbon monoxide

C | Each molecule of carbon dioxide contains twice as much oxygen as each molecule of carbon monoxide.

6 Write the chemical formulae for:
a| carbon monoxide   b| copper oxide.

7 How many atoms in total are in a molecule of carbon dioxide?

8 Draw a diagram of the substances with the following chemical formulae:
a| SO_2 b| O_2 c| Ar   d| NH_3

9 What are the formulae of the compounds in diagram E?

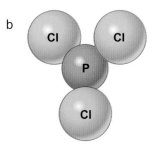

E

5 a| The ratio of oxygen to carbon in carbon dioxide is 2:1. What is the ratio of these elements in carbon monoxide?
b| In diagram B, what is the ratio of copper atoms to oxygen atoms in copper oxide?

Chemical formulae

The ratio of elements in a compound is shown in a **chemical formula**. The ratio is shown using small numbers after the symbols. For example, H_2O is the formula for water. There are two hydrogens (shown by the 2 after the H) and one oxygen (there is no number after the O). So, the ratio of hydrogen to oxygen is 2:1.

Some compounds exist as individual molecules (e.g. water). For these compounds, the chemical formula shows the ratio of elements *and* the exact number of each atom in a molecule. Some elements (e.g. nitrogen) exist as molecules too and so these also have chemical formulae. Nitrogen is N_2.

D | chemical formulae

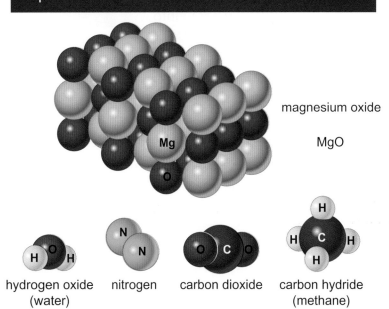

magnesium oxide

MgO

hydrogen oxide (water)

H_2O

nitrogen

N_2

carbon dioxide

CO_2

carbon hydride (methane)

CH_4

I can ...

- explain the difference between physical and chemical changes and properties
- use atomic theory to explain what happens during chemical reactions
- write and interpret chemical formulae.

8Fc MENDELEEV'S TABLE

HOW ARE ELEMENTS ARRANGED IN THE PERIODIC TABLE?

Many new elements were discovered during the 19th century and scientists throughout Europe began to look for patterns, to make sense of their properties.

The German chemist Johann Döbereiner (1780–1849) highlighted some groups of three elements that had similar physical and chemical properties. One of his 'triads' contained the metals lithium, sodium and potassium. Another contained the non-metals chlorine, bromine and iodine. However, most elements did not fit into any triad.

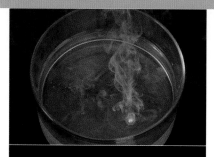

A | Lithium, sodium and potassium metals share a chemical property. They react with water to produce hydrogen and a solution of the metal hydroxide, for example:

potassium + water →
potassium hydroxide +
hydrogen

chlorine gas

iron

B | Chlorine, bromine and iodine react with most metals to form a solid compound, for example:

iron + chlorine → iron chloride

---

1 There are two triads mentioned in the second paragraph. Suggest a physical property of:
 a| the metals in one triad
 b| the non-metals in the other triad.

2 Complete the following word equations:
 a| lithium + water →
 b| copper + chlorine →

The English chemist John Newlands (1837–1898) introduced his law of octaves in 1864. By this time, many scientists had calculated the masses of different atoms and so Newlands put the elements in order of the masses of their atoms. He showed that every eighth element had similar properties. The pattern was not consistent and Newland's ideas were not believed.

In 1869, however, the Russian chemist Dmitri Mendeleev (1834–1907) published his **periodic table**. Like Newlands, he placed the elements in order of increasing masses of their atoms, forming them into groups with similar chemical properties. One of his original notes can be seen in photo C.

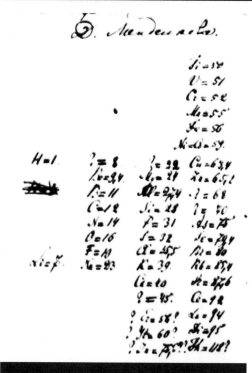

C | Even though Mendeleev's notes and ideas are hard to read, we can make out the elements because he used international symbols.

D | Mendeleev and his original periodic table

3 a| Look at photo C, and give the names and symbols of three elements in Mendeleev's notes.

b| What do the numbers represent?

Mendeleev made sure the elements all fitted into groups with similar properties by changing the order in a few places and leaving gaps for undiscovered elements. He even predicted the properties of the undiscovered elements correctly.

A modern version of the periodic table is shown on page 191. In the modern version, elements with similar properties end up in vertical **groups**. Diagram E shows an outline of the periodic table and the positions of two of Döbereiner's triads. These elements are in groups called the **alkali metals** and the **halogens**.

Mendeleev was not always correct. When argon was discovered in 1894, it did not fit into any of his groups, so he denied its existence. Later argon, along with helium, neon, krypton and xenon, was shown to belong to a new group. These very unreactive gases are now in a group called the **noble gases**.

Mendeleev put atoms in order of their mass. The modern periodic table puts atoms in order of **atomic number**. Every atom contains smaller particles called **protons**. The number of protons in an atom is its atomic number.

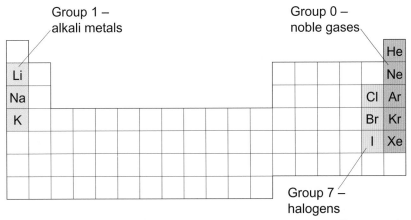

E | outline of the modern periodic table, showing some of the groups

4 Describe a chemical property of:

a| halogens   b| alkali metals

c| noble gases.

5 a| In what order did Mendeleev place the elements in his periodic table?

b| What do elements in the same group have in common?

c| In what order are elements listed in the modern periodic table?

FACT

There is now an element named after Mendeleev. See if you can find it in the periodic table.

I can ...

- use the periodic table to find elements with similar properties
- describe some typical properties of alkali metals, halogens and noble gases
- describe how the modern periodic table is arranged.

ANOMALOUS
8Fc RESULTS

WHAT HAPPENS TO ODD RESULTS?

When argon was discovered in 1894, it did not fit the pattern of Mendeleev's periodic table. He did not believe the evidence and suggested that the mass of the atoms that had been calculated was wrong.

Sometimes measurements seem odd; they do not fit the pattern or they are different from what we expect. These are **anomalous results** (or **outliers**). Their presence can affect the average and the **range** of a set of results. The range is the difference between the highest and the lowest values.

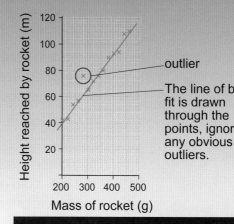

How the height a rocket reaches depends on the mass of the rocket

outlier

The line of best fit is drawn through the points, ignoring any obvious outliers.

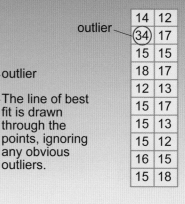

Fireworks manufacturer test: times taken for a certain rocket fuse to burn out (s)

outlier

14	12
34	17
15	15
18	17
12	13
15	17
15	13
15	12
16	15
15	18

A | Anomalous results are often ignored, especially when drawing lines of best fit.

1.
  a| Explain why the circled results in diagram A are anomalous.
  b| What is the range of rocket fuse burn times, including the outlier?
  c| What effect can removing the outlier have on this range?

2. The time taken for an aspirin tablet to dissolve in water was measured several times. The results (in seconds) were: 41; 42; 39; 29; 43; 41; 43; 40; 39; 41.
  a| Identify the anomalous result.
  b| State the range of the data, with and without the anomalous result.

Errors

Anomalous results may be caused by a **random error** (a mistake that affects only one reading). In order to ignore an anomalous result, you need to have a good reason. Some possible sources of random errors are:

- a measuring cylinder scale is read from different angles
- it is difficult to tell if a reaction has stopped or not
- someone forgets to start or stop a stopwatch promptly
- the apparatus is faulty
- the apparatus is not be set up correctly (such as a balance not being set at zero).

3. Diagram B shows some class measurements of the rise in temperature when 100 cm³ of water was heated.
  a| Explain why group 4's result is anomalous.
  b| Suggest a possible reason why group 4 obtained this result.
  c| Work out the range for:
    i| the full set of results
    ii| the results with the outlier removed.

Group	Temperature rise (°C)
1	38
2	43
3	39
4	64
5	43
6	44

B

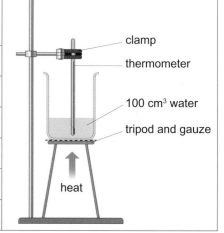

clamp
thermometer
100 cm³ water
tripod and gauze
heat

Investigating burning magnesium

When magnesium (Mg) burns it combines with oxygen (O_2) to form magnesium oxide (MgO). Some of the oxide is usually lost as smoke, which rises into the air.

The aim of this experiment is to find the change in mass when a 2 cm piece of magnesium ribbon is burned completely to form magnesium oxide.

Method

A | Wearing eye protection, place a 2 cm strip of cleaned magnesium into a crucible and put the lid on it.

B | Measure the mass of the magnesium, crucible and lid altogether.

C | Heat the crucible strongly with the lid off. When the magnesium starts to burn, use tongs to replace the lid on the crucible.

D | Every 10 seconds lift the lid to let in more air. Try not to let any smoke escape.

E | When the magnesium has burned completely, let the crucible cool and measure its mass again.

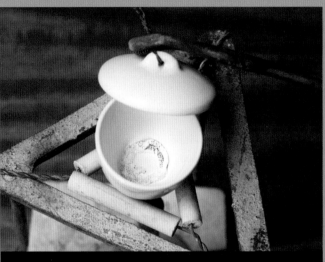

C | The white ash formed when magnesium burns is magnesium oxide (MgO).

Results

The results obtained by 10 different groups of students are shown below.

Group	1	2	3	4	5	6	7	8	9	10
Mass of crucible + Mg + lid (g)	9.12	9.10	9.09	9.11	9.13	9.12	9.18	9.14	9.10	9.12
Mass of crucible + MgO + lid (g)	9.17	9.15	9.15	9.16	9.19	9.13	9.25	9.20	9.17	9.17
Change in mass (g)	+0.05	+0.05	+0.06	+0.05	+0.06	+0.01	+0.07	+0.06	+0.07	+0.05

D

4
a| Identify an anomalous result in table D.
b| Describe a possible cause for this particular anomalous result.
c| Suggest two other possible sources of error in this experiment.

I can ...

- explain what is meant by an anomalous result (outlier)
- identify anomalous results and the range of readings in data
- suggest reasons for anomalous results/outliers/random errors.

PHYSICAL TRENDS
8Fd

WHAT KINDS OF TREND OCCUR IN PHYSICAL PROPERTIES?

When a solid is heated, its temperature rises until it reaches its **melting point**, where it melts (changes from a solid into a liquid). If the heating continues, the liquid's temperature rises and it starts to evaporate into a gas. When it reaches its **boiling point**, rapid evaporation occurs throughout the liquid. Note that the melting point of a substance is also its **freezing point**. Melting, boiling and freezing points are all physical properties of substances.

The changes in temperature, state and particle arrangement that occur as a substance is heated are shown in graph B. Melting points and boiling points can be used to work out a substance's state at a particular temperature.

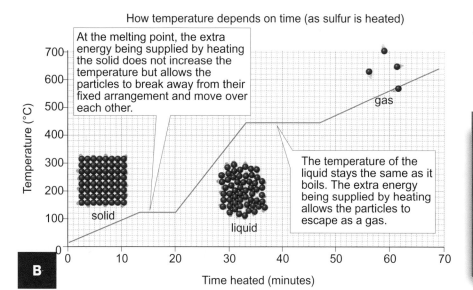

How temperature depends on time (as sulfur is heated)

At the melting point, the extra energy being supplied by heating the solid does not increase the temperature but allows the particles to break away from their fixed arrangement and move over each other.

The temperature of the liquid stays the same as it boils. The extra energy being supplied by heating allows the particles to escape as a gas.

solid

liquid

gas

B

A | The melting point and freezing point of water are both exactly 0 °C.

FACT

The kelvin temperature scale (symbol K) was developed by Lord Kelvin in 1848. The zero point in the scale is −273.15 °C, which is the lowest temperature possible. The boiling point of water on the kelvin scale is 373.15 K.

---

1 Look at graph B.

a| Give the melting and boiling points of sulfur.

b| What state is sulfur in at:
i| 75 °C ii| 140 °C?

2 a| Describe what happens to the movement and spacing of the particles as sulfur melts.

b| Explain why the temperature of the liquid does not change as it boils.

Looking for trends

A trend is a pattern of changes, which shows an increase or a decrease. We can find trends in the periodic table.

In the modern table, the vertical columns are called groups and the horizontal rows are called **periods**. There are eight main groups, separated by the block of elements called the **transition metals**. Table C shows the main group elements with information about their physical properties.

The data in table C shows clear trends in properties down many of the groups: for example, the melting points of the alkali metals decrease from lithium to rubidium.

3 Name and give the symbol for an element that is:

a| in the same group as carbon

b| in the same period as sulfur.

4 Look at table C.

a| What is the freezing point of nitrogen?

b| When heated from 20 °C, would aluminium or magnesium melt first?

c| What state would magnesium be in at:

i| 100 °C ii| 1000 °C?

5 a| Describe the trend in melting point down groups 7 and 0.

b| Estimate the melting points of caesium (Cs) and astatine (At). Caesium is in group 1 and astatine is in group 7.

	group 1	group 2	group 3	group 4	group 5	group 6	group 7	group 0
	hydrogen −259 *−253*							helium −272 *−269*
	lithium 181 *1347*	beryllium 1278 *2970*	boron 2300 *4000*	carbon *3642 *4000*	nitrogen −210 *−196*	oxygen −218 *−183*	fluorine −220 *−188*	neon −249 *−246*
	sodium 98 *883*	magnesium 649 *1090*	aluminium 660 *2467*	silicon 1410 *2333*	phosphorus 44 *280*	sulfur 115 *445*	chlorine −101 *−35*	argon −189 *−186*
	potassium 63 *739*	calcium 842 *1484*	gallium 30 *2403*	germanium 937 *2830*	arsenic *614 *—*	selenium 217 *685*	bromine −7 *59*	krypton −157 *−152*
	rubidium 39 *688*	strontium 769 *1384*	indium 157 *2080*	tin 232 *2602*	antimony 631 *1750*	tellurium 452 *988*	iodine 114 *184*	xenon −112 *−107*

element name
melting point (°C)
boiling point (°C)

*sublimes (changes directly from a solid to a gas)

C | looking for trends

The trends are not so obvious in the periods across the periodic table, where large differences in properties can be seen between certain neighbouring elements. These changes help us to split the elements into metals and non-metals. Some elements have properties in between those of metals and non-metals and these are sometimes called semi-metals.

Table E compares the main properties of metals and non-metals.

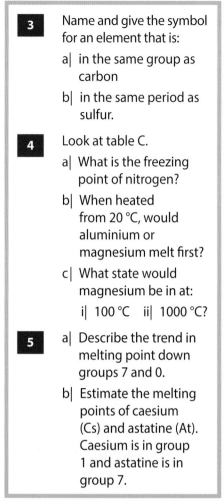

metal
semi-metal
non-metal

transition metals

D | Note the positions of the metals, semi-metals and non-metals in the periodic table.

6 Which properties in table E best splits metals from non-metals? Explain your choice.

7 Explain why silicon (Si) and germanium (Ge) are described as semi-metals.

E	**Metals**	**Non-metals**
	▪ high melting points	▪ low melting points
	▪ strong, ductile and malleable	▪ **brittle** (when solid)
	▪ shiny (when polished)	▪ dull
	▪ good conductors of heat and electricity	▪ insulators (poor conductors of heat and electricity)

I can ...

▪ explain melting, freezing and boiling points and use them to predict the state of a substance

▪ describe and identify trends in physical properties within the periodic table

▪ identify metals and non-metals by their properties and position in the periodic table.

HOW DO TEACHERS COMMUNICATE THEIR KNOWLEDGE TO STUDENTS?

There are about 90 elements in the periodic table that occur naturally. The other elements have been made by scientists.

The most recent elements have atomic numbers from 113 to 118. They were produced by teams of scientists from Russia, Japan and the USA. Each was made using a particle accelerator, in which two atoms are fired at each other at speeds of over a 1 000 000 km/h. Sometimes the atoms combine to form a new bigger atom.

> **1** What do the numbers 113 and 118 tell you about an element?
>
> **2** Look at the periodic table on page 191.
> a | Describe the position of elements 113 to 118.
> b | Write down their names and symbols.

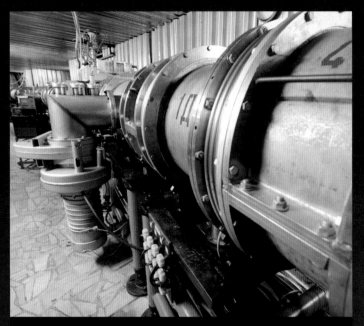

A | This particle accelerator is in Dubna, Russia (where many new elements have been made). It uses advanced technology and engineering to smash atoms together.

B | Kosuke Morita led the Japanese team that made element 113 and were allowed to name it. They called it nihonium (Nh), after a Japanese word for Japan (日本 'nihon').

Only a few atoms of these new elements have been made, and they only existed for a very short time because their atoms break apart quickly. Elements that have atoms that do not last very long are in the bottom period of the periodic table. The atoms towards the right of the period generally break apart quicker than those further to the left.

Once scientists think they have made a new element, their data is checked by scientists from around the world working at IUPAC (the International Union of Pure and Applied Chemistry). If IUPAC think the results are valid, they let the scientists suggest a name. IUPAC then agrees the name.

> **3** a | Use the periodic table on page 191 to find an element named after Mendeleev.
> b | Explain whether you think this element has atoms that break apart quickly or not.

Teaching

Many people are inspired to become research scientists by their teachers. Key skills of teachers include communicating knowledge clearly, and an enthusiasm for their subjects. Most teachers have a degree in their subject and a teaching qualification.

Mendeleev was a chemistry teacher and created the periodic table to communicate the elements to his students! His idea was extremely clear because he organised items in a logical manner and used symbols (rather than element names).

4   a | Explain how symbols make periodic table D on page 31 clear to understand.

     b | Describe one other way in which information is communicated without using many words in this periodic table.

5   Describe how an inspiring teacher might teach science.

C | Diagrams and symbols allow us to communicate information to many different people, more quickly and clearly than using words.

John Dalton used picture diagrams for the elements. With more elements, this got a bit complicated and so Swedish scientist J. J. Berzelius (1779–1848) proposed our current system of letters in 1813. Using symbols rather than words makes it easy to communicate with people all over the world, who speak many different languages.

6   List at least four ways in which your teachers communicate information.

ACTIVITY

Instructions are sometimes given without words.

1   Work in a group to draw a diagram explaining how new elements are made. Do not use words.

2   Look at table E on page 31. Work in a group to convert the table into symbols, showing the same information. Use as few words as possible.

D | These furniture building instructions contain no words.

8Fe CHEMICAL TRENDS

WHAT KINDS OF TREND OCCUR IN CHEMICAL PROPERTIES?

Elements in the same group of the periodic table have similar physical properties. For example, the alkali metals are all soft with low melting points.

Elements in the same group of the periodic table also share similar chemical properties. All the alkali metals must be stored under oil because they react quickly with water and with oxygen. They produce metal hydroxides and hydrogen with water, and they produce metal oxides with oxygen.

For example:

sodium + water → sodium hydroxide + hydrogen

lithium + oxygen → lithium oxide

metal melts into a ball

A | the reactions of three alkali metals with water

1   State three properties that all alkali metals have.

2   a| Describe the reactions of the three alkali metals with water in photo A.
     b| Write word equations for the reactions of:
        i| sodium with oxygen
        ii| potassium with water.

There is a trend in the reactions of Group 1 elements (the alkali metals) with water. Moving down the group, the reaction becomes faster and more violent. We say that the **reactivity** of the elements increases. Trends in reactivity like this can be used to predict how other elements might react.

3   Look at photo A.
     a| Why are alkali metals stored under oil?
     b| Which of the alkali metals is the least reactive?

4   The fourth alkali metal, rubidium, also reacts with water.
     a| Name the two products formed.
     b| What would you expect to see during this reaction?

B | Universal indicator shows that the hydroxide solution formed when an alkali metal reacts with water is alkaline.

FACT

A mixture of liquid sodium and liquid potassium is used to transfer heat in nuclear power stations. This dangerous mixture of metals works well as it stays liquid over a large temperature range.

Finding trends in chemical properties across the periodic table is more difficult. Photos C, D and E show the reactions with oxygen of three elements in one period and the **oxides** that are formed.

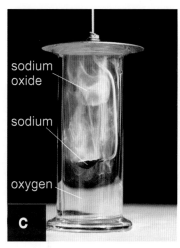

C

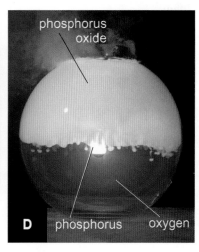

D

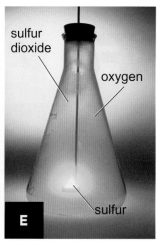

E

When we mix the oxides in water and test with **pH indicator**, there is a trend (shown in table F). Further to the left the oxides are more **alkaline**, and further to the right they are more **acidic**.

Some metal oxides form alkalis called hydroxides with water (e.g. sodium oxide forms sodium hydroxide solution). Other metal oxide are insoluble. However, all metal oxides are **bases**, which means that they react with acids to form a **salt** and water. The reaction is called **neutralisation.**

> **5** Write word equations for the reactions shown in photos C, D and E.

acid + base → salt + water

acid + metal oxide → salt + water

e.g.

sulfuric acid + copper oxide → copper sulfate + water

> Hydrochloric acid forms chloride salts, sulfuric acid forms sulfate salts and nitric acid forms nitrate salts.

F | There is a trend in acidity (pH) of element oxides across the periods in the periodic table.	Group 1	Group 2	Group 3	Group 4	Group 5	Group 6
	lithium			carbon	nitrogen	(oxygen)
	sodium	magnesium			phosphorus	sulfur

← oxides are more alkaline   oxides are more acidic →

> **6** The product of the reaction in photo C is mixed with water and then dilute hydrochloric acid is added. Write a word equation for this neutralisation reaction.
>
> **7** Describe the trend in the chemical properties of the oxides of elements across the periodic table.
>
> **8** Oxides of elements X and Y were dissolved in water. The solution of element X oxide was pH 13, that of element Y oxide was pH 11.
>   a| Describe how to test the pH of a solution.
>   b| What can you say about the positions of X and Y in the periodic table?
>
> **9** Hot iron wool produces a yellow flame when it reacts with chlorine. However, iron just glows red when it reacts with bromine.
>   a| Suggest what the reaction of hot iron wool with fluorine might look like.
>   b| Explain how you made your prediction.

I can ...

- describe the reactions of some elements with water and oxygen
- identify trends and make predictions about chemical properties using the periodic table.

SHOULD FIREWORKS BE BANNED?

The chemicals that are used in fireworks are also used in weapons. Bangers and bombs both contain black powder. The difference between them is a matter of size and use.

Every year fireworks cause injuries and sometimes even death. Rockets cause the most injuries, burns being the most common. However, all fireworks are dangerous and even sparklers can cause serious burns.

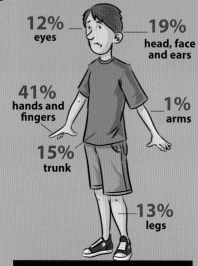

12% eyes

19% head, face and ears

41% hands and fingers

1% arms

15% trunk

13% legs

B | the types of injury caused by fireworks

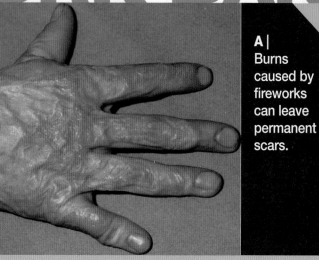

A | Burns caused by fireworks can leave permanent scars.

1
a| Which part of the body is most often injured by fireworks?
b| What is the most common type of injury?
c| Which kind of firework causes most injuries?
d| Suggest how an accident might occur with:
   i| sparklers   ii| rockets.

2 List the names and symbols of five elements found in fireworks.

3 Lithium and sodium compounds are used in fireworks.
a| Why did Mendeleev put sodium in the same group as lithium?
b| Name the group and describe the trend in reactivity as you go down the group.

4 When black powder burns it produces carbon dioxide and sulfur dioxide. Both these gases form acids when dissolved in water.
a| Write word equations for the formation of these oxides.
b| When the oxides are dissolved in water, which do you think will have the lower pH? Explain your answer.

Inside fireworks

Inside fireworks different substances are used to produce different effects. Black powder burns quickly to cause explosions or lift fireworks into the air. Flash powder produces bright flashes of light. Different metal compounds produce different colours of flame. All put together they can produce amazing displays for our entertainment.

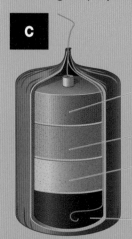

C

Red stars produced from black powder and lithium nitrate.

Yellow sparkle produced by sodium nitrate and iron filings.

Flash mix containing magnesium and aluminium powder produces bright flashes of light.

Black powder containing carbon, sulfur and potassium nitrate launches the firework into the air.

HAVE YOUR SAY

It has been suggested that fireworks should be banned in the UK for private use and only allowed at public, organised displays. What do you think?

8Ga BUILDING UP

For nearly 600 years, cathedrals were the tallest human-made structures on Earth. Built of wood and stone, their size was limited by the materials available, rather than the builder's imagination.

When it opened in 1889, the Eiffel Tower became the tallest human-made structure. At over 300 metres, it was twice the height of any other building. It was built mainly from iron, which could be moulded into strong, stiff girders and rolled into flat sheets.

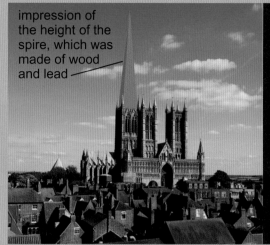

impression of the height of the spire, which was made of wood and lead

A | At 160 metres, the spire of Lincoln Cathedral was the tallest human-made structure on Earth from 1311 until it collapsed in 1549.

1 Why was iron not used in buildings in the 1300s?

2 Name two properties of iron that make it suitable for building tall structures.

The discovery and development of new materials changed building techniques. Steel replaced iron and new uses were found for other **metals**, for example: lead roof joints, aluminium windows and wall panels, titanium pipes and roofs. Modern 'supertall' buildings are built using different construction techniques as well as new materials. Steel is still used, but constructions now often rely on new **composite materials**. These mixtures of metals and non-metals can be cheaper, stronger and lighter than any steel. Diagram B shows some of the tallest buildings throughout history.

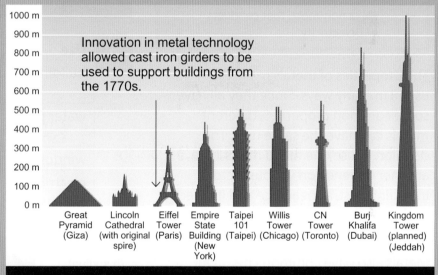

Innovation in metal technology allowed cast iron girders to be used to support buildings from the 1770s.

| 1000 m, 900 m, 800 m, 700 m, 600 m, 500 m, 400 m, 300 m, 200 m, 100 m, 0 m |

Great Pyramid (Giza) | Lincoln Cathedral (with original spire) | Eiffel Tower (Paris) | Empire State Building (New York) | Taipei 101 (Taipei) | Willis Tower (Chicago) | CN Tower (Toronto) | Burj Khalifa (Dubai) | Kingdom Tower (planned) (Jeddah)

B | Buildings got taller as new materials were developed.

C | The Burj Khalifa in Dubai is 830 m tall and became the world's tallest building when it was completed in 2009.

3 Name three metals, apart from iron, used in building houses, and state what they are used for.

4 The metals gold and silver have been used for thousands of years. Suggest a reason why they were not used to build tall structures.

5 Describe one advantage and one disadvantage of very tall buildings.

8Ga METAL PROPERTIES

WHAT MAKES METALS USEFUL?

Metals are elements. You can tell the difference between metals and **non-metals** by their common **physical properties**.

> **1** List four physical properties of a typical metal.
>
> **2** For each of the following, name the element and explain why it is unusual:
> a| a liquid metal
> b| a non-metal that conducts electricity.

The properties of metals make them useful in many ways. Since they all have some common properties, different metals can have the same uses. The decision to use one metal rather than another depends on various factors, including cost, appearance and its precise properties. Table B lists some reasons for using particular metals in house building.

Metals also have common **chemical properties**. For example, most metals react with oxygen. They also react with **halogens** and other non-metals. When metals react, they often form a single solid compound. For example:

lithium + oxygen → lithium oxide

zinc + fluorine → zinc fluoride

Although the reactions are similar, not all metal reactions occur at the same speed, as shown in photo C.

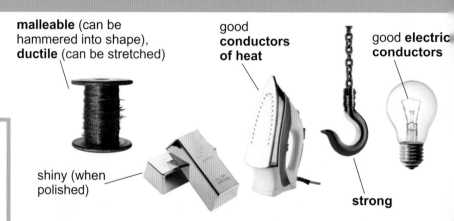

malleable (can be hammered into shape), **ductile** (can be stretched)

good **conductors of heat**

good **electric conductors**

shiny (when polished)

strong

A | the properties of metals

B	Use	Metal	Reason for choice
	building frames	iron	strong, relatively cheap
	water pipes	copper	unreactive, non-poisonous, malleable
	window frames	aluminium	strong, light
	electrical circuits	copper	good conductor of electricity, unreactive

(i) sodium burns brightly in oxygen to form sodium oxide

(iii) silver reacts with oxygen and turns black

(ii) magnesium burns in chlorine gas

(iv) iron and sulfur glow red when they react

C | Remember, in compounds that contain just two elements, the name of the element furthest to the right in the periodic table is placed last, with its ending changed to -ide.

3 a| What makes copper suitable for use in electrical wiring?

   b| Iron is stronger and cheaper than copper, so why is it not used for water pipes?

4 What is the difference between a physical and a chemical property?

5 a| Write a word equation for each reaction in photo C.

   b| Which reactions were fast and which were slow?

Catalysts

Metals are also used as **catalysts** to speed up chemical reactions. A catalyst is a substance that changes the speed of a reaction without being permanently changed itself. Photo D shows how copper metal can be used to speed up the reaction of zinc and sulfuric acid:

zinc + sulfuric acid → zinc sulfate + hydrogen

The test tube containing the copper catalyst produces hydrogen gas faster. At the end of the reaction, the copper metal can be recovered unchanged.

Catalysts are important in everyday life and many chemical industries, and some of the metal catalysts used are very expensive. Platinum, palladium and rhodium are all used in catalytic converters in cars, such as the one shown in diagram E. Only tiny amounts of catalyst are needed and, because they are unreactive and unchanged by the reaction they catalyse, they can be recovered and used again and again.

zinc + sulfuric acid alone   zinc + acid + copper catalyst

D | The copper acts as a catalyst to speed up the reaction.

6 a| What is a catalyst?

   b| Why are only tiny amounts of the metal catalysts used in car exhaust systems?

7 Describe how a catalyst is used in an exhaust system. Name the catalyst and the chemical reaction involved.

8 List five useful metals and explain why each is useful.

E | The catalytic converters in car exhausts speed up reactions that change dangerous gases into harmless ones.

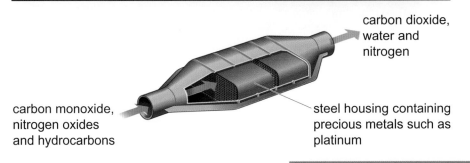

carbon dioxide, water and nitrogen

carbon monoxide, nitrogen oxides and hydrocarbons

steel housing containing precious metals such as platinum

I can ...

- describe some common properties and uses of metals
- write word equations for the reactions of metals and non-metals
- describe what a catalyst is and some uses of catalysts.

8Gb CORROSION

WHAT HAPPENS DURING RUSTING AND CORROSION?

Rust is a problem for all structures built from iron, and they often need to be painted to stop them rusting. Painting started on the Forth Rail Bridge as soon as it opened in 1890 and it was famous as the painting job that never finished. Now, with a new three-layer paint system, the painting is not needed for a few decades.

Corrosion is when the surface of a metal reacts with oxygen (an **oxidation** reaction). Many metals form an oxide layer when exposed to air:

tin + oxygen → tin oxide

Rusting refers specifically to the corrosion of iron.

A | In Scotland, the Forth Rail Bridge's new paint job should last for at least 30 years.

> **1** Which element in the air reacts with tin?
>
> **2** Explain the difference between rusting and corrosion.

Aluminium and titanium are used to make roof panels and windows. Both metals corrode naturally in air, forming a surface layer of metal oxide. The oxide coating sticks to the surface, does not affect the strength of the metal and protects it from further corrosion.

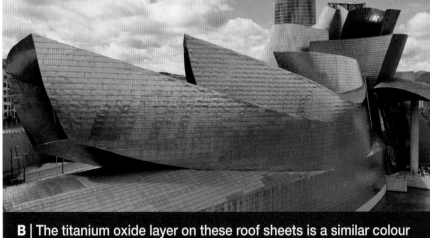

B | The titanium oxide layer on these roof sheets is a similar colour to the titanium metal.

> **3** Name one metal that reacts with oxygen:
> a| quickly
> b| slowly
> c| not at all.
>
> **4** Give two reasons why the corrosion of titanium roofs is not a problem.

Word and **symbol equations** can be written for these reactions.

C

Word equation:	titanium	+	oxygen	→	titanium oxide
Symbol equation:	Ti	+	O_2	→	TiO_2

The symbol equation uses a **formula** for each reactant and product, rather than their names. The formulae for most elements are just their symbols, so titanium is written as Ti. Oxygen gas, however, is written as O_2 because it exists as molecules containing two oxygen atoms.

Most solids, such as TiO_2, do not exist as molecules but as huge networks of atoms joined together. In this case, the formula shows the ratio of the atoms in the compound. TiO_2 tells us that the ratio of titanium to oxygen is 1:2, so in this compound there are two oxygen atoms for every titanium atom.

---

5 The ratio of lead to oxygen in lead oxide is 1:1.

a| What is the symbol for lead?

b| What is the formula for lead oxide?

6 The symbol equation for the corrosion of tin is:

$$Sn + O_2 \rightarrow SnO_2$$

a| Write the word equation for this reaction.

b| What does the formula of tin oxide tell us?

oil layer

water and air

boiled water (no air)

dry air (water removed by a drying agent)

D | What causes rusting?

The rusting of iron is more complex than the corrosion of titanium or lead. The experiment in photo D shows that both oxygen and water must be present for iron to rust. Rust is a complex compound but can be described as iron hydroxide:

iron + oxygen + water → iron hydroxide

Rust is a fragile substance that can weaken and destroy iron structures. The main way of preventing rusting is to use a barrier, such as paint, to keep air and water away from the metal. Some other examples are shown in photo E.

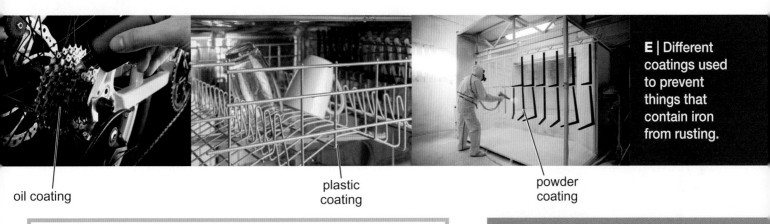

oil coating

plastic coating

powder coating

E | Different coatings used to prevent things that contain iron from rusting.

---

7 a| Name the two other reactants needed for iron to rust.

b| What elements are there in rust?

c| Suggest a reason why metal objects left abandoned in the desert are not usually very rusty.

8 Describe four barrier methods for preventing corrosion. Explain how each works and why we need to use them.

I can ...

- describe what happens during corrosion and rusting
- explain how metals can be protected from corrosion
- identify the products and reactants using a symbol equation.

8Gc METALS AND WATER

HOW DO METALS REACT WITH WATER?

Some metals are just too **reactive** to use in the building industry. Metals on the far left of the periodic table (such as lithium, sodium, potassium and calcium) all react quickly with cold water and so would be destroyed by the first shower of rain.

When metals react with water they form hydrogen gas and a metal hydroxide. This is the word equation for the reaction of sodium with water:

sodium + water → sodium hydroxide + hydrogen

A | A bridge made from calcium would not last long in wet weather.

hydrogen (H₂)

water (H₂O) containing sodium hydroxide (NaOH)

sodium (Na)

B | Sodium and water react forming hydrogen gas. The indicator turns purple, showing that an alkali, sodium hydroxide, has been formed.

---

1 Name three metals that are too reactive to use for building bridges.

2 What are the formulae for the products of the reaction between sodium and water?

calcium

C | Calcium and water reacting: if the gas is collected, it burns with a squeaky pop so proving that it is hydrogen.

Many metals do not appear to react with cold water. However, most will in fact react, just very slowly. The reaction of magnesium is shown in photo D:

magnesium + water → magnesium hydroxide + hydrogen

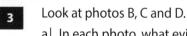

D | In water, bubbles slowly form on the surface of magnesium ribbon.

---

3 Look at photos B, C and D.

a | In each photo, what evidence tells you that a reaction is taking place?

b | Describe the test for hydrogen gas.

4 Write word equations for the reactions of potassium and calcium with water.

The reactivity series

The reactions of metals with oxygen and water form similar products and general equations can be written for them. General equations help us remember what happens in chemical reactions:

metal + oxygen → metal oxide

metal + water → metal hydroxide + hydrogen

FACT

The most reactive metals in the periodic table are caesium and francium of group 1. Francium, however, is very rare – it is estimated that there is at most only 30 g of the metal in the Earth's crust.

E | Caesium is so reactive it can explode when dropped into cold water.

In the reactions of metals with water and oxygen, some metals react faster or give out more energy than others. These differences in **reactivity** can be used to place the metals in a **reactivity series**, as shown in table F. Knowing the order of the reactivity series can help us make predictions about other reactions.

Metal	Reaction with oxygen in air	Reaction with cold water
potassium	can catch fire	can catch fire
sodium	can catch fire	✓✓✓
lithium	can catch fire	✓✓
calcium	can catch fire	✓✓
magnesium	can catch fire	✓
aluminium	✓✓✓	●●●
zinc	✓✓	●●●
iron	✓✓	●●●
tin	✓	●●●
lead	✓	●●●
copper	✓	✗
mercury	●●●	✗
silver	●●●	✗
gold	✗	✗
platinum	✗	✗

Increasing reactivity

Key

🔥	can catch fire	✓✓✓	reacts very quickly	✓✓	reacts quickly
✓	reacts	●●●	slow or partial reaction	✗	no reaction

5 Write the following metals in order of increasing reactivity: lithium, copper, tin, zinc.

6 Use the information in this topic to name a metal that:

a| does not react with water or oxygen

b| is more reactive than potassium

c| reacts with oxygen but not at all with water.

7 Metal X burns in air and reacts slowly with water.

a| Where would you place metal X in the reactivity series? Explain your answer.

b| Name the products formed when metal X reacts with:

i| oxygen   ii| water.

I can ...

- describe the reactions of metals with water
- place metals in order of reactivity
- write word and symbol equations for reactions.

8Gd QUALITY EVIDENCE

HOW CAN WE IMPROVE THE QUALITY OF EVIDENCE?

Good-quality evidence is needed to make the correct conclusions from experimental results. Good-quality evidence needs to be both **accurate** and **reliable**.

Accuracy

This describes how close a measurement is to its real value. Accuracy depends on a number of factors including using the correct measuring device, controlling variables and the skill of the experimenter. Consider the examples that are shown in diagrams A, B and C.

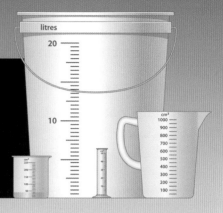

A | The best choice for measuring 40 cm³ of liquid is the 50 cm³ measuring cylinder. The scales on the other devices are too large to measure this volume accurately.

B | To compare the reactivity of these two metals in a fair way, you must control all other variables (e.g. the type and concentration of acid, the form and mass of metal).

Reliability

Repeating measurements allows you to be more certain about them. If the results measured by one experimenter are all very close together, then we say they are **repeatable**. If other people can get similar close values, we say the data is **reproducible**.

The best-quality data will be both repeatable and reproducible, with a small **range** of values and few or no **anomalous results**. Data that is repeatable and reproducible is said to be reliable: you can depend on it being correct.

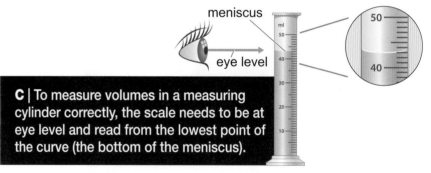

C | To measure volumes in a measuring cylinder correctly, the scale needs to be at eye level and read from the lowest point of the curve (the bottom of the meniscus).

1. a| Why would a 2 cm³ syringe be unsuitable for measuring the volume of liquid in figure A?
   b| List four variables in diagram B that should be controlled.
   c| What is the correct reading on the scale in diagram C?

2. What is an anomalous result?

3. Explain the difference between repeatable and reproducible data.

Investigating the reactivity of metals

The aim of the investigation described on the next page is to find the order of reactivity of three metals with hydrochloric acid.

D | Many metals react with acids to produce hydrogen gas.

Method

 Wear eye protection when carrying out this method.

A | Set up the apparatus as shown in diagram E using clean glassware.

B | Add 25 cm³ of dilute hydrochloric acid (0.4 M max.) to the conical flask.

C | Add a small piece of clean magnesium metal to the flask. Immediately replace the stopper and start the stop clock.

D | Measure and record the volume of gas formed after 20 seconds.

E | Clean all apparatus and repeat steps A to D one more time.

F | Repeat the whole experiment with small amounts of calcium and zinc metals. Use the same amount of metal as you used in step C.

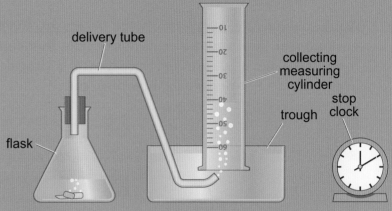

E

F

Group X	
Metal	**Volume of gas in 20 s (cm³)**
magnesium	22
magnesium	23
calcium	33
calcium	30
zinc	10
zinc	12

Group Y	
Metal	**Volume of gas in 20 s (cm³)**
magnesium	23
magnesium	23
calcium	31
calcium	31
zinc	11
zinc	19

Group Z	
Metal	**Volume of gas in 20 s (cm³)**
magnesium	23
magnesium	22
calcium	30
calcium	31
zinc	5
zinc	11

Three groups of students, X, Y and Z, investigated the reactivity of metals. Their results are shown in table F.

4 List all the variables that they needed to control.

5 State the order of reactivity for the metals and explain your answer.

6 a| Are all the results from magnesium reliable? Explain your reasoning.

b| When comparing all the results, what single value would you use for magnesium?

7 What is the range of results for zinc?

8 Identify and suggest a reason for the anomalous result obtained by group Z.

I can ...

- explain what is meant by accurate data
- identify data that is, or is not, reliable, repeatable or reproducible
- explain how to improve the quality of data collected during an investigation.

METALS AND ACIDS
8Gd

WHAT HAPPENS WHEN METALS REACT WITH ACIDS?

Acidic solutions are found in the home, in industry and in our environment. Even ordinary rainwater is acidic. Therefore, since many of the metals we use come into contact with acids, it is important for us to understand how they react.

A | The acid in rainwater reacts with copper, turning it green.

1 Explain how you can protect iron structures against acid rain.

2 Explain how you would test rainwater to see how acidic it was.

Diagram B shows the reactions of different metals when added to water and to acid. The order of reactivity is the same for both types of reaction, even though the products of the reactions are different.

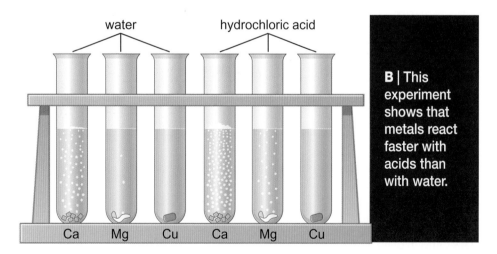

B | This experiment shows that metals react faster with acids than with water.

3 When added to dilute acid, name one metal that might:

a| explode

b| not react.

4 Place these metals in order of increasing reactivity: zinc, sodium, iron, copper.

5 Explain how you could use a metal to tell the difference between water and a dilute acid.

Metal	Increasing reactivity	Reaction with acids	Reaction with water
potassium		explosive, dangerous with dilute acids	catches fire in water
sodium			reacts quickly with water
lithium			
calcium		reacts very quickly with dilute acids	
magnesium			reacts slowly with water
aluminium			
zinc		reacts slowly with dilute acids	very slow or partial reaction with water
iron			
tin			
lead			
copper		does not appear to react with dilute acids at all	does not appear to react with water at all
mercury			
silver			
gold			
platinum			

C | the reactivity series of metals, with acids and water

When a metal reacts with an acid, **effervescence** occurs and the metal seems to disappear into solution. The gas we see given off is hydrogen, but the other product, called a **salt**, seems invisible. This is because most salts are colourless and soluble, so they stay dissolved in solution. We can only see the salt when we evaporate the water. The general equation for this reaction is:

metal + acid → salt + hydrogen

The salt formed depends on the metal and the acid used. Hydrochloric acid forms chloride salts, sulfuric acid forms sulfate salts and nitric acid forms nitrate salts. For example:

magnesium + sulfuric acid → magnesium sulfate + hydrogen

$$Mg + H_2SO_4 \rightarrow MgSO_4 + H_2$$

Photos D, E and F show how a dry sample of a soluble salt can be obtained.

Table G shows some other examples of salts, along with their formulae.

D | When magnesium (Mg) is added to hydrochloric acid (HCl), the hydrogen gas (H_2) forms bubbles, while the magnesium ($MgCl_2$) stays in solution.

G	Metal	Acid	Salt formed
	iron (Fe)	hydrochloric acid (HCl)	iron chloride ($FeCl_2$)
	barium (Ba)	sulfuric acid (H_2SO_4)	barium sulfate ($BaSO_4$)
	sodium (Na)	nitric acid (HNO_3)	sodium nitrate ($NaNO_3$)

E | The solution is filtered to remove excess magnesium.

F | Heating evaporates the water, leaving the solid salt magnesium chloride. Heating is stopped as soon as crystals start to form.

6   Name the salt formed by the reaction between:
   a| calcium and nitric acid
   b| lithium and hydrochloric acid.

7   Name the products formed when acid rain, containing sulfuric acid, falls on an unprotected iron structure.

8   Zinc reacts with sulfuric acid (H_2SO_4) to form zinc sulfate ($ZnSO_4$).
   a| Write a word equation and a symbol equation for the reaction.
   b| Describe how you could obtain a solid sample of the salt.

FACT

The most acidic rainwater ever recorded, with a pH of 1.5, fell in West Virginia, USA in 1979. Acid rain of this strength can cause iron and steel structures to rust more than 10 times faster than normal.

I can ...

- describe the reactions of metals with acids
- place metals in order of reactivity
- write word and symbol equations for reactions.

8Ge PURE METALS AND ALLOYS

WHAT MAKES ALLOYS SO USEFUL?

Most of the metals we use are not **pure**, but have had small amounts of other elements added to them. These **mixtures** of metals are called **alloys**. They are useful because they have properties that are more desirable than those of the pure metal. Some examples of alloys are given in table A.

> **1** Explain the difference between a mixture and a pure substance.
>
> **2** List the main properties of a typical metal.

A	Alloy	Main metal	Added elements	Improved properties	Example of use
	solder	lead	tin	lower melting point than lead	
	duralumin	aluminium	copper and magnesium	lighter and stronger than aluminium	
	stainless steel	iron	carbon, chromium, nickel, etc.	stronger and more resistant to corrosion than iron	

FACT

Pure gold is not hard enough to be used in jewellery, so an alloy of gold, silver and copper is used. The purity of the gold is measured in carats. Pure gold is 24 carat, while 18-carat gold jewellery contains 75 per cent gold and 25 per cent other metals.

> **3** Look at table A.
> a| Which alloy has been made to be less reactive?
> b| What is solder used for?
> c| Explain why the properties of duralumin make it suitable for the use shown.

The difference in properties can often be explained by looking at the arrangement of atoms in the pure metal compared with the alloy. Duralumin is less **malleable** and keeps its shape better than pure aluminium or copper. Diagram E shows why the addition of copper atoms changes the properties of the metal.

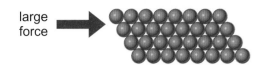

large force →

Metal atoms are arranged in layers.

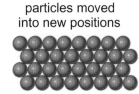

particles moved into new positions

A large force will move the layers.

In an alloy, the different atoms block the structure so the layers cannot slide so easily.

E | A model of the atoms in a metal and an alloy can be used to explain the change in properties.

4 Bronze is an alloy of tin and copper. It is harder than either of those pure metals.

a| What is an alloy?

b| Explain the difference in properties between this alloy and the metals it is made from in terms of the arrangement of atoms.

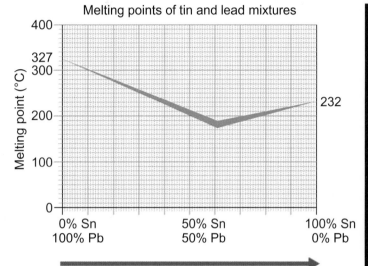

Melting points of tin and lead mixtures

Melting point (°C): 400, 327, 300, 232, 200, 100, 0

0% Sn / 100% Pb — 50% Sn / 50% Pb — 100% Sn / 0% Pb

Increasing percentage by mass of tin

F | The melting points of pure tin and pure lead are very precise. There is a range of temperatures over which the alloys melt.

When a pure substance is heated, its temperature rises until it reaches its **melting point**, where it turns into a liquid. The temperature then continues to rise until the **boiling point**, where rapid evaporation occurs throughout the liquid. The melting points and boiling points of pure substances are fixed and occur at precise temperatures. They can be used to identify substances (for example, the test for pure water is that it boils at 100 °C). Mixtures, such as alloys, melt and boil over a range of temperatures. These temperature ranges depend on the percentages of the different metals in the alloy.

Forming alloys can change chemical properties as well as physical properties. Stainless steel is less reactive than most iron alloys and so it does not react or corrode easily.

5 a| Use graph F to identify the melting points of pure lead and pure tin.

b| Which mixture produces the solder with the lowest melting point?

6 Two old pieces of iron were tested. Iron X melted at exactly 1535 °C. Iron Y melted between 1400 °C and 1450 °C.

a| Which sample was pure iron? Explain your answer.

b| Suggest why most structures are made from iron alloys rather than pure iron.

G | The Chrysler Building in New York was opened in 1930. The stainless steel on it is still bright and shiny.

I can ...

- explain what alloys are and why they are used
- use models to explain the properties of alloys
- identify pure substances by their melting points and boiling points.

HOW DO SCIENTISTS DISCOVER NEW USEFUL ALLOYS?

Thousands of years ago alloys like bronze, a mixture of copper and tin, would have been discovered by accident. Today, scientists use their knowledge and skills to develop different alloys with surprising properties and new uses. For example, shape memory alloys that return to their original shapes after being stretched or twisted.

Cables made of memory alloy are being investigated for use inside the concrete of buildings and bridges in earthquake areas. After being bent or twisted the wires would return to their original shape and close any cracks that have appeared in the concrete.

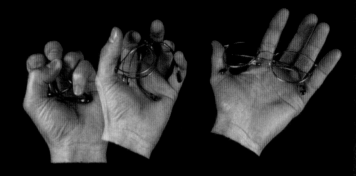

A | These spectacles, which are made from shape memory alloys, return to their original shape after being squashed.

1. Look back at page 112.
   a | What is an alloy?
   b | Name three examples of alloys and the main metal in each.

2. Why are alloys often more useful than the pure metals?

3. Look at photo A. Explain why spectacle frames made of shape memory metal are useful.

Metallurgy

Metallurgists are scientists that study the structure and properties of metals, and design new alloys. Recently, metallurgists around the world have been working on using magnesium to develop ultra-light, strong alloys that do not corrode. Magnesium is 75% lighter than steel and 33% lighter than aluminium, so these alloys could revolutionise car and building designs.

To develop a new alloy, the metallurgists need to be innovative and inventive. They may start the process with some questions. For example:

- What properties do we need a new alloy to have?
- What alloys with similar properties are available now?
- Can we adapt an existing alloy by adding something?
- Can we adapt an existing alloy by taking something away?
- Are there other materials that could be adapted to have the properties we want?

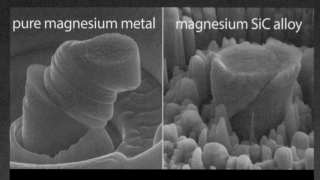

pure magnesium metal | magnesium SiC alloy

B | Research metallurgists use high power electron microscope technology to study metal structures.

Answers to these questions will help them to decide if they can innovate (further develop) using an existing alloy or whether they must invent a completely new alloy.

Research teams also use brainstorming techniques, where people are encouraged to think up as many ideas and possible answers as they can in a short time. Many of the ideas produced may be nonsense, but some can be useful.

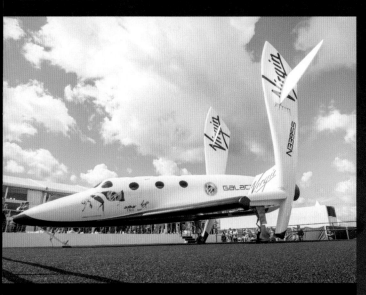

C | New ultra-light but strong magnesium alloys will have uses in all sorts of everyday items, such as aeroplanes, cars, phones and laptops.

4 Give the name of a scientist that studies metals.

5 Imagine you have been asked to find a new alloy for industrial ovens.

a | Suggest two properties the new alloy will need to have.

b | Suggest two examples of questions you might ask to start the development process.

6 Graph D shows how the strength of a copper/nickel alloy varies with composition.

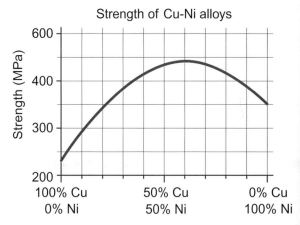

D

a | Which pure metal is stronger, copper or nickel?

b | What does the graph tell us about the copper/nickel alloy?

ACTIVITY

Metallurgists need to test the properties of the alloys that they develop. Work in a group to design a device that will test one of these properties: strength, ductility, malleability or heat conductivity.

1 Start by asking questions to see if you can use an existing piece of equipment or if you need to invent a new device.

2 Then hold a brainstorming session, making sure that everyone gets time to suggest ideas.

3 Create a presentation for your class, explaining how your device works and how your group developed it. Use drawings or models to help with your explanation.

HOW ARE METALS USED IN PUBLIC ART?

Large public works of art have been part of the landscape of our towns and cities for centuries. Many of these sculptures use alloys or special metal coatings to improve their appearance or protect them from damage. These artworks can be expensive to build but they are often greatly valued by the people who live and work near them.

1. *17 Acute Unequal Angles* looks like it is made of rusty iron.
   a| What is rust and what causes it?
   b| What is an alloy?
   c| Why was this work made from an alloy rather than iron?

2. a| Explain how adding tin to copper makes the bronze alloy harder (photo B).
   b| Why would tools be better made of bronze than made of copper?

3. The iron used to make the *Kelpies* is coated in zinc.
   a| How does coating the iron stop it from rusting?
   b| Name the products of the reaction between zinc and sulfuric acid.

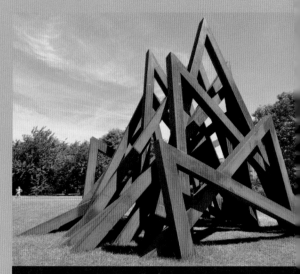

A | This public artwork is called *17 Acute Unequal Angles*. It was built with a special steel alloy, including copper, which forms a strong rust-coloured coating on its surface.

B | This fountain sculpture sits in a public square in Hong Kong. It is made of bronze, a hard alloy of copper and tin that does not corrode easily.

C | Many iron and steel structures, like the *Kelpies* in Falkirk, Scotland, are **galvanised** to prevent corrosion. Galvanising coats the iron with zinc, a reactive metal that protects the iron even if the coating becomes broken.

HAVE YOUR SAY

Some people say that spending millions of pounds on large public sculptures is a waste of money. What do you think?

8Ha DISASTER!

The **eruption** of Mount Tambora, Indonesia, in April 1815 was the deadliest volcanic eruption in recorded history. The explosion was heard over 2000 km away and killed over 10 000 people directly. Around two million tonnes of ash, rock fragments and sulfur compounds entered the atmosphere.

Over 60 000 more people died in Indonesia from starvation as the ash covered crops. Ash and sulfuric acid in the atmosphere reduced the amount of sunlight reaching the surface of the Earth. This affected the climate around the world and 1816 was known as 'the year without a summer' because of the cool, wet weather. There was famine in many countries, killing hundreds of thousands more people.

B | Volcanoes still cause problems in many parts of the world. These crops in Indonesia have been spoiled by ash from a nearby volcano.

C | Ash from volcanoes can cause spectacular sunsets around the world. The sunsets following 1815 are thought to be the inspiration for some of J.M.W. Turner's paintings.

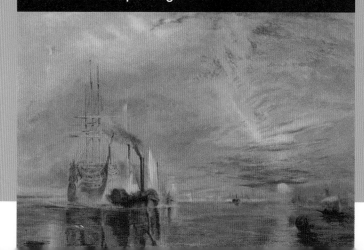

A | Ash from an eruption can be shot over 40 km into the atmosphere and spread around the world.

1 Lava from volcanoes forms rocks when it solidifies.

a| Write down some uses for rocks.

b| Describe the properties of rocks that make them suitable for these purposes.

2 a| How can sulfuric acid in the atmosphere damage crops?

b| How are similar effects caused by human activities?

3 Volcanoes also produce a lot of carbon dioxide when they erupt.

a| What effect does carbon dioxide have on the temperature of the Earth?

b| Name one human activity that adds carbon dioxide to the atmosphere.

4 a| The rocks inside a volcano and its surroundings can be very different. Describe some differences between different rocks.

b| Name any rocks you can think of.

8Ha ROCKS AND THEIR USES

HOW CAN WE DESCRIBE ROCKS?

Natural disasters range from **earthquakes** and volcanic eruptions to the sudden appearance of **sinkholes**. These disasters cannot usually be prevented, but if **geologists** know where and when they may happen, people can be moved out of the danger area. To do this, geologists need to study rocks and how they are formed.

Rocks are made of different **grains** that fit together. Grains are made from one or more chemical **compounds**. The compounds in rocks are called **minerals**. Rocks are **mixtures** of different minerals.

> **1**
> a| What is a mineral?
> b| What is a grain?

A | Sinkholes form when rocks such as **limestone** react with substances in water in the ground.

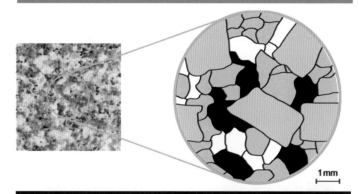

B | **Granite** is a rock made from three or four main minerals. It has interlocking grains. The scale bar helps you to see how big the grains are.

1 mm

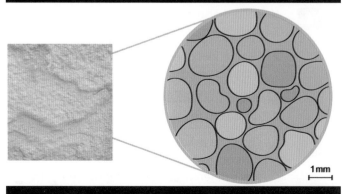

C | **Sandstone** has rounded grains made of a mineral called **quartz**.

1 mm

The grains in rocks can be different sizes and shapes. The combination of sizes and shapes of grains is called the **texture** of the rock. Geologists classify rocks by the minerals they contain and by looking at the texture. The properties of a rock depend on its texture and the minerals it contains.

In some rocks the grains all fit together with no gaps. We say that the grains are **interlocking**. Interlocking grains are sometimes called **crystals**. Rocks made of interlocking grains are usually hard and do not wear away easily.

In other rocks the grains are more rounded and there are gaps between them. Rocks like this are not usually as strong as rocks made from interlocking crystals and wear away more easily.

> **2** Write down the name of a rock that has:
> a| rounded grains
> b| interlocking grains.

3 Look at photo D. Which type of rock wears away most easily? Explain your answer.

Rocks made of rounded grains can absorb water because it can get into the gaps between the grains. These rocks are said to be **porous**. Most porous rocks are also **permeable** (water can run through them).

4 Write down three ways in which granite is different from sandstone.

5 Why do rocks made from rounded grains absorb water?

6 Describe how you could investigate whether some rocks are more permeable than others.

D | The gentle hills in the foreground are made from rocks with rounded grains. The higher hills beyond them are made from rocks with interlocking crystals.

FACT

Rocks are transparent if you slice them thinly enough. Geologists use microscopes to look at thin sections of rocks to learn about the minerals in them.

E | a thin section of **gabbro** seen through a microscope (× 11)

Rocks are used to make buildings and also as the base for roads and railways. Many buildings and monuments are made from stone because it looks attractive. Limestone is quarried to use as a building material, but it is also used to make **cement** and to neutralise acidic soils. **Concrete** is used for the foundations of houses. It is a mixture of cement, sand and **gravel** (small pieces of stone).

7 Suggest the two most important properties for a rock used to make:

a| a statue

b| a house.

8 Oolite is a type of limestone made of rounded grains of a mineral called calcite. Explain whether oolite is more like sandstone or granite.

I can ...

- describe the textures of some different rocks
- explain how some of the properties of rocks are related to their texture
- recall some uses of rocks.

8Hb IGNEOUS AND METAMORPHIC

HOW ARE IGNEOUS AND METAMORPHIC ROCKS FORMED?

We live on the **crust** of the Earth. Underneath the crust is a layer called the **mantle**. The Earth is very hot inside. Sometimes parts of the mantle and crust become so hot that they melt. The molten rock is called **magma**.

Igneous rocks

When molten rock cools down it freezes to form **igneous rocks**. If molten rock cools down fast, it forms rocks containing small crystals, such as **basalt**. This can happen when magma flows out of the Earth's crust in a volcano. Magma that reaches the Earth's surface is called **lava**. Lava cools quickly in the air or under water. Rocks formed from cooling lava are called **extrusive** igneous rocks.

FACT

The tallest volcano in the Solar System is Olympus Mons, on Mars. It is 25 km high.

B | The high temperature of this lava in Hawaii has set the house on fire.

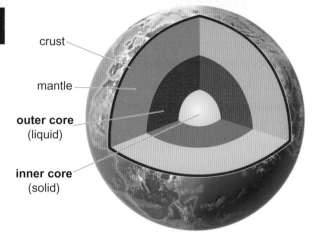

A

crust

mantle

outer core (liquid)

inner core (solid)

1 What is the difference between lava and magma?

Large volumes of magma trapped underground will cool very slowly. This forms rocks containing large crystals, such as gabbro or granite. If the magma has been forced into narrow gaps in existing rocks it can cool quickly and form rocks with small crystals. Igneous rocks that form underground are called **intrusive** igneous rocks.

Magma or lava can contain different combinations of substances. The kind of rock that is formed depends on the substances and on how fast it cools.

2 Explain how the same magma can form either gabbro or basalt.

We can explain differences in crystal sizes by thinking about **particles**. When the rock is a liquid, the particles are free to move about. As the liquid cools down, forces between the particles slowly start to form the particles into a regular grid pattern, which grows and grows.

C | A thin section of basalt at a magnification of × 11: basalt contains the same minerals as gabbro. Compare the sizes of the crystals with photo E on page 55.

If the rock cools slowly, there is plenty of time for a large grid pattern to form. This makes large crystals. If the rock cools down quickly, there is much less time for the particles to become ordered and so smaller crystals are made.

3 Why do some rocks have bigger crystals than others?

4 Why does magma usually cool more slowly than lava?

Metamorphic rocks

Earth movements can bury rocks and **compress** (squash) them. Rocks moved down into the Earth or near magma can also become hotter. High temperatures and pressures can cause changes in the minerals in rocks, and new crystals form. Rocks changed in this way are called **metamorphic rocks**. Metamorphic rocks are always made from interlocking crystals, which may be lined up to form coloured bands. Metamorphic rocks usually have different properties to the rocks from which they were made.

5 Look at diagram D. At which of the numbered places will you find metamorphic rocks? Explain your answer.

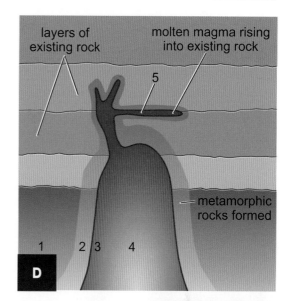

layers of existing rock

molten magma rising into existing rock

5

metamorphic rocks formed

1   2 3   4

D

- increasing temperature and pressure when rock was formed
- increasing crystal size and thickness of layers

2 cm

Granite is an igneous rock. It does not have layers.

2 cm

Schist (pronounced '***shist***') often looks shiny because flakes of a mineral called mica in the rock are lined up.

2 cm

Gneiss (pronounced '***nice***') usually has bands of different coloured minerals.

E | Granite can turn into schist or gneiss, depending on how high the temperature and pressure get.

6
a| In diagram D, the rocks that form at positions 3 and 4 have the same chemical composition. Explain how their textures will be different.

b| Explain what size crystals you would expect to find in the rock that forms at position 5 in diagram D.

I can ...

- describe the structure of the Earth
- describe how igneous and metamorphic rocks are formed
- explain how the grain size is evidence for the speed of cooling.

HOW CAN VOLCANIC ERUPTIONS BE PREDICTED?

The Nevado del Ruiz volcano in Colombia erupted in 1985, causing mud flows that buried the town of Armero. More than 23 000 people died. Scientists had warned an eruption was about to happen, but they could not predict exactly when. Despite the warnings most people decided not to evacuate the town.

Today, some countries have teams of expert volcanologists who can travel around the world to provide help where it is needed. They try to predict when an eruption might happen and identify the villages and towns that should be evacuated.

Volcanologists are scientists who use their knowledge of physics, chemistry and geology to study volcanoes. They study at university and get more training at work. They also need good communications skills to explain their findings and predictions to other scientists and to governments and other officials.

A | This village in Indonesia was destroyed when Mount Merapi erupted in 2010. Warnings from volcanologists allowed up to 20 000 lives to be saved.

1. Suggest why volcanologists need a knowledge of physics and chemistry.

2. Explain why good communication skills are essential for volcanologists.

3. Suggest what problems may be caused if an eruption does not happen at the time scientists predict.

Predicting eruptions

In an active volcano, magma moving underground can give off gases, change the shape of the volcano and cause small earthquakes. Volcanologists use many different types of technology to detect these changes.

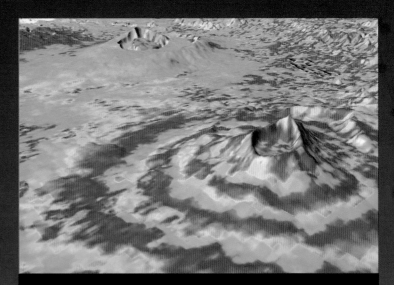

B | This image of the Mount Longonot volcano in Kenya was made by comparing two sets of satellite radar measurements taken 3 years apart. Each complete band of colours (yellow to blue) shows the ground has risen by about 3 cm during that time.

C | Tiltmeters buried on the volcano measure changes in its shape. GPS receivers on the volcano can also be used.

When scientists cannot change an independent variable, they often build **models** to experiment on. Volcanoes are so complicated that volcanologists need to use computer models.

Measurements from many different instruments are used to build a computer model of a volcano, to help the scientists to work out what is happening inside. They use the model to make predictions and test those predictions by gathering more data. If the predictions are wrong, the model is changed.

4 Look at photos B and C.

a | Suggest two advantages of using satellite data to study volcanoes.

b | Suggest why volcanologists also need to visit volcanoes to study them.

5 Suggest why a volcano grows bigger before it erupts.

6 Suggest two ways in which volcanoes can differ from one another.

7 Write a list of all the different kinds of measurements volcanologists could make to study a volcano.

PRACTICAL

Another use for models is to help to explain complicated ideas. Geologists use an instrument called a seismometer to measure earth movements. You can build a model seismometer to help you to understand how these instruments work.

1 Work in a team to build a model seismometer, like the one in diagram E.

2 One person shakes the box gently while another pulls the paper strip slowly. Describe what you see on the paper.

3 Volcanologists are studying a volcano near a remote village. Your model is going be used as part of a display to explain what the volcanologists are doing. Write a short information poster to go with your model to explain how a seismometer works.

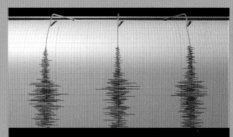

D | A seismograph trace shows earth movements.

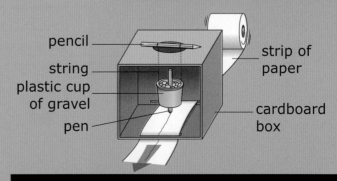

pencil
string
plastic cup of gravel
pen
strip of paper
cardboard box

E | a model seismometer

8Hc WEATHERING AND EROSION

HOW DO ROCKS WEAR AWAY?

Weathering

Limestone is mainly calcium carbonate. Metal carbonates react with acids to form a salt, water and carbon dioxide:

acid+metal carbonate → salt+water+carbon dioxide

This reaction has formed the gaps in the 'limestone pavement' in photo A. Rain contains dissolved gases from the air that make it slightly acidic, and this reacts with the calcium carbonate. This process is called **chemical weathering**.

The new substances formed may be soluble and wash away or they may be very crumbly.

A | Limestone pavements take millennia to form.

> **1** Why is rainwater acidic?
>
> **2** Give the products of the reaction between sulfuric acid and copper carbonate.

The tree in photo A can also help to break up the rock. Plant roots can grow into cracks in the rocks. When the roots grow bigger they make the cracks wider and the rock can break apart. This is called **biological weathering**.

Rocks can also be weathered by **physical changes**. Rocks **expand** (get bigger) and **contract** (get smaller) when the temperature changes. If the rock is heated and cooled over and over again, cracks can form. This kind of **physical weathering** is common in deserts and often causes sheets of rock to come off.

> **3** Describe how temperature changes can crack rocks.

Physical weathering also occurs when water gets into cracks in rocks and then freezes. Water expands as it freezes, forcing the cracks to get bigger. This is called **freeze–thaw action**.

B | Physical weathering like this is often called **onion-skin weathering**.

> **4** Predict what kind of weathering you would expect in the following places and explain your answers:
>
> a| Scotland (it rains a lot and is cold in the winter)
>
> b| the Sahara Desert (it is very hot in the day and gets cold at night, but it hardly ever rains)
>
> c| the Antarctic (it is very cold all the time).

Erosion

Pieces of rock broken up by **weathering** usually get moved away from the place where they were formed. This movement of bits of rock is called **erosion**.

If rocks fall into a stream or river, they can get **transported** (carried away). As the water moves them, the rock fragments knock against each other and wear away. This is called **abrasion**. The bits of rock and sand, in streams or rivers, are called **sediment**.

The size of sediment particles that can be carried by a river depends on how fast the water is moving. Faster-moving water can carry bigger pieces of rock. Sediments can also be carried by the wind. The wind can only move very small particles.

> **5** What is sediment?
>
> **6** How do rock fragments get worn away in streams and rivers?

C | Gravity can also cause erosion. Sometimes a lot of rock is moved at once, in a **landslide**.

Glaciers are rivers of ice. They move very slowly, but can transport very large pieces of rock. Rocks carried by glaciers also scrape and remove bits of rock from the land they move over. Rocks below the glacier are broken down into very small particles.

> **7** a| What happens to the shape of rocks that are transported in streams?
>
> b| What do you think happens to their masses? Explain your answer.
>
> **8** You can model rocks being carried by water by shaking sugar cubes in a jar. Explain how this models abrasion and evaluate the model.

FACT

An 'erratic' is a rock moved by glaciers and left up to hundreds of miles from its original location. This 40 tonne granite boulder is balancing because the softer rocks beneath it have been weathered and eroded.

D

I can ...

- describe the reaction between metal carbonates and acids
- describe how weathering can break up rocks
- describe how weathered rocks are eroded.

8Hd SEDIMENTARY ROCKS

HOW ARE SEDIMENTARY ROCKS FORMED?

When moving water or air slows down, it **deposits** any sediments it is transporting. Some sediments get moved again, but some form layers. Over a long period of time, more layers of sediment are deposited. The newer layers on top begin to squash the bottom layers. The pressure from these newer layers forces the grains of sediment closer together. This squashing (called **compaction**) squeezes the water out from the gaps between the grains.

If the water in the sediment contains dissolved minerals, these minerals can be left in the gaps and act as 'glue' to cement the grains together. Compaction and **cementation** together change sediments into **sedimentary** rocks. Sedimentary rocks are made from grains, not from interlocking crystals. Their properties depend on the types of sediment they were made from.

A | The mud and stones were deposited when fast-moving flood water slowed down.

5 cm

conglomerate

5 cm

mudstone

B | sedimentary rocks with very different grain sizes

1. What do the following words mean:
   a| compaction
   b| cementation?

2. Where does the 'glue' come from that holds the grains together in a sedimentary rock?

3. Look at the two rocks in photo B.
   a| Describe their textures.
   b| Suggest how the large pieces in the conglomerate became rounded.

FACT

C

This tomb in Petra, Jordan, is carved out of the solid sandstone cliff. The layers of sandstone were deposited by rivers flowing across the land millions of years ago.

Fossils form when dead plants or animals become covered in a layer of sediment before they rot away. If the sediments that are covering the remains change into sedimentary rocks, the remains of the organisms can also turn into rock, but they keep their shapes.

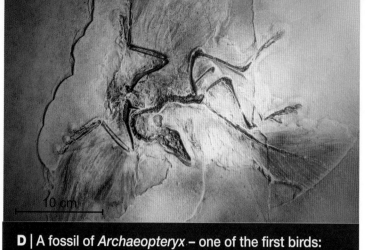

D | A fossil of *Archaeopteryx* – one of the first birds: these animals lived around 150 million years ago.

10 cm

4 What is a fossil?

5 Look at photo C. Suggest why we can see layers in the sandstone.

Sedimentary rocks that are heated or compressed can turn into metamorphic rocks. For example, a crumbly sedimentary rock called **mudstone** can turn into **slate** when it is heated and compressed. Slate is hard and can be split into layers. The slate can turn into schist or gneiss if the temperatures and pressures are high enough.

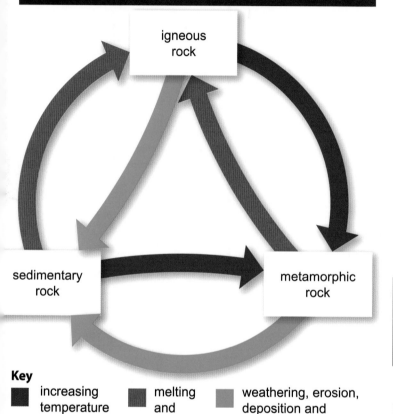

Key

- increasing temperature and pressure
- melting and cooling
- weathering, erosion, deposition and cementation

F | the rock cycle

igneous rock

sedimentary rock

metamorphic rock

E | This statue is made from **marble**, which is metamorphosed limestone. Marble has smaller crystals than the grains in limestone, which allows very fine details to be carved.

If any kind of rock is buried deeply enough, it can melt to form magma. If this magma solidifies, new igneous rocks form. The processes that make sedimentary, metamorphic and igneous rocks are linked together, forming a cycle that is never-ending. Some processes in the **rock cycle** are quick, such as landslides or volcanic eruptions, but most are so slow that we do not notice that they are happening.

6 Name two sedimentary rocks and the metamorphic rocks they can turn into.

7 Sandstone turns into a metamorphic rock called quartzite when it is heated and compressed.

   a| Suggest how the texture of quartzite will be different from the texture of sandstone.

   b| How will the other properties be different?

8 Describe what evidence you would look for to decide whether a rock was sedimentary, igneous or metamorphic.

I can ...

- describe how sedimentary rocks are formed
- describe the texture of some sedimentary rocks
- use the rock cycle model to link the three types of rock.

THEORIES IN GEOLOGY
8Hd

HOW ARE THEORIES ABOUT THE EARTH DEVELOPED?

The '**scientific method**' used in most sciences is shown in diagram A. In some sciences, such as geology or astronomy, it is difficult to carry out experiments. Most of the data used to test hypotheses is collected by observation.

> **1** How is investigating the Earth different from investigating chemical reactions or electricity?
>
> **2** Draw a new version of diagram A to show the scientific method for a geologist.

One idea about how the Earth's rocks were formed was suggested by Abraham Werner (1750–1817), who was a professor of mining in Germany. He published a book in 1787 that classified rocks by their ages rather than by the minerals in them. He worked out the ages from the order of layers of rocks in his region.

Werner based his hypothesis on some earlier ideas, and adapted them to explain the evidence he found around him in Germany. His theory was that most of the Earth had originally consisted of water with minerals mixed in it. Over time, materials settled and formed a series of layers. The oldest, hardest layer was granite. This contained no fossils because there was no life at the time. Layers that settled afterwards were softer and contained fossils.

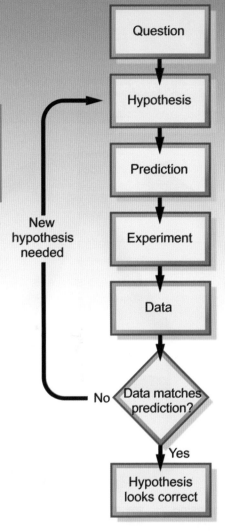

A | the standard 'scientific method'

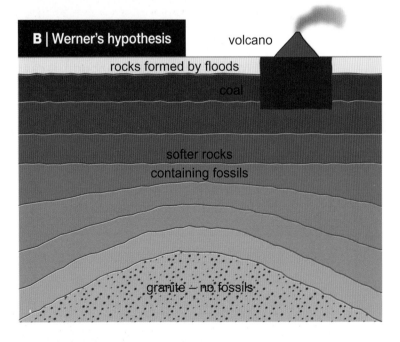

B | Werner's hypothesis

volcano
rocks formed by floods
coal
softer rocks
containing fossils
granite – no fossils

Floods that happened later, after the Earth was formed, added more layers of rock. Basalts, Werner said, had been deposited by crystallising from the vast ocean that once covered the Earth. Volcanoes were recent formations, caused by coal burning beneath the ground. They had played no part in forming most of the rocks on the Earth.

3 If Werner was correct, predict what you would find if you could drill:

a| to the rocks beneath a volcano

b| a very deep hole in a place without volcanoes.

4 What kind of rock did Werner think basalt is: igneous, sedimentary or metamorphic? Explain your answer.

Scientists can never prove that a scientific hypothesis is true. They make predictions using the hypothesis and test the predictions. If many tests show the predictions are correct, the hypothesis becomes a theory. Most geological hypotheses have to be tested by making more observations.

James Hutton (1726–1797) was a Scottish geologist who made many detailed observations of the rocks in the UK. He found one place where granite seemed to be going *through* metamorphic rocks. He decided that the granite must have been molten when it was forced through the existing rocks. He found similar examples in other places in Scotland. He used these examples to support a hypothesis that was very similar to our current ideas.

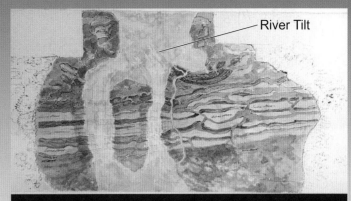

C | A sketch map of the rocks that James Hutton observed in the River Tilt, Scotland. The pink rocks are granite, formed when molten magma was forced through the grey metamorphic rocks.

5 Look at drawing C.

a| Which rocks are older: the metamorphic rocks or the granite?

b| Explain whether this observation supports Werner's hypothesis.

6 Look at photo D. Explain whether the following support Werner's hypothesis:

a| the age of the basalt

b| the way that the basalt cuts through existing rocks.

D | A dyke is formed when magma is forced through cracks in existing rocks. The basalt is younger than the existing rocks.

E | A granite 'intrusion' on the Torres del Paine mountains, Chile: Werner and Hutton would not have known about this evidence.

F | The High Force waterfall in the UK flows over a horizontal sheet of dolerite (like basalt but with larger crystals). The rocks above and below the dolerite are limestone.

7 Look at photos E and F. Do these features support or disprove Werner's hypothesis?

8 Hutton also found that no basalt he observed ever contained fossils. Explain whether this disproves Werner's hypothesis.

I can ...

- describe how the scientific method is used by geologists
- use a hypothesis to make predictions
- explain how evidence disproves a certain theory.

8He MATERIALS IN THE EARTH

HOW DO WE GET METALS FROM THE EARTH?

A | Gold often occurs near granite rocks. When the granite is weathered, tiny bits of gold get washed into streams. This man is panning for gold in France.

C | Kalgoorlie Super Pit gold mine, Australia

Rocks are important building materials, but most of the things around us also rely on metals. A few metals, such as gold and silver, are found as pure elements in rocks. We say they are found in their **native state**. However, most metals occur as compounds (minerals). A rock that contains enough of a metal or metal compound to be worth mining is called an **ore**.

> **1** What is the difference between a mineral and an ore?
>
> **2** What differences are there between the atoms in a piece of gold and in a piece of iron pyrite (photo B)?

B | Iron pyrite is a mineral. It consists of iron sulfide (FeS_2) crystals. It is also known as 'fool's gold' because some prospectors finding it thought they had found gold.

5 cm

Ores are obtained by **mining**. This involves tunnelling under the ground or digging huge pits (quarries). The ore is crushed to obtain the minerals that contain the metal. Chemical reactions are then used to obtain the pure metal.

Mining can damage the environment by destroying habitats and causing pollution. Many of these problems can be avoided, but reducing pollution costs money and means that the metals become more expensive.

> **3** State two ways in which mining can harm the environment.
>
> **4** Why don't all mine owners take steps to reduce pollution from their mines?

D | The red colour of the water is due to acids draining from an old copper mine in Romania.

Many modern devices such as smart phones, wind turbines and **solar cells** need small quantities of metals such as neodymium, terbium and tellurium. Some of these metals are quite rare and only found in one or two countries. This makes them hard to obtain and expensive. If we **recycle** devices that contain these metals, the supply of them will last longer. If we put these things into landfill sites instead of recycling them, some of the metals react and form **toxic** compounds that enter the water supply.

Recycling:

- cuts down on pollution caused by mining and quarrying
- reduces pollution from landfill sites
- will allow supplies of metals to last longer
- often needs less energy than obtaining the metal from an ore.

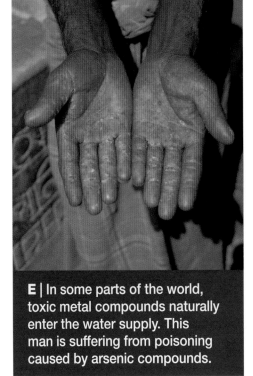

E | In some parts of the world, toxic metal compounds naturally enter the water supply. This man is suffering from poisoning caused by arsenic compounds.

F | recycling phones

FACT

It takes about 20 times as much energy to extract a kilogram of aluminium from its ore compared with extracting it from recycled waste metal.

5 Describe one physical change needed to obtain metals from rocks.

6 Write down two ways in which recycling metals can:

a| reduce pollution

b| help to reduce climate change by cutting our use of fossil fuels.

I can ...

- describe how metals are obtained
- describe some advantages of recycling metals.

131

WHY DO SOME PEOPLE LIVE IN DANGEROUS PLACES?

One of the most famous volcanic eruptions happened in CE 79, when the eruption of Mount Vesuvius destroyed the Roman towns of Pompeii and Herculaneum. The volcano has erupted many times since, sometimes killing many people and destroying nearby villages. It has not erupted since 1944, but it is possible that it could erupt again with very little warning. Today there are over three million people living near the volcano. There are plans to evacuate people if the volcano erupts, but it could take weeks to remove everyone from the danger zone.

The people around Vesuvius were killed by hot gases and ash, but volcanoes can kill in other ways. In 2018, the volcano Anak Krakatau erupted. This volcano sticks out of the sea between two large islands in Indonesia. During the eruption, an undersea landslide on the volcano caused a tsunami that killed over 400 people and injured thousands.

A | Vesuvius is still an active volcano.

B | The ash from Mount Vesuvius set hard around the people and animals that were killed in the eruption in CE 79. The bodies later decomposed. Plaster casts, such as this one, were made by filling the gaps with plaster.

1 a| What kind of rock is formed when volcanoes erupt?

   b| Describe how two other types of rock are formed.

2 If a volcano stopped erupting, it would eventually get smaller.

   a| Describe two ways in which the rocks could be weathered.

   b| Describe two ways in which the weathered fragments could be transported.

3 Suggest why people choose to live near hazards such as volcanoes.

HAVE YOUR SAY

Should people be allowed to live in areas where they might be killed by volcanoes or other natural disasters?

Throughout time we have used chemical reactions to produce new materials to help improve our lives. Today, scientists continue to discover and invent new materials with special properties and uses. Recently scientists have produced carbon nanotubes that are 100 times stronger than steel, and flexible aerogels that are lighter (less dense) than any other known solid.

The discovery and development of any new material is extremely expensive, and teams of scientists compete with each other to get money for research from governments and large corporations. Great care is taken in examining ideas for research before any money is given out.

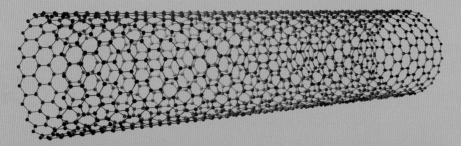

A | Aerogels are incredibly light but can support heavy loads and are excellent thermal insulators. This block of aerogel has a mass of only 2 g but can support a brick with a mass of 2.5 kg. Aerogels are used in sports racquets but could have many applications.

B | Carbon nanotubes are made only of carbon atoms. They can be several millimetres in length but have diameters that are about 50 000 times smaller than the width of a human hair. They are extremely light and strong, and are very good thermal and electrical conductors.

C | Carbon nanotubes could have thousands of different applications. Their strength, lightness and open structures means that they may be able store hydrogen under high-pressure for use in mini fuel cells (which could replace batteries).

1 What is formed in all chemical reactions?

2 Name four examples of physical properties of a solid.

3 Name two substances that are conductors of electricity and two that are insulators.

4 a| What are all substances made up of?

b| What is a chemical bond?

5 Describe one possible future use for electronic clothing.

9Ea ABOUT CERAMICS

WHAT MAKES CERAMICS USEFUL?

Ceramics are a range of hard, long-lasting, non-metallic materials, which are generally unaffected by heat. Often formed by heating and then cooling, ceramics include traditional bricks, china and glass as well as more modern materials used to make artificial bones and protective coverings for spacecraft.

Ceramics all have similar physical properties, which may make them useful:

- hard, stiff, strong when compressed, and **brittle**
- high melting points and **heat resistant**
- good **insulators** of heat and electricity
- very **unreactive**.

A | Different ceramics and their uses. (i) Glass is hard, rigid, unreactive and can be transparent, making it ideal for windows, bottles and jars. (ii) Porcelain is rigid, strong when compressed and an electrical insulator; it is used to support the electrical cables on pylons and stop electricity flowing through the pylons. (iii) Ceramics are heat resistant and so are used for the brakes in high-performance cars.

1 Porcelain is an electrical insulator.

a| Explain what this means.

b| Why does this make porcelain a useful material for use in metal electricity pylons?

c| Give the name of another electrical insulator.

2 Name two properties of ceramics that make them useful for making artificial bones.

3 Ceramics are used for making cups and mugs.

a| Name two properties of ceramics that make them useful for this purpose.

b| Name one property of ceramics that is not so useful for this purpose.

FACT

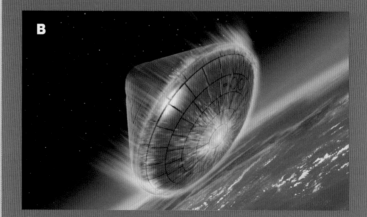

A spacecraft's surface when re-entering the Earth's atmosphere can reach temperatures of over 3000 °C. Special heat-insulating ceramic tiles are used to prevent the heat travelling into the spacecraft.

Making ceramics

The raw materials for traditional ceramics are **clays** (for making pottery) and **sand** (to make glass).

C | China, porcelain and pottery items are moulded out of different types of clay and heated in kilns to temperatures of around 1000 °C.

D | Glass is made by heating sand with other substances to temperatures above 1600 °C. Different kinds of glass will be formed depending on what substances are added to the sand.

When clay is heated, chemical reactions occur and new compounds, such as china and porcelain, are formed. During cooling, **crystals** form and bind together in the ceramic. The size of the crystals depends on the speed of cooling. Slower cooling produces larger crystals because the atoms have more time to form a grid-like **lattice structure**. This is similar to the formation of large crystals in granite when magma cools slowly.

In a lattice structure there are a large number of atoms, in a fixed regular pattern, all joined to each other by strong **bonds**. An example is shown in diagram E. One reason why ceramics are stiff is because there are so many atoms bonded to each other, with strong bonds, in a rigid structure. The high strength of the bonds is the reason why ceramics have such high melting points. Note that glass is slightly different because its atoms do not form a regular pattern, although the atoms are still held together by many strong bonds.

E | This ceramic lattice, which has no set size, contains billions of atoms of silicon, oxygen, aluminium and other elements joined together by strong chemical bonds.

4 Name three ceramic materials and a use for each one.

5 a| Name two raw materials used to make ceramics.

b| Describe one similarity and one difference in the manufacture of china and glass.

6 a| Porcelain X has much smaller crystals in it than porcelain Y. Suggest a reason for this.

b| Explain why larger crystals form if the porcelain is made differently.

7 a| What one word describes the structure (how the atoms are arranged) in most ceramic materials?

b| What do the different coloured spheres represent in diagram E?

8 Explain why ceramics like china are hard and have high melting points.

I can ...

- name some examples of ceramics and their uses
- explain why certain ceramics have particular uses
- explain how the properties of ceramics can depend on their structure

135

9Eb POLYMERS

WHAT MAKES POLYMERS SPECIAL?

Diagram A shows a typical **polymer**. These substances have molecules made of long chains, which contain repeated groups of atoms.

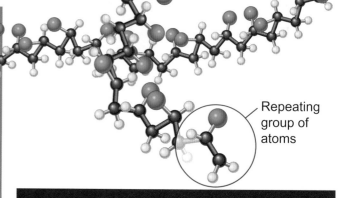

1 What is a polymer?

2 In the polymer shown in diagram A:

a| how many different types of atom are there

b| how are the atoms held together?

3 Draw up a table with the following headings.

Object	Polymer name	Properties that make polymer suitable for use

Complete the table, choosing three different objects from photo B.

Repeating group of atoms

A | Molecules usually have a set number of atoms, but the repeated groups of atoms in a polymer mean that they can vary in length. We call these 'long-chain molecules'.

poly(propene)
PVC
rubber
nylon
poly(ethene)

B | These items are all made of polymers. Many have similar properties: strong, hard-wearing, flexible, waterproof, unreactive, and insulators of heat and electricity.

Rubber is a polymer obtained from certain trees. It is soft and sticky when hot, but it is hard and brittle when cold. We use this rubber to make some glues, but we cannot use it to make things like car tyres.

The properties of rubber can be changed by **vulcanisation**. The rubber is heated with sulfur and a reaction occurs that forms cross-links between the long molecules. These cross-links make the rubber much harder and tougher, and stop its properties changing with temperature.

C | Natural rubber is produced from rubber trees.

FACT

Silly Putty®, a polymer based on silicon chains, can flow, stretch, bounce, snap and take imprints. Apollo 8 astronauts used it to stop their tools floating about inside the spacecraft.

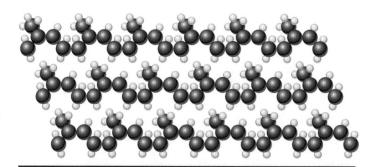

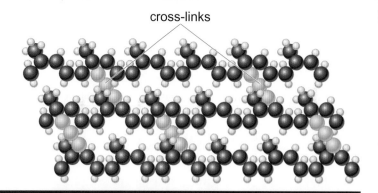

cross-links

D | When natural rubber is warmed its molecules can slide over each other, so the rubber does not go back to its original shape after stretching. A material that keeps a new shape is said to be **plastic**.

In vulcanised rubber, the cross-links stop the molecules sliding past each other, so the rubber goes back to its original shape when the stretching force is removed. A material that does this is said to be **elastic**.

4 a| Explain why vulcanised rubber is elastic but not plastic.

b| Explain what you think would happen to rubber if too many cross-links are formed. Use the word 'molecules' in your answer.

Rubber is a natural polymer. Other examples include DNA, proteins, starch and cellulose. Scientists have developed a range of synthetic polymers, mainly using **raw materials** obtained from **crude oil**. These are often made in laboratories and factories by **addition polymerisation** reactions in which lots of small molecules called **monomers** are added to form chains of an **addition polymer**. Diagram F shows how poly(ethene) is formed from ethene.

Addition polymerisation reactions like this transfer energy to the surroundings, making the surroundings warmer. Reactions that transfer energy to the surroundings are **exothermic**. (Reactions that absorb energy from the surroundings, making them cooler, are **endothermic**.)

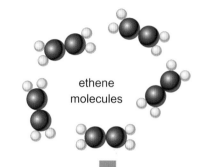

ethene molecules

polymerisation

poly(ethene) molecule

E

Synthetic polymer	Monomer	Properties	Uses
poly(chloroethene) (PVC)	chloroethene	cheap, good insulator	shrink wrap, drain pipes, wire insulation
poly(propene)	propene	strong, waterproof, flexible, hard-wearing	textiles, ropes and car body parts
poly(tetrafluoro-ethene) (Teflon®)	tetrafluoro-ethene	hard, heat-resistant, low friction surface	non-stick surfaces for saucepans and baking trays

F | During addition polymerisation ethene molecules join to form poly(ethene), which is also called polythene. Note that the name of the polymer is based on the name of the monomer with the prefix 'poly'.

5 a| What is the link between crude oil and synthetic polymers?

b| Identify a natural polymer in photo B.

6 a| Describe what happens in the reaction in diagram F.

b| Draw the monomer used to make the polymer in diagram A.

7 Choose a polymer from the table above that would make a good carpet for a hotel. Explain your choice.

8 Why is the making of poly(ethene) said to be 'exothermic'?

9 Describe the differences between a lattice, a molecule and a long-chain molecule.

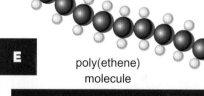

I can ...

- name some examples and uses of polymers
- explain some of the main properties of polymers
- describe how polymers are made.

9Eb PEER REVIEW

HOW ARE SCIENTIFIC DISCOVERIES CHECKED?

Scientists communicate their discoveries by:

- speaking at meetings and conferences
- writing and posting papers on the web
- writing books
- publishing **scientific papers** in **journals**.

A scientific paper is a detailed investigation report. It contains details of the **aim**, **hypothesis**, **method**, **results** and **conclusion**. **References** are included to list the sources of information used.

> **1** State two ways that a scientist can tell others of their findings.
>
> **2** Explain what is meant by a *hypothesis* and a *conclusion* in a scientific investigation.

Most scientific papers are **evaluated** before being published. This means that someone else judges them (usually by finding good and bad points and using those points to say whether overall the paper is good or not).

Scientific papers are evaluated on:

- the method (e.g. if variables were controlled)
- the results (e.g. if measurements are repeatable)
- the conclusion (e.g. if the conclusion is valid and can be made using the results).

This process, known as **peer review**, is outlined in diagram B. It is important because scientists can make mistakes and make the wrong conclusions. There have also been a few occasions when scientists have been found to have changed or misinterpreted their results to fit their ideas. It is important that other scientists check results and even try to repeat the experiments. Scientists are more likely to accept findings if they have been repeated by others.

Peer review can be time-consuming and expensive. Sometimes research papers by well-respected scientists can be passed by reviewers, with little or no inspection. This can cause problems, if incorrect ideas are published.

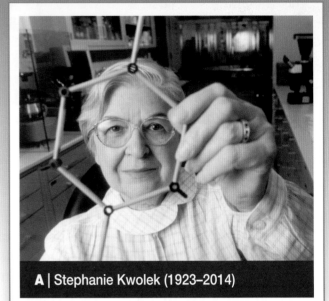

A | Stephanie Kwolek (1923–2014)

There are many scientific journals, including some devoted to science education. Stephanie Kwolek, who invented the polymer Kevlar®, discovered a way of making nylon in a beaker in 1959. She wrote a paper and submitted it to the *Journal for Chemical Education*. The paper was peer reviewed and then published. This brought her method to the attention of chemistry teachers all around the world in a time long before the Internet.

> **3** Why do scientists need to give exact details of the experiments they have carried out?
>
> **4** a| What is meant by peer review?
>
> b| Explain why peer review is important.

B | The purpose of peer review is to check the methods, results, conclusions and originality of a scientific paper.

Scientists carry out investigations to test an idea (hypothesis). Then they write a paper describing what they have done, their results and conclusions.

If there are problems, it will be recommended for revision and sent back to the journal to return to the scientist. The paper is then revised and sent back to the journal to be checked again.

If everything is correct, the paper will be recommended for acceptance. The journal then publishes the paper.

The experts review the science content and check that it is original (not copied from another scientist's work). They will also check that the conclusions are valid. Sometimes they will test the reliability of the data by repeating some of the experiments.

The paper is sent to a scientific journal. Editors at the journal read the paper and if it seems interesting and worthwhile it is sent to expert scientists for 'peer review'.

In 2012, it was discovered that scientist Hyung-In Moon had found a way of peer reviewing his own papers. He had given them glowing reviews! The papers were later retracted (withdrawn) when his deception was discovered.

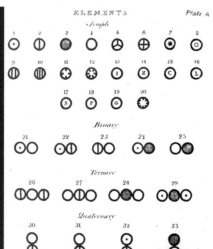

C | John Dalton published his ideas on the way elements combine in the early 1800s, before peer review was used. Scientists have now shown that Dalton's data cannot be reproduced using his methods. Some think that Dalton did not record his methods accurately but others think that he cheated and made his results fit his theory on atoms.

5 Suggest reasons why some papers are never properly peer reviewed.

6 Why might scientists write papers containing made-up data?

7 Draw a table to compare the benefits and drawbacks of peer review.

I can ...

- describe the process of peer review
- describe the advantages and disadvantages of peer review.

9Ec COMPOSITE MATERIALS

HOW ARE COMPOSITE MATERIALS USED?

Composite materials (e.g. concrete, paper, plywood) are combinations of two or more materials, with some of the properties of each. For example, laminated glass combines layers of glass with a clear polymer. The glass is hard and rigid and the polymer is flexible. The laminated glass is rigid and hard-wearing, but holds together under impact (it does not break up into pieces).

Many composite materials are made by mixing **fibres** into a liquid resin which then sets hard. Different types of fibres and resins produce different composite materials with different properties and uses.

A | Composite safety glass helps prevent injuries from flying pieces of glass.

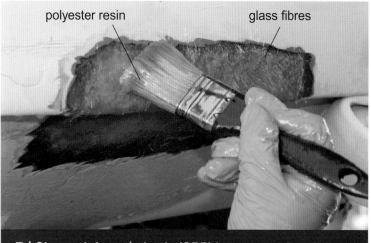

polyester resin   glass fibres

B | Glass-reinforced plastic (GRP) is a composite of glass fibres in a polyester resin. It is often used to build and repair boats because it is strong, light and slightly flexible. The glass fibres are easily moulded into complex shapes, which set hard with the resin.

C | Kevlar®, one of the strongest known polymer fibres, can be combined with polymer resins to form extremely strong and light materials. Kevlar® composites are often used for racing car and speedboat bodies, such as this wave-piercing trimaran.

1 What is a composite material?

2 What is glass-reinforced plastic (GRP)?

3 Why are the properties of GRP useful in boat hulls?

4 What properties would be needed in a composite used for racing car bodies?

Concrete

Concrete is a composite material that has been used for thousands of years. It is made from a mixture of **cement**, sand, **aggregate** (crushed rocks) and water. The cement powder and water form a material that can be moulded into shapes and then sets hard. However, hardened cement is not very strong and so aggregate is added to give concrete its strength. In building projects, steel rods are also added; this reinforced concrete is even stronger, so will not crack under pressure.

Cement is mainly calcium oxide (lime). It is made by roasting calcium carbonate (limestone), which breaks down in a **thermal decomposition** reaction:

$$CaCO_3(s) \rightarrow CaO(s) + CO_2(g)$$

calcium carbonate → calcium oxide + carbon dioxide

Very high temperatures are needed because this is an **endothermic reaction**. This means that it absorbs energy from the surroundings, and this energy is stored in the products.

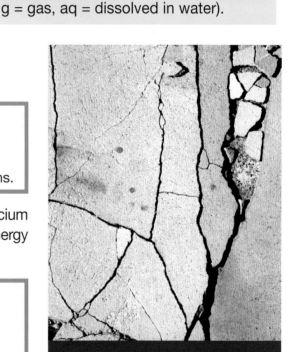

D | Concrete is strong, hard-wearing and easily moulded. It is used in roads, bridges and buildings. Different mixes have different properties and uses.

This equation shows the formulae for the substances. The letters in brackets are **state symbols** (s = solid, l = liquid, g = gas, aq = dissolved in water).

5 Explain why concrete is a composite material.

6 When zinc carbonate is heated, an endothermic decomposition reaction occurs. Explain what this means.

When water is added to the concrete mixture it reacts with the calcium oxide in an **exothermic reaction**. During exothermic changes energy is transferred to the surroundings, so their temperature rises.

7 Look at photo D. Explain why a steel grid is needed to reinforce the concrete in this particular use.

8 When GRP resin is setting, it gets hot.

a| What type of reaction is happening?

b| Explain what has happened in terms of energy transfer.

E | As concrete sets it gets warmer due to exothermic reactions. The heat can cause the concrete to expand and crack.

FACT

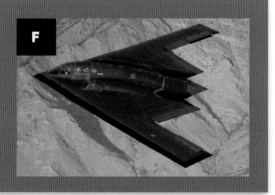

The body of this aircraft is made of a special graphite fibre composite that absorbs radio waves and helps make it almost impossible to detect by radar.

F

I can ...

- explain composite materials, giving examples
- describe and justify the uses of some composite materials
- explain what happens in thermal decomposition, and exothermic and endothermic reactions.

HOW ARE MATERIALS CHOSEN TO MAKE CARS?

Many different materials are needed to make a car. Materials scientists and designers work together to choose the best materials for each part. They need to know about the properties of materials, and what properties are needed for different parts of the car. The materials used can affect the car's efficiency, as heavier cars use more fuel.

A | The bodies of these cars are made from steel.

1. Write down two properties materials should have for each of these components.
   a | windows
   b | tyres
   c | seat covers

2. Use your knowledge of properties to suggest a material for each component in question 1. Explain your choices.

Materials science

Materials scientists study subjects such as materials science, chemistry or physics at university. They may specialise in particular materials, such as metals, ceramics, polymers or composites. They need to be good at analysing information and applying their knowledge, and they need to be able to communicate well.

Materials scientists choose the materials to use for a project, using their knowledge and understanding of material properties. They may develop new materials, or find new uses for existing materials. Some scientists investigate when materials fail, so they can work out how to improve the material or how to use it in a car so it will not fail.

Choosing materials

The main body of most cars is made from steel, but some manufacturers use aluminium alloy. Some components may be made of ceramics, polymers or composite materials.

Material	Density (kg/m³)	Strength (MPa)	Maximum temperature (ºC)	Relative cost
aluminium alloy	2700	270	150–250	$$$$
carbon fibre composite	1600	1730	80–215	$$$$$$$$$$ $$$$$$$$$$
ceramic	3800	170	1500	$$$$$$$$$$
poly(propene)	1100	33	50–80	$
steel	7900	585	500–650	$

B | properties of some materials used in cars

C | The body of this car is made from carbon fibre composites. It has a mass of 1200 kg, and a top speed of 400 km/h (248 mph). It costs over 70 times as much as a family car.

STEM

3 Suggest why the chassis (the main frame) of a car needs to be strong.

4 Use the data in table B and your knowledge of material properties to:

a | give some advantages and disadvantages of using aluminium alloy instead of steel for car bodies

b | suggest two reasons why poly(propene) is often used to make car bumpers, even though it is not a strong as steel

c | explain why ceramics are not used to make car bodies.

5 Explain why the car in photo C costs many times more than a normal car.

PRACTICAL

The properties of a carbon fibre composite material depend on the number of layers of carbon fibres, how they are laid, and the type of resin that binds the fibres. Materials scientists design ways of collecting and analysing data about material properties. They also evaluate their data to ensure it is good enough to use in designing new products.

Papier mâché is a composite material made from paper and glue. You are going to investigate some of the properties of papier mâché.

1 a Work in a group to make papier mâché samples and test them.

b Make several samples approximately 20 cm × 5 cm. Each of your samples should have a different number of layers of paper.

c When the strips are dry, compare how flexible they are (diagram D).

d Write a conclusion for your investigation.

e Evaluate the evidence you collected. Was it easy to make a fair comparison of your strips? Could you improve your method if you repeated the investigation?

2 Now plan another investigation. You could investigate the type of paper or the type of glue.

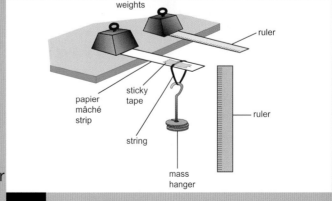

D

9Ed PROBLEMS WITH MATERIALS

WHAT ARE THE PROBLEMS OF MAKING AND USING MATERIALS?

Manufacturing materials usually uses energy released by the combustion of fossil fuels. This can damage the environment:

- carbon dioxide (CO_2) – helps trap the Sun's energy and so increases the **greenhouse effect**, leading to **climate change**

- carbon monoxide (CO), unburnt fuel and soot particles caused by **incomplete combustion**, due to lack of oxygen

- sulfur dioxide gas (SO_2) (caused by sulfur **impurities** in fuels) and nitrogen oxide gas (caused by high combustion temperatures) – dissolve in moisture in the air forming sulfuric and nitric acids, which cause **acid rain**.

Acids react with metal carbonates (such as calcium carbonate in limestone buildings).

acid + metal carbonate → salt + water + carbon dioxide

For example:

sulfuric + calcuim → calcium + water + carbon
acid   carbonate   sulfate   dioxide

$$H_2SO_4(aq) + CaCO_3(s) \rightarrow CaSO_4(aq) + H_2O(l) + CO_2(g)$$

Incomplete combustion can be reduced by increasing the amount of oxygen during combustion. Removing sulfur impurities reduces the amounts of acidic pollutants formed. Reducing the quantities of fossil fuel used will slow down the increase of atmospheric carbon dioxide, as will increasing the use of **carbon capture technology**.

acid rain reacts with limestone · soot blackens buildings

A | Air pollution affects organisms and buildings (especially those made of limestone (calcium carbonate)).

1 a| Write a word equation for the combustion of sulfur.

b| Write the equation using formulae and state symbols. Remember that oxygen is O_2.

2 State the salt produced when nitric acid reacts with calcium carbonate.

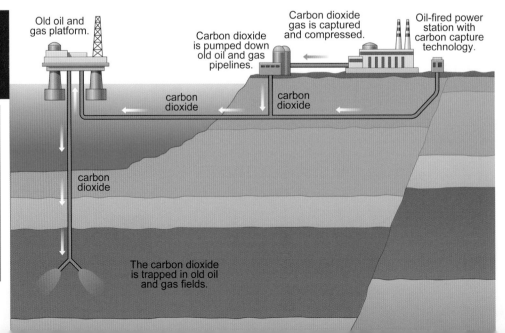

B | Carbon capture involves removing carbon dioxide from waste gases in power stations and storing it underground.

Old oil and gas platform.

Carbon dioxide is pumped down old oil and gas pipelines.

Carbon dioxide gas is captured and compressed.

Oil-fired power station with carbon capture technology.

carbon dioxide

carbon dioxide

carbon dioxide

carbon dioxide

The carbon dioxide is trapped in old oil and gas fields.

3 Suggest reasons why the stonework in photo A has become both blackened and worn away.

4 Explain how carbon capture technology could help protect our Earth.

Toxic substances

Factories can release toxic substances into the environment. In 1956 doctors in Minamata, Japan, saw an increase in people with serious nervous system problems. This was traced to a factory producing chemicals for the polymer industry, which was releasing mercury compounds into the sea. These were absorbed by microorganisms and passed up the food chain. The toxins did not break down and, because the larger animals ate many smaller animals, the concentration of the compounds increased in animals further up the food chain. This process is called biomagnification.

> **5**
>
> a| Explain how water pollutants from factories can get into humans.
>
> b| Why do the levels of poisons increase up a food chain?

Biodegradability

Many modern materials are designed to last for a long time and not to break down naturally. They are **non-biodegradable** and can cause pollution problems. For example, when plastic bags made of polythene are thrown away, they take a long time to break down, are unattractive and can also harm organisms on land and in the sea.

Burning non-biodegradable polymers could reduce the waste and produce useful energy. However, the combustion of polymers releases toxic gases that can pollute our atmosphere.

A better solution is to use **biodegradable** materials, which break down in the soil. Many new biodegradable polymers are made using renewable resources from plants. This also helps to save our limited resources of crude oil.

new biodegradable bottle cap

similar cap after 60 days

E | Biodegradable polymers break down in landfill sites.

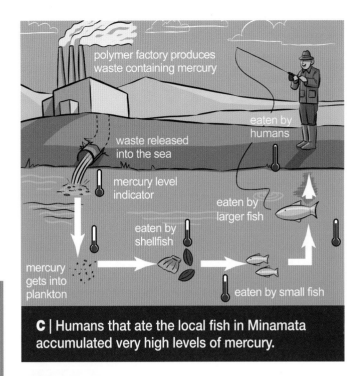

polymer factory produces waste containing mercury

eaten by humans

waste released into the sea

mercury level indicator

eaten by larger fish

eaten by shellfish

mercury gets into plankton

eaten by small fish

C | Humans that ate the local fish in Minamata accumulated very high levels of mercury.

FACT

Each of the 13 billion polythene bags made each year is only used for about 20 minutes, but takes over 1000 years to rot away. Turtles and seals can mistake plastic bags for jellyfish and choke by swallowing them.

D

> **6** Explain one advantage and one disadvantage of non-biodegradable plastics.
>
> **7** Describe two advantages of using biodegradable plastic bags made from corn starch.

I can ...

- explain how making and using materials can cause problems
- suggest ways of reducing these problems.

9Ee RECYCLING MATERIALS

WHICH MATERIALS SHOULD BE RECYCLED?

The more materials we manufacture, the faster we use up Earth's **finite** resources. Some resources could even run out this century. In addition, the more materials we use, the more waste we create.

Recycling means using the same materials again. By recycling materials we reduce our use of limited resources, save fuel and energy costs and reduce the use of **landfill sites**.

B | Dumping waste in landfill sites is unattractive, a poor use of land, and sometimes dangerous because it can leak toxic substances and even catch fire.

How the time varies for different fuels

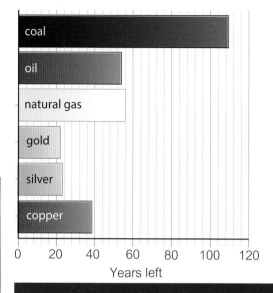

A | Some resources will eventually run out.

FACT

A tonne of ore from a gold mine produces about 5 grams of gold. However, a tonne of discarded mobile phones can produce at least 150 grams of gold, 3 kilograms of silver, 150 kilograms of copper and other metals.

Recycling metals

Metals are extracted from naturally occurring substances called minerals that are found in rocks called ores. As we use up these supplies of metal ores, we will need to dig more quarries to get new supplies. This destroys habitats and causes pollution. We will also have to use ores that are harder to obtain and contain less metal. This will require more time and energy, and be more expensive. Recycling metals will help save our resources of energy and ores. It is usually fairly easy to recycle metals. Once they are separated from other materials, the metals can be melted down and used again.

Recycling glass

Many ceramics are not easy to recycle, but glass is different. Once it has been collected and separated by colour, it can be crushed and easily melted to be moulded into new glass objects. Although the raw materials for making glass are fairly cheap and plentiful, it takes much less energy to make recycled glass, so it reduces the amount of fossil fuel used.

1. Explain why metal ores are a finite resource.

2. How much longer are our reserves of fossil fuels expected to last?

3. a| Suggest one way we can reduce our use of landfill.

   b| Describe two problems of using landfill sites.

Recycling polymers

A symbol is stamped on objects made from polymers to make recycling easier. Even with the symbols it is difficult and expensive to separate the different polymers, so recycling levels are still quite low.

C	symbols for recycling		
Symbol	**Polymer**	**Commonly found in ...**
♻ 01 PET	polyethylene terephthalate	bottles for water, soft drinks and cooking oil
♻ 03 PVC	poly(chloroethene) (also called polyvinyl chloride)	food packets, wire insulation and water pipes
♻ 05 PP	poly(propene) (also called polypropylene)	bottle caps, straws and medicine bottles

Recycling paper

Wood is a composite containing fibres of cellulose and a natural adhesive called lignin. Paper is made by boiling wood chips with water to form a pulp, which is spread out on grids to dry. This forms a new arrangement of cellulose and lignin, in sheets.

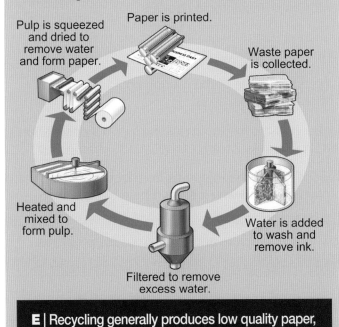

Pulp is squeezed and dried to remove water and form paper.

Paper is printed.

Waste paper is collected.

Water is added to wash and remove ink.

Filtered to remove excess water.

Heated and mixed to form pulp.

E | Recycling generally produces low quality paper, which is used to make newsprint and cardboard.

4 Describe two advantages of recycling materials.

5 Suggest why glass is separated into different colours for recycling.

6 a| Suggest one reason why the amounts of polymers recycled are low.

b| It has been suggested that, instead of using recycle labels, each kind of polymer is made in a particular colour. Suggest one advantage and one disadvantage of this idea.

Recycling concrete

Concrete from demolished buildings was often dumped in landfill sites. Now much of it is recycled using large crushing machines. The aggregate produced by these machines is used for the foundations of roads and buildings.

D | Machines crush concrete and sort the aggregate into different sizes.

7 a| How is concrete recycled?

b| What is recycled concrete used for?

8 Draw a flow chart to show the stages involved in recycling paper.

I can ...

- explain the advantages of recycling
- describe the recycling of some materials.

147

MATERIAL FAILURES?

WHAT UNFORESEEN PROBLEMS HAVE MATERIALS CAUSED?

Sometimes new materials have unexpected properties that can cause problems. A composite material containing asbestos, a natural ceramic fibre, was widely used in buildings because of its good insulating and fireproof properties. Unfortunately breathing in asbestos fibre dust can cause asbestosis, leading to permanent lung damage. New ceramic materials have now replaced asbestos for many uses.

Chlorofluorocarbons (CFCs) are non-toxic and non-flammable. They were developed to be safe to use in aerosol sprays and fridges. Later, it was discovered that CFCs were reducing ozone levels in the upper atmosphere. Ozone absorbs harmful ultraviolet radiation from the Sun, and so with less ozone more of this radiation reaches the Earth.

A | Great care has to be taken when handling asbestos because it easily produces a dust.

B | The increase in ultraviolet radiation has been linked to increased skin cancer in young people.

C | The adhesive in sticky-notes can be reused again and again.

Not all unexpected properties are a problem, however. In the 1960s, scientists were working on a super-strong polymer to be used as an adhesive for aircraft. One of those polymers was very weak and was ignored. Then someone noticed that it could be peeled off easily and reused, and so the sticky-note was invented.

1 Describe one advantage and one disadvantage of using asbestos as an insulator in cookers.

2 a| Name four different groups of waste that can be sorted for recycling.

b| Suggest how one of the groups could be sorted further to help recycling.

3 a| For each of the following materials give a description and an example: ceramics, polymers, composites.

b| Choose one of the materials from question 3a. Explain how and why it should be recycled.

c| Choose another example from question 3a. Describe how its manufacture and use can cause problems.

HAVE YOUR SAY

Some people think that people who do not recycle properly should be fined. What do you think?

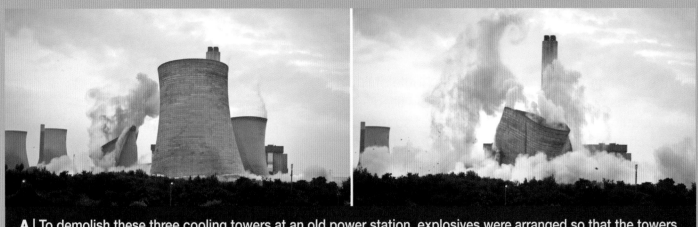

A | To demolish these three cooling towers at an old power station, explosives were arranged so that the towers imploded (collapsed in on themselves).

Large buildings and tall chimneys that are no longer wanted can be demolished by **implosion** using **explosives**. Once the explosives are detonated (set off), the implosion is very fast and usually takes just a few seconds. An expert makes sure that the building falls into itself so that other buildings nearby are not damaged.

Occasionally, the demolition does not work as expected. There is always a risk that some of the debris could fly out and hit spectators. Sometimes the building may not collapse completely and it may be left unstable and tilting at a dangerous angle. If there are some undetonated explosives left in it, it is dangerous for workers to make it safe.

When the explosives are detonated, a large amount of energy is transferred to the surroundings. Gases are produced and they expand quickly, creating a high **pressure**. This produces a shock wave and the very loud noise that we hear.

B | This tower block in China was only partly demolished by the implosion.

1   The detonation of explosives is a chemical reaction but the implosion is a physical change. State two differences between physical changes and chemical reactions.

2   State three hazards associated with demolition.

3   What causes a gas to exert a pressure?

4   State three ways to increase the pressure of a gas.

9Fa TYPES OF EXPLOSION

HOW DOES AN EXPLOSION HAPPEN?

For the 'trashcano' in photo A, a plastic bottle of liquid nitrogen was put at the bottom of a dustbin filled with water. Liquid nitrogen boils at −196 °C and so there was a rapid change of state. The gas pressure in the bottle increased until the bottle split, causing an explosion.

As with all explosions, there was a sudden increase in volume (due to the release of the nitrogen gas) and a huge transfer of energy to the surroundings (forcing the water and bin into the air).

This explosion was caused by a **physical change**. No new substances were made and there was no change in mass. Physical changes can cause natural explosions too, such as in volcanoes and geysers (see photo B).

> **1** a| What physical change happens in a geyser?
>
> b| Why is this a physical change?
>
> c| Why is this an explosion?

A | A 'trashcano' can only be made under strictly controlled conditions.

B | In a geyser, superheated water suddenly changes into a gas, increasing its volume by 1500 times and exploding out of the ground.

C | The explosion of this petrol storage tank was heard over 100 km away.

The explosion in photo C was caused when a large petrol storage tank was overfilled. Petrol escaped from the tank and some evaporated. The petrol vapour formed a cloud that spread out and mixed with the air. A spark caused the **flammable** petrol to explode.

This explosion was caused by a **chemical reaction**. New substances were formed as the petrol vapour suddenly ignited and produced large amounts of hot carbon dioxide gas and water vapour. However, as for all chemical reactions, the mass of the reactants was the same as the mass of the products.

2 Identify the following changes as physical or chemical. Give a reason for each answer:

a| heating solid wax until it changes to a liquid   b| burning coal   c| frying an egg.

3 What physical change happened before the explosion shown in photo C?

4 Explain whether a physical change or a chemical reaction is occurring in photo C?

5 What happened to the temperature of the surroundings when energy was transferred to them during the explosion shown in photo C?

In a chemical reaction, the bonds between atoms in the reactants are broken. The atoms are rearranged and new bonds are formed, to make new products with different properties. For example, hydrogen **combusts** with oxygen to form water. Hydrogen and oxygen are gases but water is a liquid at room temperature. We can show what happens using equations (see diagram D).

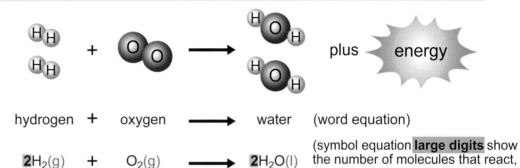

hydrogen + oxygen ⟶ water   (word equation)

$2H_2(g)$ + $O_2(g)$ ⟶ $2H_2O(l)$

(symbol equation **large digits** show the number of molecules that react, letters in brackets are state symbols (g = gas, l = liquid))

D | Particles are rearranged in a chemical reaction. We can show what happens using models, such as word and symbol equations.

6 Write word and symbol equations for the combustion of one atom of carbon.

FACT

In 2008, there was a massive explosion in the Imperial Sugar Refinery in the USA. Very fine sugar dust in the air was ignited by a spark. Fourteen people died.

Increasing pressure

The **particle model** explains how the forces of particles hitting the walls of a container cause pressure in gases. This model can also explain how gas pressure is increased by:

- increasing the number of gas particles (so more particles hit a surface)

- decreasing the size of the container (so particles hit a surface more often)

- increasing the temperature (so the particles move faster and hit more often and with more force).

7 Explain how pressure builds up in the trashcano (photo A).

8 Draw a diagram and use it to explain how an increase in the number of particles in a container increases the pressure.

gas particles in a container at room temperature   gas particles in a smaller container   higher temperature

E | increasing the pressure of a gas

I can ...

- identify and explain the differences between physical changes and chemical reactions
- model reactions using words and formulae
- use particle theory to explain gas pressure and how it can be changed.

9Fb REACTIVITY

HOW DO YOU COMPARE THE REACTIVITY OF METALS?

Some metals are more reactive than others. Caesium is one of the most reactive metals, and it blows up the trough when a small amount reacts with water! Gold is very unreactive; nothing happens if you put it in water.

The **reactivity series** is a list of metals in order of reactivity, with the most reactive at the top.

Metal	Reaction with oxygen in air	Reaction with cold water	Reaction with dilute acid
potassium	🔥	🔥	💥
sodium	🔥	✓✓✓	💥
lithium	🔥	✓✓	✓✓✓
calcium	🔥	✓✓	✓✓✓
magnesium	🔥	✓	✓✓
aluminium	✓✓✓	●●●	✓✓
zinc	✓✓	●●●	✓✓
iron	✓✓	●●●	✓
tin	✓	●●●	✓
lead	✓	●●●	✓
copper	✓	✗	✗
mercury	●●●	✗	✗
silver	●●●	✗	✗
gold	✗	✗	✗
platinum	✗	✗	✗

Increasing reactivity ⬆

Key

💥 explosive	🔥 can catch fire	✓✓✓ reacts very quickly
✓✓ reacts quickly	✓ reacts	●●● slow or partial reaction
✗ no reaction		

B | the reactivity series

A | Caesium reacts violently with water.

> **1** Name a metal that:
>   a| reacts with water and dilute acids
>   b| reacts with oxygen but not water
>   c| does not react with dilute acids or water, but reacts slowly with oxygen.
>
> **2** What is the 'reactivity series'?

To decide where to put a metal in the reactivity series, we look at how vigorously it reacts. For example, the reactions with water and acids can produce bubbles of hydrogen gas, and the more bubbles formed the more reactive the metal is.

Metals that react with water:

metal + water → metal hydroxide + hydrogen

Metals that react with dilute acids:

metal + acid → salt + hydrogen

The salt (e.g. chloride, sulfate, nitrate) depends on which acid is used.

Metals that react with oxygen:

metal + oxygen → metal oxide

This is an **oxidation** reaction. The rusting of iron is also an oxidation reaction (but needs oxygen and water).

Atoms

Metals are on the left and in the middle of the **periodic table** (see page 194). Lithium, sodium, potassium and caesium are all in the first **group**. These metals become increasingly reactive going down the group.

There are also trends in the **periods**. For example, sodium, magnesium and aluminium are all in the same period and become less reactive, from left to right.

We can explain these trends by looking at the **sub-atomic particles** found in atoms.

The central **nucleus** contains **protons** and **neutrons**. Atoms of each element have different numbers of protons, and so each element has its own **proton number** or **atomic number**. In the periodic table, elements are in order of atomic number.

The **mass number** is the number of protons and neutrons. The atom in diagram C has four protons and five neutrons; its mass number is 9. Element symbols are often shown with their mass and atomic numbers (diagram D).

Neutrons have no electrical charge, but each proton has a positive charge (+1). Each **electron** has an equal but opposite negative charge (−1). The numbers of protons and electrons in an atom are the same and so atoms have no overall charge.

Chemical reactions take place due to electrons. The electrons in some atoms take part in reactions more easily than in others (because of their numbers or distance from the nucleus). This causes differences in reactivity.

---

3 Write word equations for:

a| sodium reacting with water

b| magnesium reacting with sulfuric acid

c| zinc reacting with oxygen.

4 Barium reacts steadily with water. Rubidium reacts explosively with water. Cobalt does not react with water.

Write these metals in order of reactivity (most reactive first).

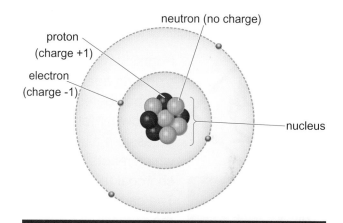

C | sub-atomic particles in a beryllium atom and their charges (not drawn to scale)

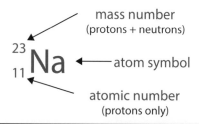

D | The atoms of an element are commonly shown in this format.

---

5 a| In which part of an atom are neutrons found?

b| State one way in which neutrons differ from electrons.

6 a| State the number of neutrons in the nucleus of a sodium atom (shown in diagram D).

b| Explain the overall charge on a sodium atom.

7 A lithium atom contains four neutrons. Use the periodic table on page 194 to help you show this type of atom using the format shown in diagram D.

I can ...

- describe the reactions of metals with water, dilute acids and air
- explain how metals are placed in the reactivity series
- describe the structure of an atom.

9Fc ENERGY AND REACTIONS

HOW DO WE GET ENERGY FROM A CHEMICAL REACTION?

Many chemical reactions that cause explosions need oxygen. This can come from the air but explosives usually have an oxidiser or **oxidising agent** mixed with them. During the reaction, this substance releases oxygen. The more oxygen, the quicker the reaction.

B | hazard symbol for oxidising

Potassium nitrate, KNO_3, is the oxidising agent that is mixed with powdered charcoal to make gunpowder for fireworks. The potassium nitrate releases oxygen, which reacts with the carbon in the charcoal to form carbon dioxide. The carbon is therefore oxidised by the potassium nitrate.

A | In this test, probes measure the temperature increase with different mixtures of reactants and oxidiser for a mining explosive.

> **1** Describe how the carbon in fireworks gets oxygen.

The solid fuel in an explosive reacts at a faster rate if it has more oxygen, and if it is in tiny pieces. Chemical reactions take place on the surface of a solid. Small pieces of a solid have a greater surface area than one large piece, so there will be more particles exposed at the surface and more reactions can take place. The **rate of reaction** (its speed) is also increased if the temperature is higher.

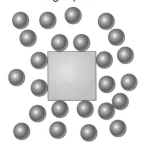
larger piece

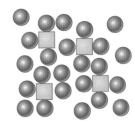
smaller pieces

smaller surface area
slower explosion

larger surface area
faster explosion

C | the effect of changing surface area

> **2** Why do you think gunpowder is made in a powder form?

Flash powder in fireworks produces loud bangs and bright sparks when tiny flecks of magnesium or aluminium combust. The oxidising agent in flash powder is potassium permanganate.

When heated, both potassium permanganate and potassium nitrate undergo thermal decomposition, releasing oxygen gas. We can confirm that the gas is oxygen by using the test shown in photo D.

> **3** Describe a test to show that a gas is oxygen.

OXYGEN

OXYGEN

D | testing for oxygen using a glowing splint

Energy transfer

Energy cannot be created or destroyed; it can only be transferred and stored in different ways.

A reaction in which energy stored in the reactants is transferred to the surroundings is an **exothermic reaction**. In the surroundings, the addition of energy causes the temperature to increase. Combustion and **neutralisation** reactions are exothermic.

A reaction in which energy is transferred from the surroundings to the reactants is an **endothermic reaction**. Thermal decomposition is endothermic.

> **4** State a type of reaction that is:
>
> a| exothermic   b| endothermic.
>
> **5** Some zinc powder was stirred into copper sulfate solution in a test tube. Use the data below to explain whether the reaction was exothermic or endothermic.
>
> Initial temperature of copper sulfate = 20 °C
>
> Final temperature of solution = 45 °C

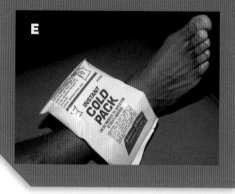

E

Many exothermic reactions need energy to start them off. Methane is a **hydrocarbon**. As it burns, the hydrogen and carbon atoms are both oxidised. A lot of energy is transferred to the surroundings during the reaction, so methane is used as a fuel.

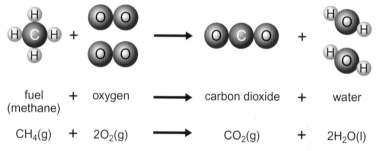

| fuel (methane) | + | oxygen | → | carbon dioxide | + | water |

$$CH_4(g) + 2O_2(g) \longrightarrow CO_2(g) + 2H_2O(l)$$

F | Methane combusts to produce carbon dioxide and water.

However, a mixture of methane and oxygen does not burn without some energy to start the reaction (for example, from a flame or spark). This input of energy is needed to break some bonds in the reactants to separate some atoms. The reaction can then start: atoms are rearranged, new bonds are formed and energy is transferred.

Some reactions, such as thermal decomposition, are endothermic and need a continuous input of energy to keep them going.

> **6** Hydrogen gas was mixed with oxygen gas in a balloon and nothing happened. Explain:
>
> a| why nothing happened when the gases were mixed
>
> b| what you need to do to start the reaction.
>
> **7** Gunpowder will only explode when there is an input of energy from heat or a flame.
>
> a| Describe the energy transferred in the endothermic part of this process and explain why this is needed.
>
> b| Describe the energy transferred in the exothermic part of this reaction.

I can ...

- describe the test for oxygen
- explain how combustion reactions can be speeded up
- classify changes as exothermic or endothermic
- explain why some reactions need a supply of energy.

9Fc PERCENTAGE CHANGE

HOW DO WE WORK OUT PERCENTAGE CHANGES?

We often use percentages to express the amount of something present. To calculate a percentage, first express the amount as a fraction of the total amount, and then multiply by 100.

For example, diagram A shows an experiment to find the approximate percentage of oxygen in the air. 50 cm³ of air is placed in one of the gas syringes. The copper metal is heated, and the plungers are moved back and forth, passing the air over the copper. The copper oxidises and forms black copper oxide, which decreases the volume of the air. When there is no further decrease, the heat is removed from the copper. The new volume of air, can be used to work out the percentage that was oxygen, as shown in diagram A.

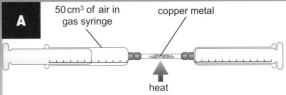

A | 50 cm³ of air in gas syringe   copper metal

heat

The plungers are used to push the air back and forth over the hot copper.

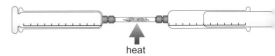

heat

When there is no further decrease in the volume of air, the remaining volume is measured.

copper + oxygen ⟶ copper oxide

$$2Cu + O_2 \longrightarrow 2CuO$$

volume decrease = start volume − end volume

$$= 10 \text{ cm}^3$$

So, 10 cm³ of oxygen has reacted.

As a percentage of the total 50 cm³ of air:

$$\frac{10}{50} \times 100 = 20\%$$

B | 1 | Look at diagram B. Explain how to use this apparatus to work out the percentage of oxygen in the air.

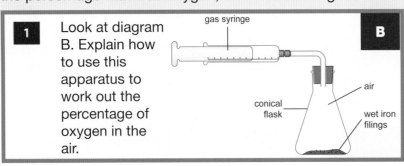

gas syringe

conical flask

air

wet iron filings

Percentage gain or loss

In the experiment above, the copper increases in mass as it gains oxygen from the air to form a solid oxide. There is, though, no change in the overall mass of substances because the air loses mass. The same thing happens when magnesium combusts in air (photo C).

When other solids are heated they appear to *lose* mass because a gas is produced, which escapes. This gas has a mass, which accounts for the decrease in the mass of the solid.

An example is the thermal decomposition of copper carbonate (photo D). All reactions obey the Law of Conservation of Mass, which states that mass cannot be created or destroyed.

C | When magnesium metal is heated in a crucible, white magnesium oxide is left behind. The contents of the crucible appear to gain mass.

$$2Mg(s) + O_2(g) \rightarrow 2MgO(s)$$

2 | 18 g of water contains 2 g of hydrogen. Calculate the percentage of hydrogen in water. Give your answer to one decimal place.

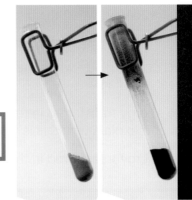

D | When green copper carbonate is heated, black copper oxide is left behind. Carbon dioxide escapes from the tube. and the contents of the tube appear to lose mass.

$$CuCO_3(s) \rightarrow CuO(s) + CO_2(g)$$

3 | What is 40% expressed as:
a| a decimal   b | a fraction in its simplest form?

We can find the mass of solids at the end of a reaction if we know the percentage gain or loss in mass.

Example 1

5.00 g of copper was heated and increased in mass by 25%. What is the mass of solid after heating?

mass gained is 25% of 5.00 g = $\dfrac{25}{100} \times 5.00 = 1.25$ g

final mass of solid = initial mass + mass gained = 5.00 + 1.25 = 6.25 g

Remember that if the solid gains mass, the final mass will be *more* than the initial mass.

Example 2

10.0 g of magnesium carbonate was heated and lost 52% of its mass. What mass of solid was left?

First find the mass lost:

mass lost is 52% of 10 g = $\dfrac{52}{100} \times 10 = 5.2$ g

Then find the mass of solid left:

mass of solid left = initial mass − mass lost = 10.0 − 5.2 = 4.8 g

Remember that if the solid loses mass, the final mass will be *less* than the initial mass.

Percentage change

We can find the percentage gain or loss in the mass of a solid when it is heated, if we know its mass at the start and the mass of the solid products at the end.

4. Calculate the percentage gain in mass when 2.4 g of magnesium are heated in air to form 4.0 g of magnesium oxide. Show your working.

5. What is the percentage loss in mass when 8.4 g of magnesium carbonate is heated if the mass of magnesium oxide left is 4.0 g? Give your answer to one decimal place.

6. What is the percentage gain in mass when 4.0 g of calcium is heated in air and forms 5.6 g of calcium oxide?

7. 100 g of calcium carbonate was heated. It lost 44% of its mass. What is the mass of solid left?

8. A piece of zinc with a mass of 4.0 g was heated. It increased in mass by 20%. What is the mass of solid formed?

Example 3

When heated, copper carbonate decomposes:

copper carbonate → copper oxide + carbon dioxide

Calculate the percentage change in mass when:

mass of copper carbonate used = 12.4 g

mass of copper oxide left = 8.0 g

- work out the difference between the mass at the start and at the end (final mass − initial mass). A negative number shows a loss in mass.
- divide this difference by the initial mass
- multiply by 100.

First find the change in mass:
final mass − initial mass = 8.0 − 12.4 = −4.4 g

Then find the percentage change:

$\dfrac{\text{mass change}}{\text{initial mass}} \times 100 = \dfrac{-4.4}{12.4} \times 100 = -35.5\%$
(to 1 decimal place)

I can ...
- express one number as a percentage of another
- calculate percentage change.

9Fd DISPLACEMENT

HOW CAN WE USE THE REACTIVITY SERIES?

Each metal will react with compounds of the metals below it in the reactivity series. Aluminium is more reactive than iron. It reacts with iron oxide and takes the place of the iron:

aluminium + iron oxide → aluminium oxide + iron

This is a **displacement reaction**. The aluminium displaces the iron.

B | Think of aluminium as 'pulling' oxygen away from iron.

This reaction needs an initial input of energy by lighting a fuse. During the reaction, aluminium forms strong bonds with oxygen. The reaction is very exothermic and the temperature increases so much that liquid iron is formed (as shown in photo A). This reaction is known as the **thermite reaction**, and is used to join sections of railway track. The molten iron runs into the gaps between the sections of rail, where it solidifies.

We can use the reactions between metals and metal oxides to arrange metals in the reactivity series, or we can use the reactivity series to predict which mixtures of a metal and a metal oxide will react.

Displacement also occurs in solutions. The order of reactivity of non-metal elements in group 7 of the periodic table (the halogens) can be worked out using displacement reactions in solutions. A solution of a more reactive halogen displaces a less reactive halogen from a solution of one of its compounds. An example is shown in photo C.

3 a| Write a word equation for the reaction in photo C.
b| Explain what this tells you about the reactivity of bromine and chlorine.

A | Aluminium reacts with iron oxide in a vigorous reaction.

— molten iron

1 Select from the word equation above:
a| two elements
b| two compounds.

2 What has been oxidised in the reaction between aluminium and iron oxide?

C | If a solution of chlorine in water is added to sodium bromide solution, the chlorine displaces the bromine. Sodium chloride is formed.

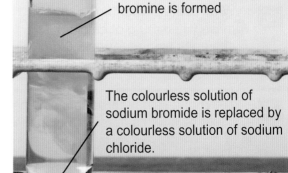

bromine is formed

The colourless solution of sodium bromide is replaced by a colourless solution of sodium chloride.

158

4 Use the reactivity series on page 12 to suggest a metal:

a| that could displace copper from copper oxide

b| that cannot displace iron from iron oxide.

— zinc strip

D | Zinc slowly displaces copper from copper sulfate solution because zinc is more reactive than copper. The blue copper sulfate solution changes to colourless zinc sulfate solution.

In a similar way, a more reactive metal will displace a less reactive metal from a solution of one of its compounds. For example, when a piece of zinc is dipped into copper sulfate solution, a coating of copper forms on the surface of the zinc. Some of the zinc takes the place of the copper and forms zinc sulfate solution. If the reaction is left for long enough, the solution will turn colourless as only zinc sulfate solution will be left.

Displacement reactions only work one way. Copper cannot displace zinc from zinc sulfate solution because copper is less reactive than zinc.

5 a| What evidence in photo D shows that a reaction occurs?

b| Write the word equation for this reaction.

c| Explain why this displacement reaction occurs.

6 Use the reactivity series on page 12 to predict whether a displacement reaction will take place in each case below. Either complete the word equation or write 'no reaction'.

a| magnesium + copper nitrate →

b| zinc + sodium chloride →

c| iron + silver nitrate →

d| copper + potassium sulfate →

e| silver + magnesium nitrate →

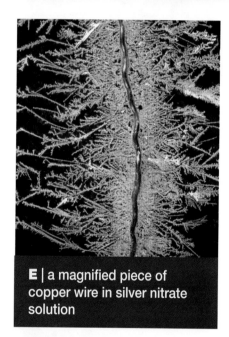

E | a magnified piece of copper wire in silver nitrate solution

7 Four metals, W, X, Y and Z, were placed in solutions of the sulfates of these same four metals. They were observed to see whether a reaction took place. The results are shown in table F.

8 Look at photo E. Suggest the name of the crystals formed on the surface of the copper wire.

F Metal sulfate solution	**Metal W**	**Metal X**	**Metal Y**	**Metal Z**
W sulfate		reaction	no reaction	reaction
X sulfate	no reaction		no reaction	no reaction
Y sulfate	reaction	reaction		reaction
Z sulfate	no reaction	reaction	no reaction	

Use the data to put the metals into a reactivity series, with the most reactive metal first.

I can …

- explain what happens in a displacement reaction
- predict whether a displacement reaction will occur.

9Fe EXTRACTING METALS

HOW DO WE GET METALS FROM THEIR ORES?

More reactive metals are more likely to form compounds than less reactive ones. Platinum and gold are so unreactive that they occur uncombined in their **native state** in the Earth's crust. Other metals are more reactive and occur as compounds. An **ore** is a rock that contains enough of a metal or metal compound (**mineral**) to be worth mining. Reactive metals need to be chemically extracted from minerals.

Iron

A lot of iron is extracted from a mineral called haematite (iron oxide) using a blast furnace (as shown in diagram B). The oxygen is removed by heating the iron oxide with carbon. Carbon is more reactive than iron so it displaces iron from iron oxide:

iron oxide + carbon → iron + carbon dioxide

The carbon is oxidised by the iron oxide. At the same time, the iron oxide is **reduced** – it loses oxygen (and forms iron). Carbon is a **reducing agent** because it has removed the oxygen from iron oxide.

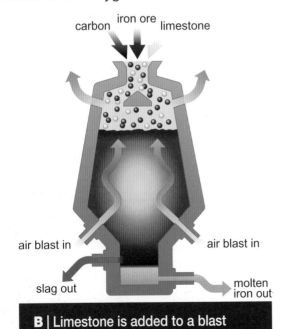

B | Limestone is added to a blast furnace to remove the impurities, which are extracted as 'slag'.

carbon   iron ore   limestone

air blast in   air blast in

slag out   molten iron out

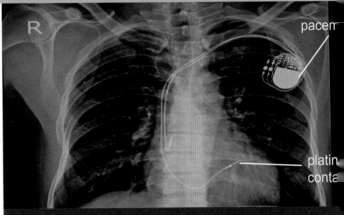

A | Some people need a pacemaker to keep their hearts beating regularly. The wires from a pacemaker are attached to the heart using platinum contacts.

1 a| Zinc can be extracted from zinc oxide in a blast furnace. Suggest a suitable reducing agent for the reaction.

b| What is added at the bottom of the blast furnace?

2 a| State the type of reaction in which carbon is changed into carbon monoxide.

b| Explain your answer.

3 State what is meant by a reducing agent.

Any reaction in which oxidation and reduction occur at the same time, is called a **redox reaction**

Carbon can be placed between aluminium and zinc in the reactivity series. It is a useful reducing agent because it oxidises to form a gas, which escapes into the air and so does not contaminate the metal that is being produced.

4 Copper can also be produced in a blast furnace.

carbon + copper oxide → copper + carbon dioxide

a| Explain why this is a redox reaction.

b| Identify each of the reactants as: is reduced, is oxidised, the reducing agent, the oxidising agent.

Aluminium

More reactive metals form more stable compounds, which are more difficult to extract the metals from. A more powerful method of reduction is needed – electrolysis. This involves passing electricity through a molten metal compound. The electricity transfers energy to the compound and splits it up to obtain the metal.

Aluminium oxide is found in an ore called bauxite. Carbon is not reactive enough to displace aluminium from aluminium oxide. So, electrolysis is used.

aluminium oxide → aluminium + oxygen

Iron could also be extracted using electrolysis but it is too expensive. A lot of electricity would be needed to heat the iron oxide to keep it molten, and the process of electrolysis also requires vast amounts of electricity. Electrolysis is only used to extract the very reactive metals that cannot be obtained by heating their oxides with carbon.

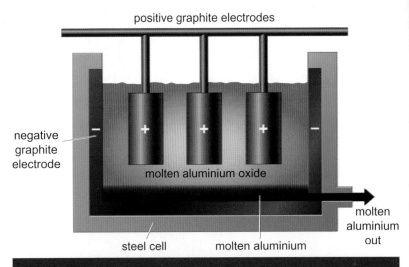

C | Electrolysis is used to extract aluminium from aluminium oxide.

positive graphite electrodes

negative graphite electrode

molten aluminium oxide

molten aluminium out

steel cell

molten aluminium

---

5   a| Name two metals, other than iron, that can be extracted from their ores by heating with carbon.

       b| Name two metals that are extracted from their ores by electrolysis.

6   Suggest why carbon is shown:

       a| between aluminium and zinc in the reactivity series in table D

       b| in brackets.

7   Suggest why the most reactive metals were not extracted from their ores before the 19th century.

Metal	Method of extraction	Ease of extraction	Date of first isolation
Potassium		hard to extract	1807
Sodium			1807
Lithium	electrolysis		1817
Calcium			1808
Magnesium			1808
Aluminium			1825
(Carbon)		getting harder to extract	before 3000 BCE
Zinc			about 500 BCE
Iron	ores are heated with carbon		
Tin			
Lead			
Copper			before 3000 BCE
Silver			
Gold	found in native state		
Platinum		easy to extract	

D | The method of extraction of a metal depends on its position in the reactivity series.

Metals that occur in their native state and those that can be extracted by heating their oxides with carbon have been known for a long time. Metals that must be extracted using electrolysis have been obtained much more recently.

FACT

In the mid-1800s, aluminium was very expensive to produce and was more valuable than gold. Emperor Napoleon III of France used aluminium plates and cutlery for his most honoured guests.

I can ...

- explain why the method used to extract a metal is related to cost and the metal's reactivity
- describe how metals are extracted from their ores by heating with carbon or by electrolysis
- explain what happens in redox reactions.

MATERIALS MANAGEMENT
9Fe

WHY ARE MATERIALS MANAGERS NEEDED IN THE CHEMICAL INDUSTRY?

The chemical industry uses chemical reactions to change raw materials into useful products. Many raw materials are obtained directly from the Earth, including coal, oil, natural gas, metal ores, salts and other minerals.

Coal is the raw material used to make coke (almost pure carbon) in a thermal decomposition reaction. Coke, iron ore and limestone are the raw materials used to produce iron metal using a reduction reaction.

---

1 Look at pages 20 and 21.

a | What do you call a raw material that is a source of a metal?

b | Name a raw material for making aluminium.

A | A vast amount of coal is turned into coke to use in extracting iron.

B | In any manufacturing process, for example when making medicines, the correct quantities of several different raw materials need to be available at the correct time.

---

2 Why are materials managers needed in the production of iron?

3 Suggest a reason why the problem shown in photo C has occurred.

Materials managers

All chemical industries need a reliable supply of raw materials to run efficiently. It is the job of a materials manager to make sure that all the required raw materials are available when they are needed.

A materials manager:

- finds sources of the materials
- negotiates prices
- checks material quality
- orders the correct quantities
- organises storage and distribution.

Materials managers need accurate information about what raw materials are needed, the quantities needed, when they are needed, how long they can be stored and how much storage space is available. Some of this information is put into an inventory.

The information in an inventory is then used to calculate the quantities of raw materials needed, when they need to be delivered and where they should be stored.

A materials manager must keep a constant supply; if just one raw material runs out, production will stop. However, the manager must not order too much because there may be no room for storage. The manager must also control delivery costs; frequent deliveries of small quantities cost more than occasional deliveries of large quantities.

Keeping an accurate and up-to-date inventory of raw materials, such as the one shown in spreadsheet D, is an essential skill for materials managers.

C | Over-ordering raw materials can cause storage problems. Some raw materials become unsuitable for use if stored for too long.

4 a | What is an inventory?
b | Suggest a problem caused if a manufacturer's inventory is inaccurate.

5 Explain why materials will usually be ordered in large quantities.

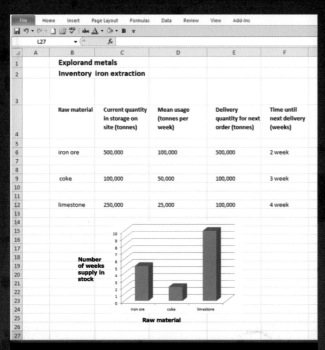

D | raw materials inventory for making iron

6 Use the information in spreadsheet D to answer these questions.
a | How much iron ore will be in storage on site one week later?
b | Use a calculation to show that coke will run out before the next delivery.
c | Calculate the mass of limestone in stock after the order is delivered in four weeks.

ACTIVITY

1 Work in a group to design an inventory for a home fridge. Only include items that are used regularly (e.g. milk, fruit juice). Discuss:
- the items you will list
- the lengths of time until certain items 'go off'
- how to make sure that items do not run out.

2 A problem with a fridge inventory is that people need to update the spreadsheet regularly. Design a 'fridge of the future' that automatically tracks and re-orders foods. Present your ideas as a labelled drawing, including how the fridge will:
- avoid food 'going off'
- trigger placing an order for more of a certain food.

SHOULD EXPLOSIVES BE BANNED?

Alfred Nobel was born into a family that manufactured tools and explosives, including iron for cannons used in the Crimean War. He devoted himself to the study of explosives, especially the manufacture of nitroglycerin.

In 1864 a shed used for the manufacture of nitroglycerin exploded, killing five people, including Alfred's youngest brother, Emil. Alfred continued to build further factories, but he concentrated on improving the stability of the substances he was developing so they would be safer and not explode unexpectedly.

A | Alfred Nobel (1833–1896) was a Swedish chemist.

Nobel invented dynamite in 1866; it was patented in 1867. This explosive is easier and safer to handle than nitroglycerin as it needs a detonator to start the reaction. Dynamite is still in daily use for constructive purposes, such as quarrying, mining, road building and demolition.

Dynamite made Nobel a very rich man but he never married. In his will he stated that his fortune should be used as prize money for the person or group of people whose work has been of the greatest good to humankind in the previous year. Since 1901, these prizes have been awarded to individuals or groups of people from around the world for outstanding achievements in physics, chemistry, medicine and literature, and for work to promote peace.

Svante Arrhenius was awarded the Nobel Prize for Chemistry in 1903 for his discovery of how compounds can carry electric currents. We can now explain what happens when metals are extracted using electrolysis.

B | Dynamite is used as the explosive in quarrying, which provides us with building materials.

In 1997, Jody Williams and a group called the International Campaign to Ban Landmines shared the Nobel Prize for Peace for their work in the banning and clearing of anti-personnel mines.

1. Many metal ores are obtained by the use of explosives in mining. Describe the energy changes that occur in this process.

2. Summarise how iron is extracted from iron oxide.

3. Summarise how aluminium is extracted from aluminium oxide.

4. Explain how the methods used for extracting iron and aluminium are related to the positions of the metals in the reactivity series.

HAVE YOUR SAY

All explosives are dangerous and should be banned. What do you think of this idea?

Artists need to know about the properties of the materials they use. Today, they have a greater choice of materials than ever before, thanks to chemists.

Many copper compounds are blue or green, which has made them useful in paints. One artists' pigment, called 'verdigris', has been made for centuries by covering copper metal in vinegar and then scraping off the green compound that forms. Naturally occurring minerals containing iron, lead and mercury have been used in paints since ancient times. Examples include brown haematite (Fe_2O_3), white cerussite ($PbCO_3$) and red cinnabar (HgS).

B | This Syrian wood panelling is from 1600. The red is vermilion – a manufactured form of cinnabar. The chemical reactions for making it were described by Arabic scientist Jabir ibn Hayyan (722–804 CE), who wrote a book on the chemistry of colours.

C | The colours on Gary Scott's bronze sculptures are developed by using a blowtorch to apply compounds such as potassium sulfide (K_2S).

A | To create this artwork, *Seizure*, Roger Hiorns filled an apartment with copper sulfate solution. After a few weeks, the solution was pumped out leaving a covering of copper sulfate crystals.

Artists also use chemical reactions. Antony Gormley often creates sculptures made out of an iron alloy that slowly develops a surface coating of rust. Colours can be applied to bronze sculptures by using a blowtorch to apply compounds such as iron nitrate ($Fe(NO_3)_3$).

1 Identify two reactions on this page that occur at different rates, and describe how the rates are different.

2 Explain whether the reaction that occurs in a blowtorch is exothermic or endothermic.

3 a | A speck of Fe_2O_3 contains 1000 iron atoms. How many oxygen atoms will it contain?

b | Write down the other four chemical formulae shown on this page and identify the elements in each compound.

4 Copper sulfate can be made by adding copper oxide (a base) to sulfuric acid.

a | State what sort of reaction this is.

b | Write out an equation for this reaction.

c | What holds atoms together in a compound?

9Ga IONS

WHY ARE IONS IMPORTANT IN CHEMISTRY?

The building in photo A is the Atomium building in Brussels. It is a giant model of the arrangement of atoms in iron. However, it does not accurately reflect how the atoms are held together.

Atoms contain a very small central **nucleus** containing positively charged **protons**, and **neutrons** (which have no electrical charge). There are also negatively charged electrons, which are outside the nucleus. There are an equal number of protons and electrons, and so the charges balance, and atoms have no overall charge. However, if an atom loses or gains electrons, the charges no longer balance. An atom that loses or gains electrons becomes an **ion**.

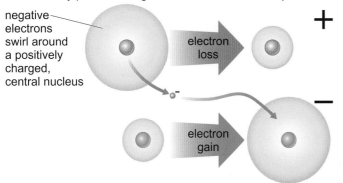

sodium atom – negative charges of electrons balanced by positive charges in nucleus

With the loss of an electron, the sodium ion has an overall positive charge.

negative electrons swirl around a positively charged, central nucleus

electron loss

electron gain

chlorine atom – negative charges of electrons balanced by positive charges in nucleus

With the gain of an electron, the chloride ion has an overall negative charge.

B | Ions are atoms that have lost or gained electrons, and so have a charge. When an ion forms, there is no change to the **atomic number** (number of protons) or **mass number** (number of protons + number of neutrons).

1   What type of charge does an electron have?

2   Explain why an iron atom has no overall charge.

3   An iron atom loses electrons. State the type of charge the ion has.

In a metal, some of the electrons become free and are shared between the atoms. You can think of this as positively charged ions of the metal surrounded by a 'sea of electrons'. The attraction between the positive and negative charges holds the structure together. We call this **metallic bonding**.

A | The Atomium building was constructed in 1958.

FACT

Thunderstorms, waterfalls and waves all create negative ions from the substances in the air.

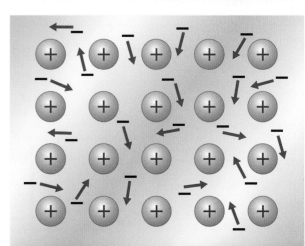

C | In metallic bonding, the electrons are able to move freely and randomly in all directions.

4 a| Look back at photo A. Suggest what the tubes in the building represent.

b| Describe one poor point about using this model for the structure of iron.

Metal conductivity

Knowing about metallic bonding allows us to understand why metals conduct electricity. If you apply a **voltage** (a **potential difference**) between two points on a piece of metal, electrons will flow in the same direction. This flow of electrons transfers energy and forms an electrical current.

5 Explain why metals conduct electricity.

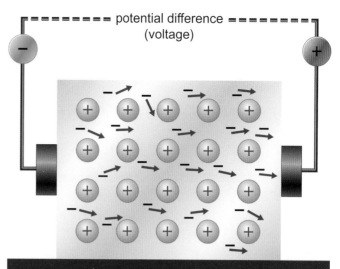

D | When a voltage is applied to a piece of metal, an electrical current flows.

Ionic compounds

Metal atoms quite easily lose electrons and non-metal atoms easily gain electrons. A positively charged metal ion and a negatively charged non-metal ion attract one another. This force of attraction is called an **ionic bond** and this is another type of bonding.

Compounds held together with ionic bonds are **ionic compounds**. Many metals in the middle of the periodic table form ionic compounds with intense colours, which are used in artists' colours.

Like electrons, ions can also carry an electrical current if they can move. So, solid sodium chloride will not conduct electricity but molten sodium chloride will, and so will sodium chloride solution.

The symbol for an ion is the element symbol with a little superscript + or − after it.

sodium chloride   lithium bromide

Different ions can have different amounts of charge, as shown by the numbers.

magnesium sulfide   iron oxide

E | some common ionic compounds

F | Ionic transition metal compounds are found in oil paints.

6 What is the symbol for the ion formed from a sulfur atom?

7 a| What charge does a magnesium ion carry?

b| Has a magnesium ion lost or gained electrons to form this ion?

8 Potassium bromide (KBr) is an ionic compound. Draw the ions in this compound.

9 Solid lithium bromide contains charged particles but cannot conduct electricity. Why not?

10 Suggest why swimmers should get out of the sea during a thunderstorm.

I can

- explain how ions are formed
- describe metallic and ionic bonding
- explain how metals and ionic compounds can conduct electricity.

167

HOW CAN WE MODIFY THE WEATHER?

We can control environmental conditions, including temperature and humidity, inside buildings such as art galleries, offices and our homes. Controlling environmental conditions outside, however, is more difficult because it means modifying the weather.

Weather modification is a new area of scientific research. In dry regions of the world, where there is no rain for long periods, making it rain on demand would provide fresh water for drinking and for growing crops. Regions that are often damaged by hurricanes and cyclones would benefit from storms being weakened or stopped altogether.

A | Typhoon Manghkut was a powerful storm that hit South China and the Philippines in September 2018.

B | Typhoon Mangkhut killed at least 134 people and caused about US$3.74 billion worth of damage to buildings and property.

1 | Give two examples of how the indoor environment might be controlled in an art gallery.

2 | Describe two weather modifications that could be helpful to people.

Weather control engineer

'Weather control engineer' may be a job of the future. Such engineers will need to understand how different weather conditions are caused. They will look for ways of controlling weather safely and without causing problems for neighbouring areas. A weather control engineer will probably need a science university degree with further training in climate science and technology.

One idea that is being tested uses ionisers that cause particles in the air to become ions. The static charge on the particles is thought to attract dust and water molecules to them, forming the 'seeds' for making large raindrops.

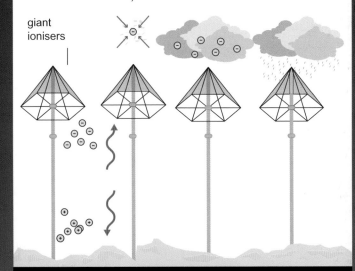

1. Ionisers turn gas molecules in the air into ions.

2. The ions stick to specks of dust, which are carried into the atmosphere (as hot air rises).

3. The negatively charged dust causes water to condense around it.

4. Clouds form, which produce rain.

giant ionisers

C | Ionisers such as these are being tested in dry parts of the world to see if they can increase the amount of rain.

Another method of seeding clouds to produce rain releases the ionic compound silver iodide into the clouds. The very fine particles of powdered silver iodide cause water to condense around the particles until they are large enough to fall as rain.

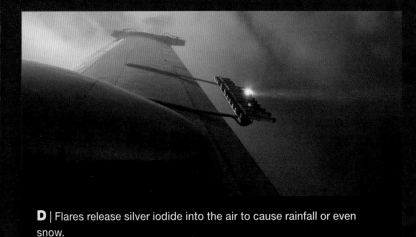

D | Flares release silver iodide into the air to cause rainfall or even snow.

3 Describe two ways that rain might be caused when no rain is forecast.

4 State what is meant by an ion.

5 Describe an advantage of causing clouds to produce rain.

6 Suggest a disadvantage of causing rain when it normally does not rain.

Evaluating new ideas

Two key points that a weather control engineer needs to consider when planning to change the weather are:

■ Should we change the weather in a given area?

■ What is the best way to change the weather?

These points need to be evaluated before any weather modification is done.

First, the possible benefits and possible disadvantages are listed. Each benefit and disadvantage can be given a score, depending on the impact of each one. Comparing the scores can help you work out whether the benefits outweigh the disadvantages. This helps make an informed decision.

Key point	Scores (−2 to +2) (positive scores are benefits of one system over the other, negatives are disadvantages)	
	Ioniser	Silver iodide seeding
chance of causing rain	−1	+2
availability of equipment	−1	+2
cost	+1	−2

E | Evaluation table for comparing methods of causing rain. More points could be added to the table to give a better comparison.

7 a | Use the scores in the table to suggest which method of seeding clouds might be better.

b | Suggest one other suitable key point that could be included in the table.

ACTIVITY

In a group, discuss what kind of weather modification could be helpful where you live. Choose one change and evaluate it.

You could think about the effects on different groups of people (e.g. farmers or office workers), how much new technology may be needed, and how expensive it might be. Use your evaluation to decide whether your weather modification should be developed for use in your area.

Write a short statement to explain your decision and be prepared to read this out to your class.

9Gb ENERGY TRANSFERS

WHAT HAPPENS TO ENERGY IN PHYSICAL AND CHEMICAL CHANGES?

Bonds affect the properties of substances. For example, the metallic bonding in magnesium is stronger than in sodium, which is why solid sodium is softer and more **malleable** than solid magnesium.

Metallic bonding is stronger if there are more free electrons and ions with more charges. The more charges, the stronger the force between opposite charges. In sodium each atom contributes one electron to metallic bonding, leaving ions with a 1+ charge. However, in magnesium the atoms contribute two electrons, leaving Mg^{2+} ions.

A | sodium – melting point: 98 °C; boiling point: 883 °C

> **1** Potassium atoms contribute one electron to metallic bonding, but calcium atoms contribute two electrons. Explain which metal is likely to be harder.
>
> **2** Explain whether sodium or magnesium will conduct electricity better.

Physical changes

To melt or evaporate a substance, energy must be supplied. The energy breaks some of the bonds between particles. The stronger the bonds, the more energy is needed to break them.

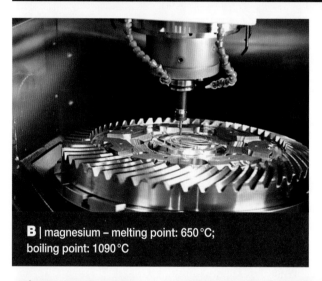

B | magnesium – melting point: 650 °C; boiling point: 1090 °C

C | Sodium melts at 98 °C and boils at 883 °C. In some street lights, electricity is passed through sodium gas to give a yellow light.

D | In some solar power stations, light is focused on a central tower to melt an ionic compound called sodium nitrate (melting point: 308 °C). This is then used to boil water and so generate electricity using a turbine.

3 Why is sodium used in some street lights but magnesium is not?

4 Aluminium atoms can each contribute three electrons to metallic bonding. Suggest how the boiling point of aluminium will compare with the boiling point of magnesium.

5 Describe the evidence on the previous page to suggest that ionic bonding is stronger than metallic bonding.

E | Making ice from water is exothermic. These ice sculptures are at a festival in China.

Melting and evaporation require an input of energy. They are **endothermic** changes. The energy that *en*ters makes the particles move faster and breaks some of the bonds holding the particles near to each other. The additional energy also means that the temperature of the substance can increase (but the temperature of things around it falls).

Freezing and condensation are **exothermic** processes. Particles lose energy and slow down, allowing bonds to form between them. The *ex*it of energy can reduce the substance's temperature (but increase the temperature of things immediately around it).

6 Draw a table to compare endothermic and exothermic changes.

Chemical reactions

Unlike in physical changes, in chemical reactions new bonds form between *different* types of atoms. This produces new substances. When bonds are broken, energy is taken in. When bonds are formed, energy is released. The difference between the energy taken in to break the bonds and the energy released when new bonds form, determines whether a chemical reaction is exothermic or endothermic.

FACT

For sweat to evaporate, an input of energy is needed. This energy comes from your skin. As it loses energy to your sweat, your skin cools down.

We can show the differences in energy between the reactants and products in a **reaction profile**.

7 In diagram F, explain which reaction profile (P or Q) shows an endothermic reaction.

8 a| A metal burns in air with a bright white light. Explain whether this is an exothermic or endothermic reaction.

b| Draw a reaction profile for this reaction.

9 When barium hydroxide is mixed with ammonium thiocyanate in a test tube, ice forms on the *outside* of the tube.

a| Explain whether the reaction inside the test tube is exothermic or endothermic.

b| The ice is formed from water vapour in the air. Is this a chemical reaction or a physical change?

c| Describe the changes that occur to water molecules as this process occurs.

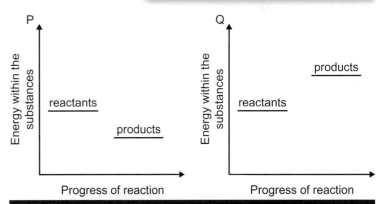

F | reaction profiles for endothermic and exothermic changes

I can

■ interpret and sketch reaction profiles
■ explain why changes are described as being exothermic or endothermic
■ explain how bonding affects the properties of some substances.

RATES OF REACTION

WHAT CONTROLS THE RATE OF A REACTION?

Some chemical reactions happen very slowly while others occur extremely quickly. The **rate of reaction** is how quickly a reaction takes place.

> **1** Compare the rates of the reactions in photos A and B.

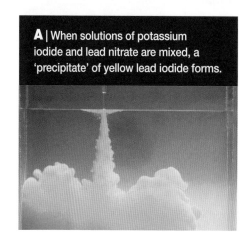

A | When solutions of potassium iodide and lead nitrate are mixed, a 'precipitate' of yellow lead iodide forms.

B | In this painting by Hieronymus Bosch (c. 1450–1516), the green pigments used for the grass and trees have slowly reacted with substances in the air and turned more yellow.

To measure the rate of reaction, we either measure how quickly the reactants are used up or how quickly the products are formed. For example, photo C shows the reaction between calcium carbonate (marble chips) and hydrochloric acid. Carbon dioxide gas is produced by the reaction. Some results from the reaction are shown in table D and graph E.

thistle funnel

trough

beehive shelf

marble chips and hydrochloric acid

C | This method of collecting a gas is known as 'collection over water'.

Time (s)	Volume of carbon dioxide collected (cm³)
0	0
10	36
20	55
30	66
40	72
50	73
60	73

D

The mean rate of reaction is calculated by dividing the total volume of gas by the time taken to collect it.

$$\text{mean rate of carbon dioxide formation} = 72 \text{ cm}^3 / 40 \text{ s}$$
$$= 1.8 \text{ cm}^3/\text{s}$$

You can see from graph E that the rate of reaction changes. It is fastest at the start and gradually becomes slower. The reaction then stops.

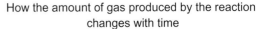
How the amount of gas produced by the reaction changes with time

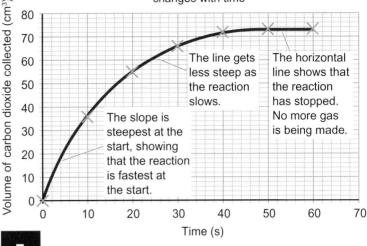

The slope is steepest at the start, showing that the reaction is fastest at the start.

The line gets less steep as the reaction slows.

The horizontal line shows that the reaction has stopped. No more gas is being made.

E

> **2** a| Describe how graph E shows when the reaction stops.
>
> b| Give a reason why the reaction stops.
>
> **3** a| Calculate the mean rate of reaction between the start and 8 seconds.
>
> b| Explain why this is a mean rate.

Changing rates

For particles to react, they need to collide with each other.

Increasing the temperature increases the rate of a reaction because the particles are moving faster and so collide more and with more energy. The harder particles collide, the more likely they are to react.

The more often particles collide, the more particles will react. One way of increasing the number of particles that collide is to increase the **surface area** of a reactant. Diagram F shows that only the blue particles on the surface of the block on the left can react with the red particles. If you split up the blue block, then more of the blue particles are on a surface and so can react.

The ratio between the surface area and volume is an important concept. We call this the **surface area : volume ratio** or **SA:V ratio**. We calculate it by dividing the total surface area of something by its volume. When a substance is split into smaller pieces, its volume does not change but its surface area increases. So, its SA:V ratio is greater. The greater the SA:V ratio, the faster the rate of reaction.

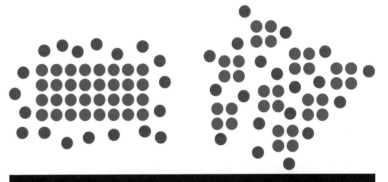

F | Increasing the surface area of a reactant increases the rate of reaction.

> **4** a| Calculate the SA:V ratio of a cube of side 3 cm.
>
> b| The cube is now split into 27 cubes of side 1 cm. Calculate the total SA:V ratio for the 27 cubes.
>
> c| How would splitting a large cube of calcium into smaller cubes affect its rate of reaction with water?
>
> **5** What has to happen for two particles to react?
>
> **6** Sketch a copy of graph E, and add a line to show the reaction if the marble chips had been smaller.
>
> **7** Explain why the reaction in graph E is fastest at the start.

FACT

On the morning of 14 October 1913, in a coalmine in Senghenydd, Wales a spark ignited a pocket of methane gas. This explosion caused coal dust to be swept into the air. Coal dust has a large surface area. The dust then exploded and this resulted in the deaths of 440 men and boys.

I can
- describe how rates of reaction change
- explain the importance of surface area : volume ratios in chemical reactions.

CHEMICAL EQUATIONS

HOW ARE SYMBOL EQUATIONS USED AND BALANCED?

A **salt** is an ionic compound produced in a **neutralisation reaction**. Some neutralisation reactions are shown by the **word equations** in the panel below.

> nitric acid + sodium hydroxide ⟶ sodium nitrate + water
>
> hydrochloric acid + copper oxide ⟶ copper chloride + water
>
> calcium carbonate + sulfuric acid ⟶ carbon dioxide + calcium sulfate + water

1 State the names of the salts found in the word equations above.

2 Write a word equation for the reaction between potassium hydroxide and hydrochloric acid.

Symbol equations

We use symbols to represent the **formulae** of elements and compounds. The formula for a compound clearly shows the elements it contains (which is not always obvious from a substance's name). For example:

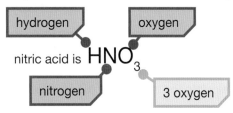

nitric acid is HNO_3 — hydrogen, oxygen, nitrogen, 3 oxygen

The small lowered numbers in a formula show the ratio of the different elements. If there is no number after an element, that element is in the ratio of 1 compared with the others. So, nitric acid contains 3 times as much oxygen as nitrogen. The ratio is 3:1. The ratio of oxygen to hydrogen is also 3:1. There are the same amounts of nitrogen and hydrogen. The ratio is 1:1.

We use formulae in symbol equations. For example:

nitric acid + sodium hydroxide ⟶ sodium nitrate + water
HNO_3 + $NaOH$ ⟶ $NaNO_3$ + H_2O

We can add **state symbols** to show the state different substances are in. State symbols are in brackets after each substance in a symbol equation: (s) for 'solid', (l) for 'liquid', (g) for 'gas' and (aq) for 'aqueous' (dissolved in water).

For example:

nitric acid + sodium hydroxide ⟶ sodium nitrate + water
$HNO_3(aq)$ + $NaOH(aq)$ ⟶ $NaNO_3(aq)$ + $H_2O(l)$

A | Limestone is mainly calcium carbonate, which reacts with acids in rainwater. This is a neutralisation reaction.

3 State the ratio of sodium to oxygen in:

a| sodium hydroxide

b| sodium nitrate.

4 Write a symbol equation for the reaction between magnesium carbonate ($MgCO_3$) and sulfuric acid (H_2SO_4). The salt ($MgSO_4$) is soluble.

5 Explain whether sodium nitrate is soluble in water or not.

6 Re-write your answer to question 4 adding in state symbols.

Balancing equations

In a chemical reaction, the **law of conservation of mass** states that the total mass of the reactants is always exactly the same as the total mass of the products. This is because atoms cannot be created or destroyed in a chemical reaction. So, when we write out symbol equations we must have the same number of each atom on both sides of the arrow. Doing this produces a **balanced equation**.

For example, this equation is balanced:

$$HNO_3(aq) + NaOH(aq) \longrightarrow NaNO_3(aq) + H_2O(l)$$

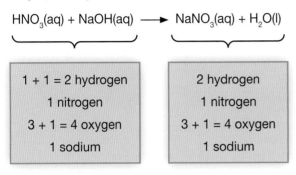

1 + 1 = 2 hydrogen	2 hydrogen
1 nitrogen	1 nitrogen
3 + 1 = 4 oxygen	3 + 1 = 4 oxygen
1 sodium	1 sodium

This equation is not balanced:

$$HCl(aq) + CuO(s) \longrightarrow CuCl_2(aq) + H_2O(l)$$

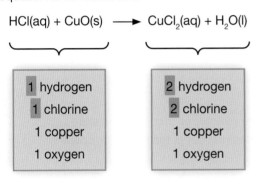

1 hydrogen	2 hydrogen
1 chlorine	2 chlorine
1 copper	1 copper
1 oxygen	1 oxygen

We need to balance equations by adding atoms. We cannot change the formulae in the equation. Instead, we can put a large number in front of a formula that then multiplies the elements after it.

For the unbalanced equation above (and in diagram C) we need another hydrogen on the left of the arrow. We can get this by doubling the 'HCl'. We write '2' in front of the HCl, meaning '2 lots of HCl'. This gives us two hydrogens. It also doubles the number of chlorines because the 2 applies to HCl as a whole (and not just the H). The equation is now balanced.

$$2HCl(aq) + CuO(s) \longrightarrow H_2O(l) + CuCl_2(aq)$$

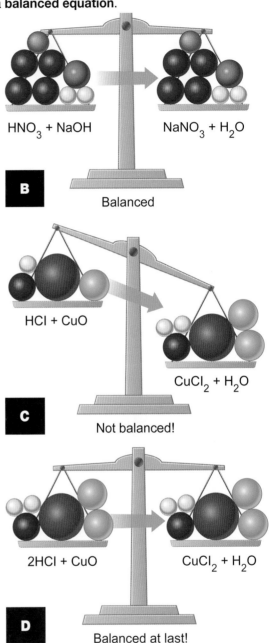

B
HNO₃ + NaOH   NaNO₃ + H₂O
Balanced

C
HCl + CuO   CuCl₂ + H₂O
Not balanced!

D
2HCl + CuO   CuCl₂ + H₂O
Balanced at last!

---

7 Write out a balanced equation, using state symbols, for:

a | magnesium burning in oxygen (O_2)

b | methane (CH_4) reacting with oxygen

c | sulfuric acid reacting with sodium hydroxide to produce Na_2SO_4(aq).

8 What are the names of the products and reactants in the two reactions shown on this page?

I can

- write balanced symbol equations with state symbols.

STANDARD FORM

HOW IS STANDARD FORM USED?

The standard SI unit of length is the metre. We often want to measure things that are smaller than a metre and so we use centimetres (cm), millimetres (mm), micrometres (μm) and nanometres (nm). Using these smaller units means that we do not end up with so many 0s in the numbers.

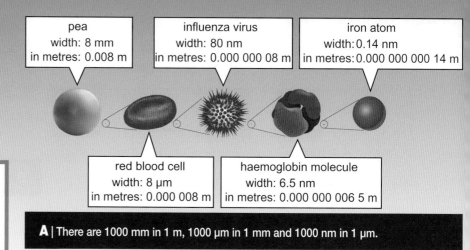

| pea
width: 8 mm
in metres: 0.008 m | influenza virus
width: 80 nm
in metres: 0.000 000 08 m | iron atom
width: 0.14 nm
in metres: 0.000 000 000 14 m |

| red blood cell
width: 8 μm
in metres: 0.000 008 m | haemoglobin molecule
width: 6.5 nm
in metres: 0.000 000 006 5 m |

A | There are 1000 mm in 1 m, 1000 μm in 1 mm and 1000 nm in 1 μm.

1

a| How many times bigger is a pea compared with a red blood cell?

b| How many times bigger is a red blood cell compared with a flu virus?

Index numbers

To measure areas we use square units, such as square metres (m^2) or square millimetres (mm^2). To measure volumes we use cubic units, such as cubic centimetres (cm^3). The small raised number is the **index** (or **power**).

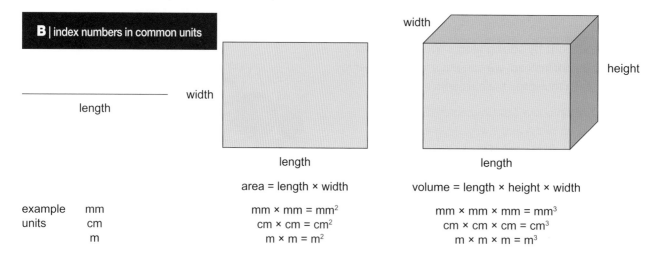

B | index numbers in common units

width

length

length

area = length × width

width

height

length

volume = length × height × width

| example
units | mm
cm
m | mm × mm = mm^2
cm × cm = cm^2
m × m = m^2 | mm × mm × mm = mm^3
cm × cm × cm = cm^3
m × m × m = m^3 |

Index numbers tell you how many times to multiply something.

For example, 5^2 means two 5s are multiplied together: $5^2 = 5 \times 5$

$3^9 = 3 \times 3 \times 3 \times 3 \times 3 \times 3 \times 3 \times 3 \times 3$

$10^{11} = 10 \times 10 \times 10 \times 10 \times 10 \times 10 \times 10 \times 10 \times 10 \times 10 \times 10$

There is an easier way to do this on a calculator rather than keying the numbers all those times! Make sure you know how to use the 'index' or 'power' function on your calculator.

When you multiply a number by 10, the digits move one place value to the left and you fill in the gaps with zeros:

$$1$$
$$1 \times 10 = \quad 10$$
$$10 \times 10 = 100$$

In positive powers of 10, the index tells you how many place values to move 1 to the left.

$$10^5 = 1\ 0\ 0\ 0\ 0\ 0$$
$$10^9 = 1\ 000\ 000\ 000$$

In negative powers of 10, the index tells you how many place values to move 1 to the right.

$$1$$
$$10^{-1} = 0.1$$
$$10^{-5} = 0.00001$$

2 Write out these multiplications in full.

a| 6^6 b| 10^3 c| 2^8

3 Write these multiplications using an index number:

a| $4 \times 4 \times 4$
b| $10 \times 10 \times 10 \times 10 \times 10$
c| $2 \times 2 \times 2 \times 2$
d| $10 \times 10 \times 10 \times 10 \times 10 \times 10 \times 10$

4 Write these as 'ordinary' numbers:

a| $10^3 = 10 \times 10 \times 10 = \ldots..$
b| 10^4
c| 10^6
d| 10^{-2}
e| 10^{-4}

Standard form

We can write very large or very small numbers as a number between 1 and 10 multiplied by a power of 10. This is called **standard form**:

$A \times 10^n$ where A is between 1 and 10 and n is the power of 10.

Standard form is another way of writing numbers without having too many zeros to deal with. For example, the beaker in photo C contains 602 000 000 000 000 000 000 000 copper atoms. We can write this in standard form:

number between 1 and 10

$$602\ 000\ 000\ 000\ 000\ 000\ 000\ 000 = 6.02 \times 10^{23}$$

power of 10

Very small numbers are shown using standard form with a negative index number. For example, the width of a carbon atom is 0.000 000 000 07 m.

In standard form:

$$0.000\,000\,000\,07 = 7 \times 10^{-11}\ \text{m}$$

C | This beaker contains 6×10^{23} atoms.

5 The Earth is about 4 600 000 000 years old. Write the number of years in standard form.

6 The Moon has a diameter of 3.474×10^6 m. Write this distance as an ordinary number.

7 An average human cell has a mass of 0.000 000 000 001 kg. Write this mass in standard form.

8 Water has a density of 1×10^3 kg/m³. Write this density as an ordinary number.

9 Light takes about 3×10^{-9} s to travel 1 m. Write this time as an ordinary number.

10 Use standard form to show the widths of each of the items in diagram A in metres.

I can

- recognise and use numbers and units with indices
- convert numbers to and from standard form.

WHAT IS A DYNAMIC EQUILIBRIUM?

In a chemical reaction, reactants form products. We show this using equations, with the reactants on the left of the arrow and the products on the right.

$$HCl(aq) + NaOH(aq) \longrightarrow NaCl(aq) + H_2O(l)$$

reactants   products

Sometimes there is only one product and sometimes there is only one reactant (such as in decomposition reactions). The equation below shows the decomposition of hydrogen peroxide (H_2O_2). A weak aqueous solution of hydrogen peroxide is used to remove stains from paintings.

$$2H_2O_2(aq) \longrightarrow 2H_2O(l) + O_2(g)$$

In some reactions, the products react together and form the reactants again. For example, if ammonium chloride is heated it will decompose to form ammonia and hydrogen chloride. However, some of the ammonia and hydrogen chloride will react together again to form ammonium chloride. There are two reactions going on at the same time:

$$NH_4Cl(s) \longrightarrow NH_3(g) + HCl(g)$$
$$NH_3(g) + HCl(g) \longrightarrow NH_4Cl(s)$$

A reaction that can go both backwards and forwards is called a **reversible reaction**. We show this in equations using half arrows that point in both directions.

$$NH_4Cl(s) \rightleftharpoons NH_3(g) + HCl(g)$$

When we read an equation like this, we say that the reaction going from left to right is the 'forward reaction', and the reaction going from right to left is the 'backward reaction'.

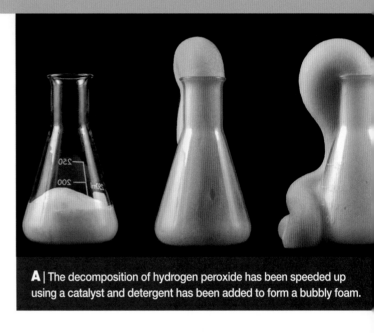

A | The decomposition of hydrogen peroxide has been speeded up using a catalyst and detergent has been added to form a bubbly foam.

---

1 State the names of the products and reactants when hydrogen peroxide decomposes.

---

2 a | What is produced by the forward reaction when ammonium chloride decomposes?

b | What is produced by the backward reaction?

3 Nitrogen (N_2) can be made to react with hydrogen (H_2) to form ammonia in a reversible reaction. Write a balanced symbol equation, including state symbols, for this reaction.

4 Sulfur dioxide (SO_2) can react with oxygen to form sulfur trioxide (SO_3) gas in a reversible reaction. Write a balanced symbol equation, including state symbols, for this reaction.

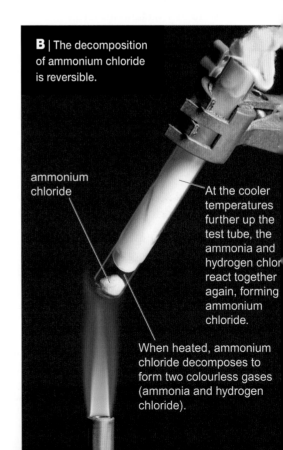

B | The decomposition of ammonium chloride is reversible.

ammonium chloride

At the cooler temperatures further up the test tube, the ammonia and hydrogen chlor[ide] react together again, forming ammonium chloride.

When heated, ammonium chloride decomposes to form two colourless gases (ammonia and hydrogen chloride).

Equilibrium

If a reversible reaction happens in a sealed container, the reactants are never totally converted into products because some of the products will always react to form the reactants again.

As the rate of the forward reaction slows down, the backward reaction speeds up. They then reach a point where the two reactions are taking place at exactly the same rate. The reaction has reached **equilibrium**.

Once equilibrium has been reached, the percentages of the different substances in the reaction mixture do not change, as shown on graph C. However, the reactions are still happening. Something that is undergoing constant change is said to be 'dynamic' and so this is called a **dynamic equilibrium**.

If a reversible reaction is exothermic in one direction, it will be endothermic in the other. The same amount of energy will be transferred in each direction.

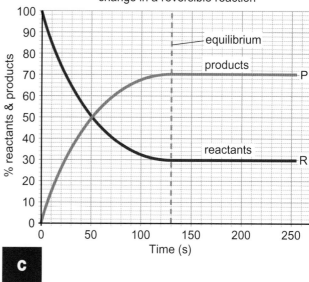

How the percentages of reactants and products change in a reversible reaction

C

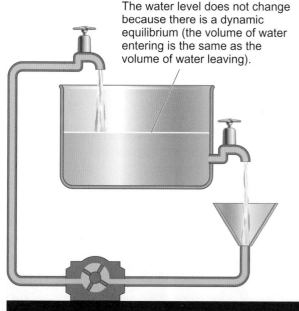

The water level does not change because there is a dynamic equilibrium (the volume of water entering is the same as the volume of water leaving).

D | a model to help think about a dynamic equilibrium

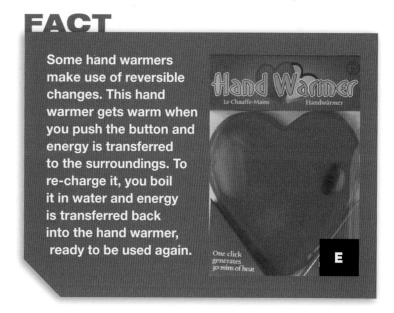

FACT

Some hand warmers make use of reversible changes. This hand warmer gets warm when you push the button and energy is transferred to the surroundings. To re-charge it, you boil it in water and energy is transferred back into the hand warmer, ready to be used again.

One click generates 30 mins of heat

E

---

5 Look at graph C. Describe what line P tells you about the forward reaction.

6 a| State the percentage of reactants when equilibrium has been reached in graph C.

b| Explain why this is a dynamic equilibrium.

7 Hydrogen and iodine vapour (I_2) can react to form hydrogen iodide gas (HI) in a reversible reaction.

a| Write out a balanced symbol equation, including state symbols, for this reaction.

b| Hydrogen iodide production is exothermic. Describe the energy transfer in the backward reaction.

I can

■ represent reversible reactions using balanced symbol equations

■ explain how a dynamic equilibrium is formed in reversible reactions.

HOW IS CHEMISTRY USED TO MAKE AND RESTORE FRESCOS?

Frescos are wall decorations created by painting on wet plaster. The plaster is made from calcium oxide mixed with water, which forms calcium hydroxide in an exothermic reaction. Once on the wall, the plaster is painted. The calcium hydroxide reacts with carbon dioxide in the air to form solid calcium carbonate ($CaCO_3$). This reaction traps the paint pigments.

Frescos, like all artworks, react slowly with substances in the environment. Acidic gases, such as sulfur dioxide (SO_2), are a particular problem. Sulfur dioxide, formed by the burning of sulfur impurities in fossil fuels, reacts with oxygen in the air to form sulfur trioxide gas (SO_3). This then reacts with water vapour to form sulfuric acid (H_2SO_4).

The sulfuric acid can react with the calcium carbonate to produce 'gypsum' (calcium sulfate), which forms big crystals in a fresco. This causes the fresco to bubble and flake.

Restorers can remove 'gypsum' by cleaning a fresco with ammonium carbonate:

$$CaSO_4 + (NH_4)_2CO_3 \rightleftharpoons (NH_4)_2SO_4 + CaCO_3$$

Other substances are used to remove layers of soot and grime from frescos, and faded areas can be restored by repainting using the original pigments.

1
a| State the type of reaction used to remove 'gypsum'.

b| Reactions like this form a 'dynamic equilibrium'. Give a definition for the term 'dynamic equilibrium'.

2 Describe the direction of energy transfer when calcium oxide reacts with water.

3 State the ratio of the different elements in 'gypsum'.

4 Write out balanced symbol equations for the two reactions that produce sulfuric acid from sulfur dioxide, including state symbols.

5 Calcium oxide is an ionic compound. Describe the bonding in this compound.

A | This fresco has been damaged by the formation of 'gypsum'.

before   after

B | The Sistine Chapel ceiling fresco in the Vatican was restored between 1980 and 1999. Some people think that the restoration removed too much of Michelangelo's original work.

HAVE YOUR SAY

Should we restore art? Write an argument for or against.

BEING
9H OBJECTIVE

If you are being objective about something, you do not allow your personal feelings or opinions to influence what you say.

When scientists write papers, they try to be objective. They state all their results and describe how the evidence supports their hypotheses. Other scientists can easily see what they have done.

Not everyone reports science like this. Newspapers and advertisers may choose words to add extra importance to a point. Or they may only describe part of the evidence. This causes bias – a shift away from the correct meaning.

Some scientific reports are paid for by companies, and might be biased in favour of the company. It is important to think about who has written or paid for the investigations and reports, and whether all the evidence has been included.

A

GreenCar

Climate Friendly
Worried about climate change? Our new GreenCar can help you save the planet. An electric motor drives you smoothly and quietly, with no carbon dioxide emissions. Contact your local dealer for details.

B

Electric cars
the facts

While it is true that electric cars do not emit CO_2, the electricity used to charge their batteries has to be generated somewhere. Only if this electricity is produced by renewable resources can the car claim to be truly 'climate-friendly'.

1 Look at the car advert in A.

a| Which words in the advert encourage you to buy the car?

b| Write down part of a sentence from the text that could be described as showing bias.

2 Look at the magazine article in B. Identify a fact that has not been mentioned in the advert in A, and suggest why it has not been mentioned.

9H1 CARBON CAPTURE

NEWS

| Home | UK | World | Business | Education | Technology | Science | Health | Entertainment | More |

Carbon Capture and Storage gets going

Press release: CarbOilCo

CarbOilCo is excited to announce our new carbon capture and storage (CCS) plant comes online today. Maintaining the supply of energy is vital in our world, and fossil fuels provide the only widely available reliable energy resource. CarbOilCo is reducing the effect of carbon dioxide on climate change by working with power stations to capture CO_2 and store it in our underground reservoirs.

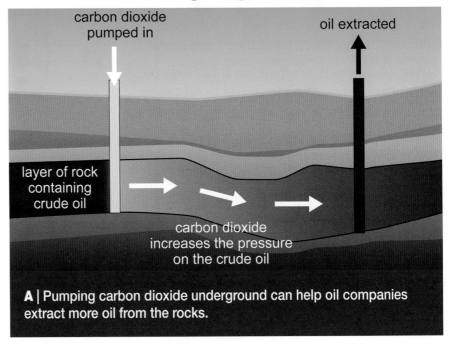

carbon dioxide pumped in

oil extracted

layer of rock containing crude oil

carbon dioxide increases the pressure on the crude oil

A | Pumping carbon dioxide underground can help oil companies extract more oil from the rocks.

---

1 This story is from an online news site. The editor wants readers' questions to be answered, explaining the science. Use your communications skills to write a detailed answer for one of the following questions.

a| Coal consists mainly of carbon. How is coal formed and why is it a non-renewable resource?

b| What is the carbon cycle? (*Hint:* It may be easier to answer this question using a labelled diagram.)

c| Why is the amount of carbon dioxide in the Earth's atmosphere increasing and why is this likely to cause environmental problems?

2 Carbon dioxide captured from power stations is often pumped into the rocks in oil fields. This process is called 'enhanced oil recovery'. Collect information to help you to explain why using carbon dioxide in this way may not help to reduce the amount put into the atmosphere.

3 Newspaper or magazine editors often write 'editorials' in which they give their own balanced opinions on things discussed in their publication. Find out more about the benefits and drawbacks of CCS plants, and use the results of your research to write a balanced editorial that shows both sides of the argument. The final part of your editorial should give your own conclusion about whether or not new CCS plants are a good thing.

9H2 ELECTROLYSIS INVESTIGATION

When a salt such as copper sulfate dissolves in water, the crystals break up and form positively charged particles of copper (called copper ions) and negatively charged sulfate ions in the water. In electrolysis, two electrodes are placed into the solution and connected to an electricity supply and the charged particles are attracted to the electrodes. Copper metal forms at the electrode connected to the negative terminal of the power supply.

Metals can be extracted from their ores using electrolysis. However, for fairly unreactive metals such as copper there are also other, cheaper, methods that can be used.

Many uses of copper require the copper to be pure. Electrolysis can be used to purify copper, by making the impure copper the positive electrode. Copper from this electrode turns into copper ions in solution, and these are deposited on the negative electrode as pure copper.

A | Copper-coated electrodes are being lifted from an 'electrolysis' bath. Pure copper has been deposited on the electrodes.

B | You can extract copper from copper sulfate solution in a school laboratory. What variables affect the amount of copper produced?

Planning

You are going to work in a team to plan and carry out an investigation of your choice to find out how different variables affect the amount of copper produced during the electrolysis of copper sulfate solution. Here are some variables you could investigate:

- the volume of copper sulfate solution
- the concentration of copper sulfate solution
- the size of the current
- the time for which the current flows
- the size (or surface area) of the electrodes.

Results and conclusion

- Present your results in a way that helps you to reach a conclusion. Other people should be able to look at your results and see why you reached that conclusion.
- Write a conclusion based on the data you have gathered.

Evaluation

- Have you gathered enough data to reach a conclusion?
- Is your data good enough to give you confidence in your conclusion?

 Copper sulfate is harmful. Wear eye protection.

9H3 NANOPARTICLES

COMMUNICATING WITH THE PUBLIC

Titanium dioxide is widely used as a white pigment, in paint and things such as toothpaste. Since titanium dioxide particles are good at reflecting all wavelengths of light, it is used in sunscreens.

Titanium dioxide crystals can be made that are much smaller than usual – only about 20 nanometres across. These are examples of **nanoparticles** (particles of 1 nm to 100 nm in diameter). Titanium dioxide nanoparticles have different properties from the larger crystals. They do not reflect all colours of light but still absorb UV light from the Sun.

Making a material into nanoparticles often changes its properties. This is mainly because the surface area of the material is greatly increased for the same mass.

Nanoparticles made of various materials have many uses. For instance, vehicle catalytic converters can now be made using less platinum if this metal is made into nanoparticles. Catalytic converters have a mesh with a large surface area, through which exhaust gases pass. For small engines, this mesh is often made of an alloy of iron, chromium and aluminium. This is coated with a layer of large titanium dioxide crystals, to give the mesh a rough surface (and more surface area), and this is covered in a fine layer of platinum nanoparticles (the catalyst). The large surface area of the catalyst speeds up the reactions that convert pollutants in exhaust gases into less harmful compounds.

A | This white sunblock contains titanium dioxide crystals that are about 300 nm across. 'Invisible' sunscreens contain titanium dioxide nanoparticles.
1 nanometre = 1 millionth of a millimetre.

B | This catalytic converter is designed for use on petrol-powered lawn mowers.

1   A motor exhibition needs a card to describe the elements used in the catalytic converters in small engines. For each element, outline how it is extracted and describe one other use of the metal, with a reason for this use.

2   In a catalytic converter it is important that the exhaust gases come into contact with a large enough surface area of catalyst. Describe how the ratio between surface area and volume changes as the particles get smaller, and explain why less catalyst can be used if it is made into nanoparticles.

HAVE YOUR SAY

Materials that come into contact with humans are tested for safety. Some people say that if previously tested materials are made into nanoparticles they must be tested again. This will increase the cost of using nanoparticles. Do you think these materials need re-testing?

GLOSSARY

Pronunciation note: A capital 'O' is said as in 'so'

abrasion	When rock fragments bump into each other and wear away.
accuracy	A measure of how close a value is to its real value.
acid (*ass*-id)	A substance that reacts with alkalis, turns litmus red and has a pH of less than 7 is acidic.
acid rain	Rainwater that is more acidic than usual, usually caused by sulfur dioxide and nitrogen oxides dissolved in it.
addition polymer	A polymer formed by adding monomer molecules together to form a long chain in an addition polymerisation reaction.
addition polymerisation	The reaction that joins monomer molecules together to form a polymer.
aggregate	Gravel, small stones or pieces of crushed rocks used in building.
aim	What you are trying to find out or do.
air pressure	The force on a certain area caused by air molecules hitting it.
alkali (*alk*-al-lie)	A substance that reacts with acids, turns litmus blue and has a pH of more than 7.
alkali metal	A group of very reactive metals in group 1 of the periodic table.
alloy (*al*-oi)	A metal mixed with one or more other elements.
analogy (an-*al*-O-jee)	A model that compares something complicated to something that is easier to understand.
anomalous result (uh-*nom*-uh-luh s)	A measurement that does not fit the same pattern as other measurements from the same experiment.
antacid (ant-*ass*-id)	An indigestion remedy that contains a base to neutralise the excess acid in the stomach.
apparatus	Pieces of equipment.
asthma	A condition in which the tiny tubes leading to the alveoli become narrow and start to fill with mucus.
atom	Atoms are small particles from which all substances are made.
atomic number	The number of protons in an atom. The atoms of different elements contain different numbers of protons.
balanced equation (eck-*way*-shun)	A symbol equation in which the numbers of atoms or ions of different types are the same on both sides of the arrow.
bar chart	A chart where the lengths or heights of bars (rectangles) represent the values of the variables.
basalt (*ba*-salt)	An igneous rock with very tiny crystals.
base	Any substance, soluble or insoluble, that neutralises an acid forming a salt and water only.
biodegradable	Capable of being decomposed (broken down) by organisms in the soil.
biofuel	A fuel made from plants or animal droppings.
biological weathering	When rocks are worn away or broken up due to the activities of living things. For example, growing plant roots can split rocks.
boiling	When there is liquid turning into a gas in all parts of a liquid, creating bubbles of gas in the liquid.
boiling point	The temperature at which a liquid boils.
bond	A force that holds some atoms tightly together.
brittle (*britt*-el)	Not easily bent, not flexible, breaks under force.

Brownian motion (*mO*-shun)	An erratic movement of small specks of matter caused by being hit by the moving particles that make up liquids or gases.
carbonate (*car*-bon-ayt)	A compound containing an element bonded with carbon and oxygen.
carbon capture technology	Technology that can be used to remove carbon dioxide from the waste gases produced by power stations and industrial processes preventing it from entering the atmosphere.
carbon dioxide	A waste gas produced by respiration.
carbon monoxide	A poisonous gas caused by carbon burning without enough oxygen. Found in cigarette smoke.
catalyst (*cat*-a-list)	A substance that speeds up a chemical reaction, without itself being used up.
catalytic converter (cat-a-*lit*-ick)	A device fitted to the exhaust pipe of a vehicle to change harmful pollutant gases into less harmful gases.
caution (cor-*shun*)	A warning to 'take care'. Some substances need to be used with caution (e.g. they may cause skin irritation).
cell (biology)	The basic unit of all life. All organisms are made of cells.
cement	A building material made from a mixture of clay and lime (calcium oxide). The word also means 'to stick things together'.
cementation	A process in which water is squeezed out of the spaces between pieces of rock leaving mineral salts behind that stick or cement the rock pieces together.
ceramic (ser-*am*-ick)	A range of hard, durable, non-metallic materials, which are generally unaffected by heat. E.g. china and glass.
change of state	When a substance changes from one state of matter (solid, liquid or gas) into another.
chemical change	A change that forms one or more new substances.
chemical energy	A name used to describe energy when it is stored in chemicals. Food, fuel and batteries all store chemical energy.
chemical formula (*kem*-ik-al)	A combination of symbols and numbers that shows how many atoms of different elements are in a particular molecule. In compounds that do not form molecules, it shows the ratio of the different elements in the compound.
chemical property	How a substance reacts with other substances.
chemical reaction	A change in which one or more new substances are formed.
chemical weathering (*kem*-ik-al)	When rocks are broken up or worn away by chemical reactions, usually with rainwater.
chromatogram (kro-*ma*-t-o-gram)	The results of chromatography (e.g. a dried piece of paper for paper chromatography), when the dissolved solids have been separated.
chromatography (*krome*-a-tog-ra-fee)	A method that separates out dissolved substances in a mixture, using a liquid or gas solvent.
clay	Very fine particles of rock.
climate change	Changes that will happen to the weather as a result of global warming.
colloid	A mixture of a solid, liquid or gas in a solid, liquid or gas, where the substances do not settle out if left to stand.
combustion	Burning, usually in air. The reaction gives out energy, which is transferred to the surroundings by heating or light.
communication	The transfer of information.

compaction	When layers of sediment or rock are squashed by the weight of sediment above them.
complete combustion	When a substance reacts fully with oxygen, such as: carbon + oxygen → carbon dioxide.
composite material (*kuh m-poz-it*)	A material made up of two or more substances. The separate materials do not react together. It has significantly different properties from the substances from which it is made.
compound	A substance that can be split up into simpler substances, since it contains the atoms of two or more elements joined together.
compress	To squeeze into a smaller volume.
concentrated (*con-cen-tray-ted*)	A solution that contains a large amount of solute dissolved in a small amount of liquid (solvent).
concentration	The amount of something in a certain volume. For example, the mass of solute dissolved in a certain volume of solvent.
conclusion (*con-cloo-shun*)	An explanation of how or why something happens, which is backed up by evidence. You use evidence to 'draw' a conclusion.
concrete	A building material made by mixing sand, cement and gravel (aggregate) with water.
condense	When a substance changes from its gas state into its liquid state.
conductor	A substance that allows something to pass through it (e.g. heat, electricity).
conservation of mass	In a chemical reaction the total mass of the reactants is the same as the total mass of the products. Mass is conserved, that is, it is kept the same.
continuous	Data values that can change gradually and can have any value (between two limits) are continuous (e.g. human height).
contract	To get smaller.
control variable (*vair-ee-ab-el*)	A variable other than the independent variable, which could affect the dependent variable and so needs to be controlled.
convention	A standard way of doing something or representing something, so that everyone understands what is meant.
correlation	A relationship between two variables. If an increase in one appears to cause an increase in the other it is 'positive'. An increase in one linked with a decrease in the other is 'negative'.
corrosion (*kur-O-zhuhn*)	When something, such as stone or metal, reacts with chemicals in the air or water and gets worn away.
corrosive (*cor-row-sive*)	Substances that attack metals, stonework and skin are said to be corrosive.
criteria (*cry-teer-ee-a*)	A set of standards by which to judge things.
crude oil	A fossil fuel formed from the decay of sea creatures over millions of years under the conditions of high heat and pressure and in the absence of air.
crust	The solid rocks at the surface of the Earth.
crystal (*kris-tal*)	Piece of a mineral with sharp edges. A solid with a regular shape and flat surfaces that reflect light.
cubic centimetre (cm³)	A unit used for measuring volume.
data	Observations or measurements collected in investigations.
density	A measure of a substance's mass per unit volume measured in grams per cubic centimetre (g/cm³)).
dependent variable (*dee-pend-ent*) (*vair-ee-ab-el*)	The variable that is measured in an investigation. The values of the dependent variable depend on those of the independent variable.
deposit	When moving water, ice or wind drops rock fragments or grains.
desalination (*dee-sal-in-ay-shun*)	To produce fresh drinking water by separating the water from the salts in salty water.
diffusion (*diff-you-zshun*)	When particles spread and mix with each other without anything moving them.
diluted (*die-loot-ed*)	A substance that has had water added to it to make it less concentrated.
discrete (*dis-kreet*)	Data that involves a limited number of values (numbers).

discontinuous	Data values that can only have one of a set number of options are discontinuous (e.g. shoe sizes and days of the week).
disperse	To spread without settling out, such as the bits in a colloid.
dissolve	When a substance breaks up into such tiny pieces in a liquid that it can no longer be seen and forms a solution.
distillation (*dis-till-ay-shun*)	The process of separating a liquid from a mixture by evaporating the liquid and then condensing it (so that it can be collected).
ductile	A ductile material can be pulled into a wire, without breaking.
dynamic equilibrium (*dy-nam-ick*) (*ek-will-ib-bree-um*)	When there are constant changes going on but these changes are equal and opposite and so do not affect the overall levels of something.
earthquake	When the ground shakes.
Earth's crust	The solid layer of rocks on the surface of the Earth.
effervescence	The production of a gas in a reaction occurring in a liquid.
efficiency (*e-fish-en-see*)	A way of saying how much energy something wastes.
electricity	A way of transferring energy through wires.
electrolysis (*ell-ek-troll-e-sis*)	Breaking down a substance using electricity.
electron	A sub-atomic particle found outside the nucleus of an atom. It has an electrical charge of −1.
element	A simple substance, made up of only one type of atom.
endothermic (*end-O-ther-mik*)	A change or reaction that absorbs energy from the surroundings making the temperature of the surroundings fall.
energy	Something that is needed to make things happen or change.
environment	The conditions in a habitat caused by physical environmental factors.
equilibrium (*ek-will-ib-bree-um*)	When things are balanced and not changing, they are 'in equilibrium'.
erosion	The movement of loose and weathered rock.
eruption	When lava or ash comes out of a volcano.
estimate	An approximate answer, often calculated from a sample or using rounded values.
ethanol	A common solvent. It is found in some cleaning products.
evaluate	Looking at the good and bad points about something, in order to reach an overall decision.
evaluation	Weighing up plus points and minus points to reach a judgement about something (e.g. how good something is, how well something does its job, how safe something is).
evaporation	When a liquid changes into a gas.
evidence	Data used to support an idea or show that it is wrong.
exothermic (*ex-O-therm-ic*)	A reaction that gives out energy that can be felt as it heats the surroundings, such as combustion.
expand	To get bigger.
explosive (*ex-plo-siv*)	An explosive substance reacts very fast, giving out a lot of energy and making a lot of noise and gas. Heating may cause an explosion.
extrusive	Igneous rocks formed when lava freezes above the ground.
fair test	An experiment in which all the control variables are controlled and only changes in the independent variable cause changes in the dependent variable.
fibre (*fY-ber*)	A long, thin continuous strand or thread.
filter	Anything, such as cloth, paper or a layer of sand, through which a liquid is passed to remove suspended pieces of solid.
filtrate	The fluid that passes out of a filter.
filtration	Passing a fluid through a filter in order to remove solid pieces.
finite	Something that is a limited resource and will eventually run out.

fire extinguisher	Something that is used to put out a fire, such as a canister of carbon dioxide, powder, water or foam.
fire triangle	A way of showing in a diagram that heat, fuel and oxygen are needed for fire.
flammable	A flammable substance catches fire easily.
flow	To move and change shape smoothly.
fluid	A gas or a liquid.
force	A push, pull or twist.
formula (chemical)	A combination of symbols and numbers that shows how many atoms of different kinds are in a particular molecule. In compounds that do not form molecules, it shows the ratio of elements in the compound.
fossil	The remains of a dead animal or plant that became trapped in layers of sediment and turned into rock.
fossil fuel	A fuel formed from the dead remains of organisms over millions of years (e.g. coal, oil or natural gas).
freeze	When a liquid turns into a solid.
freeze–thaw action	A type of physical weathering that happens when water gets into a crack in a rock and freezes. The freezing water expands and makes the crack bigger.
freezing point	The temperature at which a liquid turns into a solid. It is the same temperature as the melting point of the substance.
fuel	A substance that contains a store of chemical or nuclear energy that can easily be transferred.
gabbro (*gab*-ro)	A type of igneous rock with large crystals.
galvanisation	Coating iron or steel with a thin layer of zinc to stop the iron or steel rusting. The zinc acts as a barrier to oxygen and water.
gas	One of the states of matter. Does not have a fixed shape or a fixed volume and is easy to squash.
gas pressure	The force on a certain area of a surface caused by gas particles hitting it.
generate	To produce electricity.
geologist	A scientist who studies rocks and the Earth.
glacier	Ice that fills a valley and moves slowly downhill.
global warming	Increased warming of the Earth's surface as a result of increased amounts of greenhouse gases (e.g. carbon dioxide) in the air.
gneiss (*nice*)	A metamorphic rock formed when schist is heated and squashed more. It usually has bands of different coloured minerals.
grain	A distinct part of a rock, made of one or more minerals.
gram (g)	A unit for measuring mass.
granite (*gran*-it)	An igneous rock with large crystals.
gravel	Small pieces of rock used in building.
greenhouse effect	The warming effect on the Earth's surface caused by greenhouse gases absorbing energy emitted from the warm Earth's surface and re-emitting it back to the surface.
greenhouse gas	A gas, such as carbon dioxide, water vapour or methane, in the Earth's atmosphere, which absorbs energy emitted from the Earth's surface and then emits it back to the surface.
group	A vertical column of elements in the periodic table. Elements in the same group generally have similar properties.
halogen	An element in group 7 of the periodic table (e.g. chlorine, fluorine).
hazard	Something that could cause harm.
hazard symbol	A warning symbol that shows why something is dangerous.
heat resistant	A substance that is not easily damaged by heat.
hydrocarbon	A compound made up of only hydrogen and carbon atoms.
hypothesis (*hy-poth-uh-sis*)	An idea about how something works that can be tested using experiments. Plural is hypotheses.

igneous rock (*igg*-nee-us)	A rock made from interlocking crystals that are not in layers. Formed when magma or lava cooled down and solidified.
implosion (*im-plo-shun*)	An object is destroyed by collapsing in on itself.
impurity	An unwanted substance that is found mixed into a useful substance.
incomplete combustion	When a substance reacts only partially with oxygen, such as when carbon burns in air producing carbon dioxide, carbon monoxide and soot (unburnt carbon).
independent variable	The variable that you chose the values of in an investigation.
index	A small raised number after a unit or another number to show you how many times to multiply it by itself. For example, 10^3 means multiply 10 together 3 times $(10 \times 10 \times 10)$.
indicator	A substance that changes colour in solutions of different acidity and alkalinity.
inner core	The middle of the Earth.
insoluble (*in-sol-you-bul*)	Describes a substance that cannot be dissolved in a certain liquid.
insulator	A material that does not allow something to pass through it (e.g. heat, electricity).
interlocking	When crystals fit together with no gaps between them.
internal energy	The energy stored in the movement of particles. Sometimes called 'thermal energy'.
intrusive	Igneous rocks formed when magma freezes underground.
ion (*i-on*)	An atom that has a tiny electrical charge.
ionic bond (*i-on-ick*)	A strong force between oppositely charged ions.
ionic compound (*i-on-ick*)	A substance containing ions from two or more elements.
irritant (*irr-it-ant*)	An irritant substance causes skin and eyes to be sore or sting.
journal (scientific)	A scientific magazine in which scientists publish their findings by writing articles called scientific papers.
landslide	A sudden movement of rocks and/or soil downwards.
lattice structure (*latt*-iss)	An arrangement of many atoms or other particles, which are bonded together in a fixed, regular (grid-like) pattern.
lava (*lar*-va)	Molten rock that runs out of volcanoes.
law of conservation of energy	The idea that energy can never be created or destroyed, only transferred from one store to another.
law of conservation of mass	The idea that mass is not lost or gained during a chemical reaction. The mass of all the reactants is equal to the mass of all the products.
limestone	A sedimentary rock made from the shells of dead sea creatures, consisting mainly of calcium carbonate.
limewater	A solution of calcium hydroxide. It is clear and colourless but turns 'milky' in contact with carbon dioxide.
line graph	A graph that shows how one variable changes when another changes (usually time). The points are joined with straight lines.
line of best fit	A line drawn on a scatter graph that goes through the middle of the points, so that about half the points are above the line and about half of them are below the line.
liquid (*li-kwid*)	One of the states of matter. Has a fixed volume but not a fixed shape.
magma	Molten rock beneath the surface of the Earth.
magnetic	A material, such as iron, that is attracted to a magnet.
magnetism	A force that attracts objects made of iron or other magnetic materials.
malleable	Able to be beaten and bent into shape.
mantle (*man*-tel)	The part of the Earth below the crust.
marble	A metamorphic rock formed from limestone.

mass	The amount of matter that something is made from. Mass is measured in grams (g) and kilograms (kg).
mass number	The number of protons and neutrons in an atom.
matter	All things are made of matter. There are three states of matter: solid, liquid, gas.
mean	An average calculated by adding up the values of a set of measurements and dividing by the number of measurements.
melt	When a solid turns into a liquid.
melting point	The temperature at which a solid turns into a liquid.
metal	An element that is shiny when polished, conducts heat and electricity well, is malleable, flexible (ductile) and often has a high melting point.
metallic bonding	The type of bonding found in metals. We can think if it as positively charged ions in a sea of negatively charged electrons.
metal ore	A rock containing a compound of a metal, which can be used as a source of the metal.
metallurgist	A person who studies the properties of metals and alloys.
metal oxide	A metal that has combined with oxygen in a chemical reaction, e.g. magnesium oxide.
metamorphic rock	A rock formed from interlocking crystals that are often lined up in layers. It is formed when existing rocks are heated or compressed.
meteorologist	A scientist who studies the weather and makes weather forecasts.
method	A description of how an experiment is carried out, written in simple, well-organised steps.
mineral	A naturally occurring element or compound that can form distinct grains in rocks. Some mineral compounds are important sources of metals.
mining	Obtaining metal ores or other substances from the Earth.
mixture	Two or more substances jumbled together but not joined to each other. The substances in mixtures can often be separated from each other.
model	An example of something happening which can be used to explain how a scientific idea should be understood.
molecule	Two or more atoms joined together in a group of a set size.
monomer	A small molecule that can join with other molecules like itself to form a polymer.
mudstone	A sedimentary rock made of tiny particles.
nanoparticle	A particle of substance with a diameter of 1–100 nanometres.
native state	When a metal is found in the Earth as an element.
neutral (new-tral)	A substance that is neither an acid nor an alkali. It has a pH of 7.
neutralisation (new-tral-ise-ay-shun)	A reaction in which an acid reacts with an alkali or a base to produce a salt and water only.
neutron	A sub-atomic particle found in an atom's nucleus. It has no electrical charge.
nitrogen oxide	Acidic gas formed when nitrogen reacts with oxygen at high temperatures, such as in a car engine. There are different types of nitrogen oxide.
noble gas	A group of very unreactive non-metal gases. Found in group 0 of the periodic table.
non-biodegradable	Not decomposed (broken down) by organisms in the soil.
non-metal	Any element that is not shiny, and does not conduct heat and electricity well.
non-renewable resource	Any energy resource that will run out because we cannot renew our supplies of it (e.g. oil).
normal distribution	When many things have a middle value with fewer things having greater or lesser values. This sort of data forms a bell shape on charts and graphs.
nucleus (new-clee-us)	The central part of an atom, where protons and neutrons are found.
observation	Something that you see happening.
onion-skin weathering	A type of physical weathering that happens when a rock is heated and cooled over and over again.
opaque (O-payk)	A substance that is opaque is not possible to see through.
ore	A rock that contains enough of a certain metal, or mineral, to make it worth mining.
organic molecule	A molecule that is built using a chain of carbon atoms.
outer core	The middle of the Earth.
outlier	Another term for 'anomalous result'.
oxidation (ox-i-day-shun)	Reacting with oxygen. For example, when a fuel combusts or when a metal reacts with oxygen to form a metal oxide.
oxide	A compound of a metal or non-metal with oxygen, such as magnesium oxide or carbon dioxide.
oxidiser	A substance that supplies oxygen for a reaction.
oxidising agent (ox-id-eyes-ing)	A substance that provides oxygen to oxidise another substance.
oxygen	A gas that makes up about 21 per cent of the air.
paper chromatography (krome-a-tog-ra-fee)	Chromatography where the solvent moves through paper, carrying the dissolved solids.
particle model	Another term for particle theory.
particles (part-ick-als)	The tiny pieces of matter that everything is made out of.
particle theory	A theory used to explain the different properties and observations of solids, liquids and gases.
period	A horizontal row in the periodic table.
periodic table	An ordered list of all known elements.
permeable	Permeable rocks let water soak through them.
pH scale	A numerical scale from 1 to 14 showing how acidic or alkaline a substance is. Acids have a pH below 7, neutral substances have a pH of 7 and alkalis have a pH greater than 7.
phlogiston (flo-jist-on)	A substance that scientists once thought explained why things burn; it has since been proved that it does not exist.
physical change (fi-zi-kal)	A change in which no new substances are formed (e.g. changes of state).
physical model (fi-zi-kal)	A model that you can touch or a model that you could build.
physical property (fi-zi-kal)	A description of how a material behaves and responds to forces and energy. Hardness is a physical property.
physical weathering (fi-zi-kal)	When rocks are worn away or broken up by physical processes such as changes in temperature.
pie chart	A type of chart in which a circle is divided into sectors to represent the proportions of a total made up by different items.
plastic	A plastic material changes shape when there is a force on it but does not return to its original shape when the force is removed.
pollutant	A substance that can harm the environment or the organisms that live there.
pollution	Something that damages the environment or the organisms that live there.
polymer	A substance made up of very long molecules containing repeating groups of atoms.
porous	Porous rocks have tiny holes in them.
precaution (pre-cor-tion)	An action taken to reduce the risk of a hazard causing harm (e.g. wearing eye protection when handling an acid to prevent it splashing in your eyes).
precise	Measurements that are close to one another.
prediction	What you think will happen in an experiment.

prefix (*pree*-fix)	Something added to the beginning of a word to change its meaning. In 'kilometre', 'kilo' is the prefix.
pressure	The amount of force pushing on a certain area. A way of saying how spread out a force is.
product (**prod**-uct)	A new substance made in a chemical reaction. Products are written on the right side, after the arrow, in a word equation.
propanone	A common solvent. Found in nail varnish remover.
property	A description of how a material behaves and what it is like. Hardness is a property of some solids.
proportional (*prO-por-shun-al*)	A relationship between two variables where one doubles if the other doubles. A graph of the two variables would be a straight line through the origin.
proton	A sub-atomic particle found in an atom's nucleus. It has an electrical charge of +1.
proton number	The number of protons in an atom's nucleus. Another term for atomic number.
pure	A single substance that does not have anything else in it.
qualitative	Data that is described in words.
quantitative	Data that is described in numbers.
quartz (*kwartz*)	The mineral that forms the grains in sandstone.
random	When there is an equal chance for one event occurring as there is for any other events in the same set.
random error	An error that can be different for every reading.
range	The difference between the highest and lowest values in a set of data (usually ignoring any anomalous results).
rate	The rate at which something happens is its speed.
rate of reaction	The speed of a reaction is known as its rate.
ratio	A way of comparing two different quantities. Two numbers separated with a colon (:).
raw material	A substance used to make other substances.
reactant (*ree-**act**-ant*)	A substance that takes part in a chemical reaction. Reactants are written on the left side, before the arrow, in a word equation.
reaction profile	Graph showing the changes in energy of reactants and products during a reaction.
reactive (*ree-**ak**-tiv*)	A substance that reacts with many other substances or reacts very easily is reactive.
reactivity	A description of how quickly or vigorously something reacts.
reactivity series	A list of metals that shows them in order of their reactivity, with the most reactive at the top.
recycling (*re-**cy**-cling*)	Using a material again, often by melting it and using it to make new objects.
redox reaction	A reaction in which one reactant is reduced and another is oxidised.
reduced	If a substance has lost oxygen then it has been reduced.
reducing agent	A substance that removes oxygen from another substance.
references	Acknowledgement of any outside sources of information used when writing a scientific paper.
relationship	A link between two variables, so that when one thing changes so does the other. Best seen by using a scatter graph. Also called a correlation.
reliable	Results that are repeatable and reproducible are reliable.
repeatable	Results that are similar when repeated by the same experimenter.
reproducible	Results that are similar when repeated by different experimenters.
residue	The solid pieces that remain in a filter after filtration.
resource (*rez-**ors***)	Something needed by an organism. For example, plants need light as a resource and animals need food as a resource.
result	A measurement or observation from an experiment.

reversible reaction	A chemical reaction that can easily be reversed.
risk	The chance that a hazard will cause harm.
rock	A naturally occurring substance made of one or more minerals.
rock cycle	All the processes that form sedimentary, igneous and metamorphic rocks linked together.
rust	A weak, brown, crumbly, solid, formed when iron corrodes. (A mixture of oxides and hydroxides of iron.)
rusting	The corrosion of iron or steel (water and oxygen must be present for rusting to occur).
sacrificial protection	Using a more reactive metal to protect iron from rusting.
salt	An ionic compound (other than water or hydrogen) formed during the neutralisation of an acid with a base (or the reaction of a metal with an acid).
sandstone	A sedimentary rock made out of grains of quartz.
saturated	A solution that contains so much dissolved solute that no more solute can dissolve in it.
scatter graph	A graph in which data for two variables is plotted as points. This allows you to see whether there is a relationship between the two variables. Lines (or curves) of best fit are often drawn through the points.
schist (*shist*)	A metamorphic rock formed when slate or other rocks are heated and squashed more. It is usually shiny with platy crystals in wavy layers.
scientific method	Any way of testing that involves collecting information in order to show whether an idea is right or wrong. This is often done by developing a hypothesis that is tested by using it to make a prediction. The prediction is then tested using experiments.
scientific paper	An article written by scientists and published in a science magazine called a journal. It is like an investigation report but usually shows the results and conclusions drawn from many experiments.
sediment	Rock grains and fragments dropped by moving air or water.
sedimentary	Describes a rock formed from grains stuck together. The grains are often rounded.
sieve	A mesh used for filtration.
sinkhole	A large hole in the ground caused by limestone dissolving. Sinkholes can sometimes form in other types of rock as well.
SI unit	A standard international unit used by scientists. 'SI' stands for 'Système International d'Unités'.
slate	A metamorphic rock with tiny crystals that are lined up. It is formed from mudstone and can be split into layers.
small intestine	An organ used to break up food and get it into the blood.
sodium chloride	The chemical name for table or common salt.
solar cell (*sell*)	A flat plate that uses energy transferred by light to produce electricity.
solid	One of the states of matter. Has a fixed shape and fixed volume.
solubility	The amount of substance that dissolves in a particular solvent at a particular temperature to make a saturated solution.
soluble	Describes a substance that can dissolve in a liquid.
solute	The substance that has dissolved in a liquid to make a solution.
solution (*sol-**oo**-shun*)	When a substance has dissolved in a liquid. Solutions are transparent.
solvent	The liquid in which a substance dissolves to make a solution.
soot	A form of carbon, which is produced as very fine particles when hydrocarbon fuels undergo incomplete combustion.
standard form	A very large or very small number written as a number between 1 and 10 multiplied by a power of 10. $A \times 10^n$ where A is between 1 and 10 and n is the power of 10.
state of matter	There are three different forms that a substance can be in: solid, liquid or gas. These are the three states of matter.

state symbol	Letters in brackets after a formula in a chemical equation to show the state of a substance: (s = solid, l = liquid, g = gas, aq = dissolved in water).
steam	Water as a gas. May also be called water vapour.
sub-atomic particle	The smaller particles of which atoms are made (electrons, protons, neutrons).
sublime	When a solid turns into a gas, without becoming a liquid.
sulfur dioxide	An acidic gas released from burning fossil fuels, which contributes to acid rain.
surface area	The total area of all the surfaces of a three-dimensional object.
surface area : volume ratio	The surface area of a three-dimensional object (such as an organism) divided by its volume. Also written as SA:V ratio.
suspension (*sus-pen-shun*)	A mixture of a solid and liquid, where the solid bits are heavy enough to settle out if the mixture is left to stand.
symbol	The letter or letters that represent an element.
symbol equation	A way of writing out what happens in a chemical reaction using symbols to represent the substances involved.
systematic error (*sis-tem-at-ick*)	An error that is the same for all readings, such as when forgetting to zero a balance before using it to measure a series of masses.
table	An organisation of data into rows and columns.
texture	The scientific word used to describe the shapes and sizes of grains in a rock, and how the grains are packed together.
theory (*thear-ree*)	A hypothesis (or set of hypotheses) that explains how and why something happens. The predictions made using a theory should have been tested on several occasions and always found to work.
thermal decomposition	Breaking down a compound into simpler substances using heat.
thermite reaction	Highly exothermic displacement reaction between aluminium and iron oxide that produces molten iron.
thermometer	Any device used to measure temperature.
tissue (*tish-you*)	A part of an organ that does an important job. Each tissue is made up of a group of the same type of cells all doing the same job.
toxic (*tox-ic*)	A toxic substance is poisonous.
transition metal	One of a central group of elements in the periodic table.
transparent	Clear, can be seen through. (Note: transparent substances may be coloured or colourless.)
transport	The movement of rock grains and fragments by wind, ice or water.
universal indicator	Substance that turns different colours depending on the pH of a solution, and can detect pHs across the whole pH range.
unreactive (*un-ree-yak-tive*)	A substance that reacts with few other substances, or reacts very slowly or not at all.
volcano	A mountain that shoots out molten rock.
vacuum (*vak-yoom*)	A completely empty space containing no particles.
valid	Something is valid if it is doing what it is supposed to do. A measurement is valid if it measures what it is supposed to measure. A valid conclusion is drawn only from the data that the conclusion is supposed to be drawn from.
variable (*vair-ee-ab-el*)	Anything that can change and be measured.
vibrate (*vibe-rayt*)	To move backwards and forwards.
voltage	A way of saying how much energy is transferred by electricity.
volume	The amount of room something takes up. Often measured in cubic centimetres (cm^3).

vulcanisation	When rubber is heated with sulfur. The sulfur forms cross-links between the rubber molecules, changing the material's properties.
water of crystallisation	The water molecules that allow some compounds to form crystals.
weathering	When rocks are broken up by physical, chemical or biological processes.
word equation (*word eck-way-shun*)	An equation in which the names of the reactant(s) are written on the left side, there is an arrow pointing from left to right and the names of the product(s) are written on the right side.

							1 H hydrogen										2 He helium
3 Li lithium	4 Be beryllium											5 B boron	6 C carbon	7 N nitrogen	8 O oxygen	9 F fluorine	10 Ne neon
11 Na sodium	12 Mg magnesium											13 Al aluminium	14 Si silicon	15 P phosphorus	16 S sulfur	17 Cl chlorine	18 Ar argon
19 K potassium	20 Ca calcium	21 Sc scandium	22 Ti titanium	23 V vanadium	24 Cr chromium	25 Mn manganese	26 Fe iron	27 Co cobalt	28 Ni nickel	29 Cu copper	30 Zn zinc	31 Ga gallium	32 Ge germanium	33 As arsenic	34 Se selenium	35 Br bromine	36 Kr krypton
37 Rb rubidium	38 Sr strontium	39 Y yttrium	40 Zr zirconium	41 Nb niobium	42 Mo molybdenum	43 Tc technetium	44 Ru ruthenium	45 Rh rhodium	46 Pd palladium	47 Ag silver	48 Cd cadmium	49 In indium	50 Sn tin	51 Sb antimony	52 Te tellurium	53 I iodine	54 Xe xenon
55 Cs caesium	56 Ba barium	57 La lanthanum	72 Hf hafnium	73 Ta tantalum	74 W tungsten	75 Re rhenium	76 Os osmium	77 Ir iridium	78 Pt platinum	79 Au gold	80 Hg mercury	81 Tl thallium	82 Pb lead	83 Bi bismuth	84 Po polonium	85 At astatine	86 Rn radon
87 Fr francium	88 Ra radium	89 Ac actinium	104 Rf rutherfordium	105 Db dubnium	106 Sg seaborgium	107 Bh bohrium	108 Hs hassium	109 Mt meitnerium	110 Ds darmstadtium	111 Rg roentgenium	112 Cn copernicium	113 Nh nihonium	114 Fl flerovium	115 Mc moscovium	116 Lv livermorium	117 Ts tennessine	118 Og oganesson

- metal
- semi-metal
- non-metal

58 Ce cerium	59 Pr praseodymium	60 Nd neodymium	61 Pm promethium	62 Sm samarium	63 Eu europium	64 Gd gadolinium	65 Tb terbium	66 Dy dysprosium	67 Ho holmium	68 Er erbium	69 Tm thulium	70 Yb ytterbium	71 Lu lutetium
90 Th thorium	91 Pa protactinium	92 U uranium	93 Np neptunium	94 Pu plutonium	95 Am americium	96 Cm curium	97 Bk berkelium	98 Cf californium	99 Es einsteinium	100 Fm fermium	101 Md mendelevium	102 No nobelium	103 Lr lawrencium

STEM skills

The STEM pages in each unit focus on key STEM skills. These skills are listed and described below.

STEM skill	STEM skill description	STEM pages developing skill
Numeracy and use of maths	Using maths	7H
Generation and analysis of data	Design ways of collecting and analysing data to reach answers.	7F, 7G 9E
Critical analysis and evaluation	Give reasons why data (or proposed solutions) are or are not good enough (e.g. to answer questions, solve problems).	7H 9G
Communication	Use language and maths to communicate ideas effectively.	7E, 7G 8F, 8H
Innovation and invention	Combine ideas to reach answers.	7F 8G
Problem-solving	Use reasoning and systematic approaches to reach answers.	8H 9F

INDEX